LAND OF SECOND CHANCES

Tim Lewis is a feature writer at the *Observer* and contributing editor of *Esquire*. He has previously been the editor of the *Observer Magazine*, *Observer Sport Monthly* and the *Independent's Sunday Review*. He lives in London.

TIM LEWIS

LAND OF SECOND CHANCES

The Impossible Rise of Rwanda's Cycling Team

YELLOW JERSEY PRESS
LONDON

Published by Yellow Jersey Press 2014

2 4 6 8 10 9 7 5 3

First published in Great Britain in 2013 by
Yellow Jersey Press
Random House, 20 Vauxhall Bridge Road,
London SW1V 2SA

www.vintage-books.co.uk

Addresses for companies within The Random House Group Limited can be found at: www.randomhouse.co.uk/offices.htm

The Random House Group Limited Reg. No. 954009

A CIP catalogue record for this book is available from the British Library

ISBN 9780224091770

The Random House Group Limited supports The Forest Stewardship Council® (FSC®), the leading international forest-certification organisation. Our books carrying the FSC label are printed on FSC®-certified paper. FSC is the only forest-certification scheme supported by the leading environmental organisations, including Greenpeace. Our paper procurement policy can be found at www.randomhouse.co.uk/environment

Printed and bound by CPI Group (UK) Ltd, Croydon, CR0 4YY

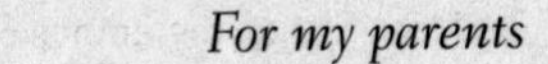

For my parents

'You can't know where you're going unless you know where you've come from.'

Rwandan proverb

CONTENTS

Prologue

A LONG RIDE

There had been a lot of odd moments in Adrien Niyonshuti's life recently. Most of them started when a group of Americans arrived in Rwanda and put on a bicycle race in September 2006. Adrien won and, as his prize, he was allowed to keep the mountain bike he had borrowed from the visitors for the event. It was a Schwinn, nothing that special by Western standards, which meant it was exponentially more advanced than anything that little, landlocked Rwanda – about the size of Wales, but with four times as many inhabitants – had ever seen. He actually didn't ride it very much. He was nineteen years old and no one else in the country had a mountain bike to go with him, so it was dull on his own. But the bike was definitely the beginning of something.

From this point on, new experiences arrived at a rattle for Adrien. Not long after, he flew on an aeroplane for the first time. In South Africa, he slept on a bed between sheets, after a couple of nights of just lying on the top because he did not dare to disturb them. He learned to use flush toilets, again after some initial confusion. He raced on his road bike against

Lance Armstrong. He saw snow for the first time, high in the Colorado Rockies.

But, for those who have followed Adrien's life for a few years, one Friday lunchtime in London in August 2012 set a new bar for incongruity. The Criterion Theatre, a Victorian-era West End playhouse that usually hosts a long-running production of *The 39 Steps*, had been commandeered for a salon called *When Clive Met Adrien*. Adrien was Adrien, who in exactly forty-eight hours' time would become the first Rwandan to compete in the men's mountain bike event at the Olympic Games. Clive was Clive Owen, the glowering British film star who had a Golden Globe and a Bafta on his shelves at home.

Adrien knew next to nothing about Clive, but it quickly emerged that Clive knew pretty much everything about Adrien. The actor strode on stage, wearing a crisp slate-grey suit and open-necked shirt, and immediately broached the question we'd all been chewing on: what was the guy from *Closer* and *Children of Men* doing hosting a talk with a Rwandan cyclist? He was, he explained, an ambassador for the Aegis Trust, a UK-based charity that raises awareness of genocide and has particularly strong links with Rwanda. More than that, though, Clive was mad about sport.

'There are thousands of athletes who have come here to compete in the Olympic Games and all of them will have extraordinary stories of dedication and commitment to their sport,' he said, glancing at diligently prepared notes. 'But I really think that Adrien Niyonshuti's story is one of the most extraordinary.'

Adrien was seven years old during the Rwandan genocide in 1994, when at least 800,000 of his compatriots – one in ten of the population – were slaughtered in a hundred days. He only escaped death by running and hiding from the Hutu mobs that were assigned to kill every last Tutsi. Sixty members of his family, including six of his siblings, were brutally hacked down in those three months. But now, just two days before the biggest moment of Adrien's life, wasn't a time to dwell on those tales of horror. The week before, Adrien had carried his country's flag at the London 2012 opening ceremony, nervously but proudly leading a delegation of seven athletes. And, as he often said, one of his dreams was that cycling would finally give the world a reference point for Rwanda that was not the genocide.

At this moment, Adrien joined Clive on the stage. He was a quiet, gentle presence – that was obvious even from the cheap seats – and he walked stiffly, like he had forgotten to remove the coat hanger from his clothes. He was not quite five and a half feet tall and slim, full of sharp angles. His hair was shaved to a stubble, as Rwandan men invariably have it, and he had finely drawn features with precipitous cheekbones. He wore a Team Rwanda gilet in the national colours of sky blue, green and yellow, black tracksuit trousers and running shoes. He didn't look out at the audience once as he took his seat.

Adrien's voice was soft and he spoke rapidly; the audience leaned forward as one to catch what he said. He ran through the creation of Team Rwanda, the racing squad that was formed not long after he won that first race in 2006. It started with five riders, but in five years had grown to nearly twenty; the country now had its own professional road race, the week-long Tour of Rwanda, and it had become one of the strongest cycling nations in all of Africa. The inspiration for the project initially had come from a Californian called Tom Ritchey, one of the inventors of the mountain bike back in the late nineteen seventies. It had been taken on and knocked into shape by a former professional road racer called Jock Boyer, who in 1981 became the first American to ride the Tour de France. Both men had complicated – some would say compromised – reasons for becoming involved in Rwanda.

Adrien first heard of the Olympics in 2007, when he was twenty years old and just starting out as a bike racer: 'I asked Jock, "What means the Olympics?"' Few Rwandans had a television, and there was only one station, but the following year he managed to find a screen and he watched the opening ceremony from Beijing and some of the events. Adrien half-smiled, 'I say, "One day I'd like to be there."'

He spent two years training, pushing, fixating on his goal. He found out that there were three cycling events for which he could qualify: the men's individual time trial, the road race and the cross-country mountain biking. His first opportunity came in the African Continental Championships in November 2010, which doubled as a selection competition for the Olympics. By coincidence, the event was being staged in Kigali, the capital city of Rwanda, and the time trial course was an undulating twenty-mile loop around streets that Adrien used to cycle on to get to his secondary school. He was competing against the best riders in Africa: the top guys from South Africa, the champion from the unlikely cycling powerhouse of Eritrea, a Namibian contracted to a team in Europe; riders from twenty countries in all. The racers set off one after another, riding alone against the stopwatch. Adrien knew that a top-three finish would send him to London. He came fourth. He shrugged. 'The rider from Algeria beat me by one second.' Adrien was exaggerating: in fact, it was only 0.11 of a second.

The next opportunity came in the road-race qualification two days later. Over a hundred African riders lined up in Kigali, the range of abilities and equipment quite something to behold; from the sleek carbon-fibre bicycles of the leading contenders to those from Burundi, which were held together just by wire, tape and the prayers of the riders. Before the start, a minute's silence was observed to commemorate the death of a Rwandan boy who had wandered onto the road in front of the Ivory Coast team car a few days earlier. Then the competitors were off, for fourteen laps of a seven-mile circuit, knowing again that the top three riders would book their tickets to London.

Everyone knew this was Adrien's best chance. Weighing just sixty-eight kilograms, he was not really built for a sustained power effort like the time trial, while his inexperience on a mountain bike would be a daunting handicap in that discipline. On a road bike, however, he was smooth and powerful, and his capacity for self-punishment when the going was really tough had become legendary. He started well and when a group of twelve favourites broke clear after ten laps he was perfectly placed among them. Then, suddenly, as he attempted to attack on a steep slope, he stood on his pedals and his chain broke. Not slipped off, but shattered – cyclists could ride for years, a lifetime even, without this fate befalling them. For it to happen in the most important race of Adrien's life was freakishly unlucky.

His rivals disappeared into the distance. Adrien stood on the side of the road, hopping from leg to leg like he needed to pee, waiting for one of his Rwandan team-mates to catch up. A minute passed, then ninety seconds – it felt like hours, he said afterwards – and finally he switched bikes. His new ride wasn't the right size, but he adjusted the seat with an Allen key as he pedalled and he raced wildly, impulsively, to make up lost time. It was to no avail: he finished eighth, exactly one minute, thirty-one seconds behind the winner, the Eritrean champion, Daniel Teklehaimanot.

As Adrien told this story, there were audible gasps in the

theatre. This was despite the fact we were in London, he was in London: we all knew there was a happy ending to this part of the story. Still, somehow, his dream remained an outrageous long shot. It was actually two weeks after this pair of disappointments that I met Adrien for the first time, during the 2010 Tour of Rwanda. He explained back then that his last chance to qualify for the London Olympics was the African Continental Championships for mountain biking in Stellenbosch, South Africa, in February 2011. At the time, I mistook his quietness for lack of confidence, even vulnerability. I wouldn't have bet someone else's money on his making it. But the more time I spent with Adrien, the more I appreciated his resilience: he got neither too high when the going was good nor too low when it wasn't, which had presumably been a useful trait throughout his life.

In Stellenbosch, the first three nationalities, rather than just the first three riders, would be allocated places in the Olympics. In the days before, Adrien, a devout Muslim, spent a lot of time in prayer: 'I say, "God, you know everything, tell me what to do,"' he recalled. Race day itself was almost anticlimactic after what he had been through before. He rode hard, there were no mechanical dramas and he finished fourth, behind two South Africans and a Namibian. 'You did it!' exclaimed Clive Owen. Impromptu cheers filled the auditorium.

During the question-and-answer session, conversation turned to the race on Sunday; one woman asked Adrien if he thought he might win a medal. 'My goal for this Olympics is to finish the race,' he replied. Everyone laughed, but for the first time Adrien looked out into the stage lights, confused. He was serious.

*

There was something unsatisfying, even defeatist, about this goal. This was a fairytale after all, the kind that only the Olympics could produce, and it demanded an iconic ending. Adrien's answer was partly a statement of uncompromising fact: mountain bike races are run on short loops of a track little wider than a set of handlebars; if a competitor lags far behind the leaders, the organisers do not hesitate to yank him off the course. But his response was revealing about the psyche of his nation, too. Nearly two decades after the genocide, Rwanda was still synonymous with death. That was often the only thing that anyone on the outside knew. Geographically, the country was a tiny pebble dropped on the Equator in the centre of Africa, the continent that the rest of the world found easiest to ignore. The middle of nowhere, then. Adrien's homeland had not been blessed with natural resources, which had made it even less essential to external interests. It didn't produce iconic writers, musicians or sportspeople. Rwanda was, in short, desperate for heroes. It craved a new identity.

Adrien could not be blamed for being cautious. Experience told him that success did not come easily to people from Rwanda. But the country was also changing faster than anyone believed possible, and Adrien had become a conspicuous part of that. From being ranked by the World Bank as the poorest country on earth after the genocide, Rwanda was refashioning itself under its ambitious leader, President Paul Kagame, as a progressive, middle-income hub determined to graft its way out of poverty. An African Gorilla to take on those Asian Tigers. These developments were driven by an unwavering faith in technology and a twenty-first-century belief in entrepreneurialism, the Internet and environmentalism. It was not just whiz-bang developments either: public resources, including aid money, had been effectively directed towards providing services, reducing inequality and keeping corruption low. In 2012, the World Bank returned to Rwanda and found that in the previous five years a million of its eleven million citizens – one in five of those considered 'poor' – had been lifted out of poverty. Paul Collier, an economist who is the director of the Centre for the Study of African Economies at Oxford University, noted: 'This rate of poverty reduction is the fastest ever achieved in Africa and equals the best achieved globally.'

But, while the country had started to buzz with talk of biotech investments and Java programing, there was one object, more than any other, that encapsulated Rwanda's past, present and future. It had a long history in the country, from the colonial days onwards, but also a dynamic modern relevance. It symbolised hope, unity and prosperity for many; it represented progress, though not fast enough for some people's tastes, and often favouring men more than women. Still, its fortunes mirrored Rwanda's own; its story shone a light onto the lives of all its citizens. It was the bicycle.

1
AMAGARE

When I think of cycling in Rwanda, I picture a boy, no more than fifteen years old, riding his bike down the hill to the grand lakeside resort of Gisenyi. From the highest point on the road, more than a mile and a half above sea level, it's a swooping descent of fully thirty miles and this kid was blowing down it as fast as a car or nearly a motorbike. It was a stunning, cloudless day and, when I took my eyes off the tarmac, Lake Kivu sparkled and shimmered seductively in the distance. To the right, the anything-goes border city of Goma, beneath the Nyiragongo volcano in the Democratic Republic of Congo, occasionally flashed into view. It last erupted in 2002, lava sweeping into the city, forcing the evacuation of 400,000 people and the loss of forty-five lives. When the molten lava set, Goma's citizens returned and simply rebuilt on top of the ink-black rock.

But mostly I was transfixed by the boy. It is a winding road and he carved elegant, plunging arcs around the bends with little heed for oncoming traffic or indeed his continued existence. I was driving a belching Land Rover rental car and when I pulled close it was clear that his bicycle was older than he was. Two large cloth sacks tethered on the back bulged with freshly picked potatoes and probably added eighty kilos. It would have been gruesome going uphill but, this way round, he must have felt like he was flying.

It was a couple of miles before I realised that his bike had no brakes. He was riding forty miles an hour *with no brakes*. When he wanted to slow down, he would languidly lower his right flip-flop from the pedal onto the road and its rubber sole would hiss and burn and his speed fractionally reduce. When the road levelled off a little, I pulled alongside the boy. I yelled something idiotic like '*Courage!*' and he looked back at me blankly. It occurred to me that this was how, at some point, most of us fall in love with cycling: we get buzzed, then a little scared, but we want to do it again; later we will be confronted by the intense suffering that comes with serious riding, but that too becomes addictive. It could be that I was watching a future Olympian, but more likely I was seeing a kid doing his job, earning a couple of thousand francs – around £2 – for an afternoon hauling spuds.

Adrien Niyonshuti started much the same way. He grew up on the other side of the country, in the Eastern Province, where the terrain is less dramatically mountainous, and he never had to haul goods for money, but he too recalled the early pleasures of careering down a long descent so fast that his eyes filled with tears. It is not an experience that you have to travel very far to find in Rwanda. This is, after all, *le pays des mille collines*, the land of a thousand hills, and anyone who has ever chosen to cross it on a bicycle will have wondered who was responsible for such a patent understatement. It has every kind of peak: spiky volcanic ones, strung-out torturous ones, creep-up-on-you spiteful ones; at the top of each of them is a vista that is reminiscent of Tuscany or Switzerland or sometimes New Zealand. Depending on how one feels about these things, it's either the perfect place in the world to ride your bike, or the worst.

'All this climbing . . . It's just bullshit,' Arnaud Ontsatsi, a rider for the Gabon national team, complained early on at the 2011 Tour of Rwanda. 'It's just too hard. We have hills at home, but nothing like this. How are we supposed to train for this?' Ontsatsi and the whole Gabon sqaud went home after just three days of competition.

The lush Edenic look of Rwanda comes as a shock, particularly to visitors from other parts of Africa. Kigali, the capital since the early sixties, sits in the middle of the country, a sprawling, modern-ish city of around one million people. From there, a handful of decent paved roads radiate out like spokes to Congo in the west, Uganda in the north, Tanzania in the east and Burundi in the south. Nine out of ten Rwandans are subsistence farmers and they compete over the most densely populated land in all of the continent. Not so long ago most of the country was forest, but now even the steepest slopes are planted, ploughed and harvested. Bananas, tea and coffee all grow well here, while copses of silver eucalyptus trees lend rural areas the smell of bath-time. Scrawny goats cling on to slanted grass and herdsmen bully long-horned Ankole cattle with wooden staffs. Despite being on the Equator, the altitude ensures it remains temperate between the two seasons of unrelenting rain. Every possible variation of green – from the dazzling chartreuse of a tea plantation to the exotic limes, olives and emeralds of the rainforest – is represented somewhere. Rwandans say that God visits other countries during the day, but always comes back at night to rest there.

Bicycles – what they call *amagare*, or *igare* in the singular – are the dominant mode of mechanical transportation in

Rwanda, an organic part of life, commerce and sometimes even recreation. They would have arrived in the country not long after the white man. In fact, from the earliest days there were strong links between central Africa and the growth of cycling in Europe.

The velocipedes of the 1860s and 1870s, known evocatively as boneshakers, then high-wheelers, had wheels made from solid iron. These became extinct overnight in 1885 with the arrival the Rover Safety Bicycle, a creation of the English inventor of James Starley. With its direct front-wheel steering and selection chain rings and sprockets, it was not far removed from the modern bicycle. Its only shortcoming was the tyres: smaller wheels were less forgiving than oversized ones and the solution of the day – solid rubber strips tacked to the wheel rim – was brutally groin-numbing. John Boyd Dunlop, a Scottish veterinary surgeon who lived in Belfast, came to the rescue of cyclists everywhere with the invention of the pneumatic tyre in 1888. When a doctor advised remedial cycling for his sickly nine-year-old son, Dunlop had a flash of inspiration: he fixed linen sleeves to the wooden wheels of a tricycle, inserted simple inflatable rubber tubes and pumped them with air. He knew immediately he had made a significant discovery; his first advertisement promised 'Vibration impossible'.

Cycling had already been popular in Europe but, now that the machines could be comfortable and fast, it boomed. This was where Africa, and particularly Rwanda's neighbour Congo, came in. King Leopold II of Belgium made his claim to the region in 1880 through his agent, the rapacious British explorer Henry Morton Stanley, and the Congo Free State was confirmed as his personal domain at the Conference of Berlin in 1884. Rwanda's fate was determined a few years later in 1890 in Brussels when it was decided that it would now belong to the

German Empire, along with Burundi, in return for the Germans handing over Uganda to the British. Curiously, no European had even set foot inside Rwanda when this decision was passed down: Stanley had been peppered with arrows when he tried; it was left to Count Gustav Adolf von Götzen, a German, to take the first steps into the country in 1894. In this way, like children trading football stickers, the fates of millions in central Africa were decreed.

King Leopold II, a megalomaniac with acute small-country syndrome, was initially interested in securing a trade route for ivory, but Dunlop's invention changed his priorities and there was now an unquenchable desire for rubber. It was first exported from the Congo Free State in 1890 and soon it was the colony's most profitable industry. Harvesting wild rubber from vines in the rainforest was an arduous business, particularly for inhabitants who were not being paid and were forced to do it because the women of their village had been taken hostage, as was often the case. The *chicotte*, a razor-sharp whip made from sun-dried hippopotamus hide, became the instrument of enforcement and so began the 'rubber terror' that would see the population of Congo reduced by half – perhaps ten million inhabitants in all – during Leopold's rule. (This was the reality of Joseph Conrad's novella *Heart of Darkness* and his murderous ivory trader Kurtz. Although Kurtz is said to have been modelled on a renegade Belgian called Leon Rom, Conrad gave him English and French ancestry and noted in the book: 'All Europe contributed to the making of Kurtz.') The European demand for rubber for bicycles, increased by the development of motorbikes and then the automobile, only seemed to intensify the brutality. Rwanda might consider itself fortunate that it did not have the right climatic conditions for rubber production. The Germans instead plundered Cameroon, another of their colonies; one of the leading companies back then was Continental, which began making bicycle tyres in the town of Korbach in 1892 and, more than a century later, still produces them for many of the world's top cyclists.

Rwanda may have been close to the source of the cycling boom at the turn of the century, but it would be a long time before *amagare* were a common sight on its rutted byways. It soon became clear that the territory contained little in the way of mineral deposits, so the Germans decided not to waste money on roads and infrastructure. After the First World War, Belgium took control of the country – then known as Ruanda-Urundi, and including both modern-day Rwanda and Burundi – on the orders of the League of Nations. In this period, bicycles were mostly limited to use by Roman Catholic missionaries. These zealous individuals covered the ground assiduously enough, however, converting Rwanda into the most Christianised country in Africa. The Church's influence on the country has been chequered – the clergy were heavily complicit in fomenting division between Hutus and Tutsis in the colonial period; then, during the genocide, churches were the sites of some of the very worst massacres – but the beliefs have stuck. In 2006, the last time anyone counted, more than half of Rwandans were Roman Catholic and a quarter were Protestants (with significant Seventh-Day Adventist and Muslim minorities). Less than two per cent said they had no religious beliefs.

Bicycles were a luxury and there were few signs of prosperity in Rwanda during colonial times. The country was hit by a drought and a severe famine in the late nineteen twenties, and then by the same one-two in the early forties. The latter Ruzagayura famine led to the death of around a quarter of a population estimated at two million. Meanwhile, with the help of their colonisers, internal divisions between Rwandans were becoming more entrenched. In 1933, the Belgians began a census that would lead to the creation of identity cards on which ethnicity was marked. On these, it was codified officially that the country was made up of three distinct groups: Hutu (eighty-five per cent), Tutsi (fourteen per cent) and Twa (one per cent).

These distinctions formalised a hypothesis put forward in 1863 by John Hanning Speke, a British Army officer turned anthropologist who stumbled upon and named Lake Victoria and proposed it as the source of the Nile River. On his travels in the region, Speke was badly wounded by a spear attack in Somalia; later he'd go blind and a little mad, attempting to gouge a beetle out of his ear with a knife. In his journals, he was dismissive of the 'negroes' he came across, by which he meant the squat, stockier, darker-skinned Africans who tended to have flat noses, full lips and prominent jaws. The only hope for the continent, he decided, was a 'superior race' who typically herded cattle rather than worked the fields and had straighter hair, lighter skin and longer limbs. Speke determined that the latter group, which included Tutsis, should be considered 'Hamitic' peoples, descended from modern-day Ethiopia and before that from Noah's son Ham, of Genesis legend, who was cursed for seeing his father naked and afterwards became the progenitor of black skin. Their deep-seated Christianity offered crumbs of hope for 'barbaric' central Africa.

It will surprise no one that Speke's theories have not stood the test of time. Historians and ethnographers do not now believe that Hutus and Tutsis should be considered separate ethnic groups. It is possible that two distinct peoples wandered into Rwanda at different times and from opposite geographical directions – everyone agrees that the Twa, itinerant pygmies, were the country's original settlers – but no one can confirm it. What is clear is that Hutus and Tutsis lived side by side for centuries and shared land, a common language and religion; Mwami, their chiefs and quasi-deities, could be either Hutu or Tutsi and the two groups would fight side by side. They inter-married, sometimes swapping ethnicity in the process, and a Hutu who owned cows might become known as a Tutsi for that reason alone; it is estimated that a quarter of modern Rwandans have great-grandparents from both groups. There are no reports of systematic ethnic violence before colonisation.

During Belgian rule, particularly with the introduction of identity cards, ethnicity came to define Rwandan life. Scientists arrived to measure the width of Hutu and Tutsi noses, bestowing the exercise with the cut-price credibility that psychologists now lend to reality television shows. Perhaps the distinction felt natural to a colonial power that had its own messy conflagration of Walloon and Flemish cultures. Still, it did not take long for Rwanda to start to unravel. With Tutsis favoured by the Church-run education system and given preference for political appointments, Hutus were reduced to a second-class existence. Forced labour on projects such as road construction often turned abusive and the policies were unpopular enough for tens or maybe hundreds of thousands of resentful Rwandans, mostly Hutus, to flee the country for Congo or to affluent, British-run Uganda.

As Rwanda tottered towards independence, the stakes were raised and the situation turned violent. After decades of Tutsi dominance, there had been a gradual but perceptible shift in power towards the Hutu masses during the nineteen-fifties. This was in part because the country had become a trustee of the United Nations, but also because of an influx of Flemish priests who perhaps sympathised, as a majority themselves back home in Belgium, with the treatment of the Hutus. In 1957, a group of Hutu thinkers unveiled the Hutu Manifesto, which asserted their right to rule Rwanda. Two years later, an uprising called Muyaga – 'Wind of Destruction' – made the case in a less academic way; Tutsi houses were razed by Hutu mobs and hundreds killed. The Belgian administrators did not intervene and indeed began the formal transfer of power. In early 1960, Tutsi chiefs were swapped for Hutus and the following year the position of Mwami was abolished and Rwanda was declared a republic. In 1962, the country gained full independence; its first president, Grégoire Kayibanda, was one of the authors of the Hutu Manifesto. Around this time, there was an exodus of around 130,000 Tutsis to neighbouring countries.

When I have come back from spending time in Rwanda, people often ask if it is easy to spot the difference between Hutu and Tutsi. Not only do identity cards no longer exist now but talking about ethnic distinctions is often awkward or at worst a criminal offence; such talk is labelled 'divisionist'. They are all Rwandans. Of course, it is possible to recognise physical archetypes. Adrien, for example, is classically lean and fine-featured; he looks like a typical Tutsi and he was indeed raised as a Tutsi. One of the other riders on Team Rwanda, Gasore Hategeka, is a tank: strong and muscular with a round face and darker skin; he lives in the north-west of Rwanda, the most fertile area for growing crops in the country. He looks like a Hutu and, true enough, he is – or used to be. Mostly, however, it was impossible to tell. Many times, I spent hours interviewing a Rwandan with one of my interpreters, Liberal or Ayuub, both of whom had lived in the country since shortly after the genocide, and neither of us would have a clue if we had been speaking to a Hutu or a Tutsi.

Ayuub, in fact, summed up the dichotomy when we were driving one day. His father was Ugandan, his mother was a Rwandan Tutsi; he had been raised in Congo, Uganda and Rwanda. When he came back to Rwanda for good, he married a Hutu woman. 'What would that make my kids?' he asked. He was relieved he didn't have to decide any more.

Back to the bicycle. The nineteen-sixties saw modest improvements for many Rwandans; the gross domestic product nudged up by around five per cent each year and the newly independent country was boosted by foreign aid, mainly from Belgium, with Switzerland another generous donor. Paul Rutayisire, a lecturer in history at the National University of Rwanda, grew up in the east of the country and he remembered as a child, in the sixties, that well-to-do people from his town would save their money, disappear to Uganda or Tanzania and return with three things: a petrol lamp, spectacles and a bicycle. 'A bicycle was a sign of civilisation, big social status,' he recalled. 'They were so proud when they came back with those objects. They would have the petrol light on, even during the day! Ah yes, it was very funny.'

In Uganda, bicycles had become indispensable as 'boda-bodas', border-to-border bicycle-taxis. These were first seen in the sixties, and proliferated in the seventies, owing to a need to transport people, contraband goods and animals between Busia, in the south-east corner of the country, and neighbouring Malaba in Kenya. There was a no man's land of a little less than a mile but, if a person went by bike, they did not need the paperwork required by motor vehicles. So young men, typically on bulky black Indian or Chinese single-speed roadsters, accessorised with plump cushions over the back wheel for passengers to sit on, would shout 'Boda-boda!' and turn a nice profit from picking up fares. Over time, they would pimp their rides with anything that might catch the eye or ear: sparkling reflectors made from tin lids, melodious bells, framed religious images and pendants from English football teams like the ones that captains exchange before cup finals. Bicycle-taxis remained popular until the nineteen-nineties when motorbikes began to take over.

The east of Rwanda, which borders with Uganda and Tanzania, was a natural spot for cycling to catch on. It is the flattest part of the country and the bikes that were coming in were cumbersome steel monsters with one lonely gear. It is also a little hotter, maybe a fraction less rainy. The other area where bicycles were taking hold was Butare in the deep south. Butare was the most urbane town in Rwanda and, if the Belgians had to stop anywhere, it was the most tolerable option – even now its restaurants serve fantastic, crisp *frites*. When the national university opened there in 1963, expatriate European teachers and the most affluent Rwandan students pootled on their bicycles along the main drag to the campus, one mile south of the town centre. On Sundays, after church, they would venture further, maybe thirty miles to Burundi and back.

Rwandans who couldn't afford a bicycle took inspiration from what they saw and decided to knock up their own. Wooden bikes, *icugutu* in local parlance, are – in a not especially strong field – perhaps Rwanda's signature innovation. They are scooters really, hacked crudely with machetes from eucalyptus trees; some have seats, but most do not, and the only concession to comfort is a thin strip of rubber around the small wheels. In the words of one American journalist, 'They look like they were stolen from Fred Flintstone's garage.' (Adrien Niyonshuti tried to explain them to Clive Owen at the event in London: 'It don't have pedals, it don't have crank, it don't have cassette, it don't have chain, it don't have brakes.' Clive looked blank: 'So what does it have?') There is basic steering, but the rider's comfort is definitely a secondary concern. They are central Africa's mules and, at this task, they are surprisingly effective: they can be loaded high with bleating goats, chattering children or kilos of bananas, tea and coffee.

A visitor to Rwanda has to look a little harder to find wooden bikes these days: President Kagame has banned them from main roads. The message is that an ambitious country such as Rwanda – which considers itself the cleanest, safest state in Africa – is no place for prehistoric scooters. (That detail always reminded me of Muammar Qaddafi ordering all of the camels within Tripoli's city limits to be shot because he thought they made Libya look backward. In a similar vein, Kagame has also ordered an 'eradication campaign' of thatched roofs on houses and Rwandans are fined on the spot if they are not wearing shoes.) But, on one point at least, it was hard to argue with the president, whose own first bike half a century ago was an *icugutu*. They are suicidally dangerous and a magnet for accidents. They have two speeds: scarcely moving and amusing-home-video out of control. Still, wander into small villages anywhere in the country and these renegade bicycles are being put to work as no-tech pick-up trucks. There are some in Congo, a smattering in Uganda, but nowhere has adopted them as enthusiastically as Rwanda.

As soon as proper bicycles became available in Africa, people raced them. These competitions were most firmly established in Italian and French colonies. In Eritrea, the inaugural Giro d'Eritrea was run in 1946: it had five stages and thirty-four riders, although Eritreans themselves were actually barred from competing. The next year, the country, which had been colonised by Italy but since 1941 had been a British protectorate, was distracted by a guerrilla war and staged a shorter event, the Giro delle Tre Valli, the 'Tour of the Three Valleys'. Eritrea would remain cycling-obsessed, but it would be more than fifty years (during most of which it was in conflict with Ethiopia) before organised racing was resurrected.

On the other side of the continent, there was similar interest in cycling in French Upper Volta. Upon independence, in December 1959, the country that would later become known as Burkina Faso decided to show off the new republic by hosting a pair of criteriums – short, fast, spectator-friendly races – in the capital Ouagadougou. New president Maurice Yaméogo invited some of the most famous European cycling stars of the day – including Jacques Anquetil and a past-his-prime Fausto Coppi – to compete against local riders and then go hunting for big game. In the first race, Anquetil sprinted in ahead of Coppi; in the second, which finished in front of the presidential palace, Coppi allowed a local amateur Sanu Moussa to take first place and win a Citroën from a sponsor. The group then flew south to Fada n'Gourma where they shot a gazelle, bought elephant tusks as souvenirs and saw local children taunt crocodiles with a dead chicken hung on a string. These would, in fact, be the last races of 'Il Campionissimo', as Coppi contracted malaria – more salacious reports mention poison or even suicide – dying on the second day of the new decade back at home in Italy.

In North Africa, meanwhile, there was a slow drip of riders into the Tour de France. The Tunisian champion Ali Neffati became the first African to compete in the race in 1913 and rode again the following year. In 1950, a pair of Algerians Abdel-Kader Zaaf and Marcel Molinès made a memorable impression on stage thirteen, a 135-mile run between Perpignan and Nîmes. They broke clear from the main pack early on and built up a lead of twenty minutes; they were helped by home-from-home temperatures of 40°C and the rest of the field stopping en masse for a dip in the Mediterranean. But with just a short distance to the finish, a long day in the sun took its toll and they stopped for a drink. Zaaf was offered a bottle of wine by spectators and, as a Muslim, this was his first taste of alcohol. He began acting erratically, eventually finding the shade of a tree and deciding to take a nap; a photograph showed him passed out, surrounded by Frenchmen mugging for the camera.

When Zaaf woke up, he had a couple more glugs of wine, climbed on his bike and headed back the way he had come, away from the finish. The organisers caught him, sent him to hospital and, against his protests, disqualified him from the race. Molinès, meanwhile, became the first African stage-winner of the world's most prestigious bicycle race, coming in five minutes ahead of the bunch. (The story doesn't end entirely tragically for Zaaf: he competed in five more Tours de France, finishing the race once, in 1951, and he profited from his new infamy by featuring in an advertisement for a wine producer.)

Rwanda, in cycling as in many other respects, lagged a few years behind the rest of the continent. Most of the bikes in the country were owned by European expatriates, civil servants or visitors involved in construction, and they were a status symbol beyond the dreams of most citizens. When I first arrived in Butare, I asked around for the oldest cyclist that anyone knew. An hour later, I was sitting in the grounds of a primary school with a driver called François Rudahunga. Born in 1956, he trained as a carpenter and in the eighties he had been one of the best racers in Rwanda. We sat on children's chairs outside a sparse classroom and he explained that, when he was growing up, a '*pneu ballon*' – or 'fat tyre' – bicycle would cost about a year's salary. A car was more money than he believed he'd ever earn in his life. 'The first thing a young man thought of buying was a bicycle,' said François. 'I bought mine from an old man who worked at the university who couldn't keep up the instalments he was paying. It showed everyone, particularly young women, that you were doing well, that you were impressive.'

The first races in Rwanda in the sixties were between *muzungus* – 'white people'; from the Swahili for foreigner, though a more evocative translation is 'aimless wanderer' – and were old-fashioned endurance tests: a challenge would be set to reach a far-flung corner of the country and an intrepid bunch of riders of differing abilities would set out to achieve it. For Rwandans to compete, they needed a benefactor. In Kigali, this would likely have been Emmanuel Mayaka, who arrived from Congo in the sixties and set up the first (and, until recently, only) cinema in Rwanda, Ciné Elmay; it offered a choice between VIP seats or 'general happiness' places and screened a mixture of Nolly-, Holly- and Bollywood films. Mayaka cycled a little himself, but mostly he sourced bicycles, which he distributed to promising youngsters to compete on. If they needed more time in the day to train, he would give them a job collecting ticket stubs in the cinema at night. In Butare, there was also a pair of Belgians who would help Rwandan hopefuls: one was a teacher and the other owned the construction company that built the university. Again, they would offer basic coaching and bring along a bunch of bananas to refuel the riders.

More serious racing in which Rwandans could compete came with the roads in the nineteen-seventies. When a rudimentary stretch of tarmac opened in 1977 between Kigali and Rusumo on the Tanzanian border, the Ministry of Youth, Sports and Culture held a bicycle race to celebrate. It was a

185-mile round-trip – later named the Tour de l'Est – and a rabble of around fifty riders completed the course over two days. In addition, there were regular sprints around Kigali, and a longer event between the capital and Butare called Ascension des Mille Collines. But a pattern soon emerged in the races: whatever length, however hard, a skinny man from Rwamagana in the Eastern Province was winning them all. In the beginning he competed on a bulky steel roadster, while his rivals rode comparatively lightweight sports bikes loaned from the Europeans. Still he thrashed everyone. His name should have been a giveaway: Emmanuel Turatsinze; his second name meaning, in the local language Kinyarwanda, 'We are victorious'.

Emmanuel was Adrien Niyonshuti's uncle.

Emmanuel came, as his family likes to remind you, from a long line of distinguished athletes. His father – Adrien's maternal grandfather – excelled at Rwanda's two national sports: archery and wrestling. In the latter, he defeated the penultimate monarch Mwami Mutara Rudahigwa, who was said to have stood six-foot seven. The family were Tutsi and during the first Hutu attacks in 1959, Emmanuel's father and grandfather were chased out of Rwamagana. Near the border with Uganda, they reached a river; they stopped, looked at their pursuers, took a few steps back and both men cleared the water in a single leap. The Hutus, unable to swim or find a canoe, could only watch. 'My grandfather was good at hunting,' Adrien's older sister Jeanne told me. 'And he was excellent at dancing.'

Emmanuel was born in 1952, as well as anyone can remember. Initially at least, he had the privileged life of a Tutsi. His father was on friendly terms with the Mwami, and the family had a farm with a few cattle, an indicator of significant wealth in Rwanda. But, when the Belgians began favouring the Hutu majority and then with the full transfer of power at independence, his opportunities diminished. He had basic schooling but was now not eligible for further education. Emmanuel went to work as a market trader and, with slick patter and hard work, he earned well. When he had saved enough, he bought a single-speed bicycle and that was what he raced on until a Kigali entrepreneur, Jacques Rusirare, the owner of Ameki Color, Rwanda's answer to the paint company Dulux, stepped in and paid for a proper racing bike. It was a royal-blue Benotto, which had long ago come out of their factory in Turin. Emmanuel was practically unbeatable in Rwanda through the late nineteen-seventies and much of the eighties too, a multiple winner of the Tour de l'Est and Ascension des Mille Collines. He trained by riding with Adrien's father buzzing alongside him on a motorbike. He competed in Burundi, Tanzania and, at the age of thirty-five, in Kenya at the 1987 All-Africa Games, but it was hard not to think that he was born a generation too soon.

In early 1987, as Emmanuel's career was winding down, his sister gave birth to her tenth child on a farm a few miles outside of Rwamagana. It was a boy and his Muslim parents named him Niyonshuti (inherited family surnames are not used in the country); it roughly translates as: 'He' – meaning God – 'is the friend.' Later he would be given the Western first name of Adrien. They didn't really call him either of those, though. As the last born – his eldest siblings were already in their late twenties – he was spoiled, so they took to calling him 'Machoncho' after a Burundian folk song about an indulged child. And his mother teasingly gave him the nickname 'Dessert'. 'After all of them you have the dessert, which is the special one,' she explained to me. 'And he turned out to be the special one.'

Adrien never saw his uncle compete, but all the old-timers at cycle events in Rwanda today agree there are uncanny similarities between the two of them. Emmanuel had a quiet humility and generosity off the bicycle, but he showed little compassion when he was riding. Adrien has that, too. Both were natural leaders. But mostly Adrien has inherited his uncle's fierce sporting intelligence. Cycling can sometimes seem a simple, repetitive sport but in any race there is intense strategising. The ability to apportion your efforts is a defining characteristic of successful riders; Emmanuel and Adrien were without peer in Rwanda in this regard. They might not be the most powerful riders in a race, but they were the smartest and they found a way to win.

Adrien's birth and his uncle's declining days – as well as the construction of a new network of excellent roads, subcontracted by the government to a Chinese company – coincided with the Rwandan cycling federation organising longer races at home. In 1988, it staged a forerunner for the Tour of Rwanda, inviting six-rider squads from Emmanuel Turatsinze's Rwamagana team, François Rudahunga's Butare and Emmanuel Mayaka's Ciné Elmay, plus a selection of riders from the rest of the country; around fifty in total, all Rwandan. It was a haphazard event that mostly stuck to the western highlands, but there was enough take-up to run a more refined version of it in 1989 and invite guests. The inaugural Tour du Rwanda (the French title was preferred in those days) had three select teams from Rwanda competing against the national outfits from Kenya, Uganda, Burundi, Tanzania and Zaire (now the Democratic Republic of Congo, as it has been known since 1997). The standard of racing was wildly variable but local riders dominated and the outstanding performer was one of Mayaka's young protégés from Kigali, Omar Masumbuko. He won the Tour du Rwanda again in 1990, too.

Rwandan society, however, was rapidly disintegrating. The

1990 Tour was severely abridged because of political instability across the country. Around a million Rwandan Tutsis were living outside its borders, most in Uganda, and a small number of these formed a modest rebel force called the Rwandan Patriotic Front (RPF). On 1 October, around fifty men from the RPF's armed division, the Rwandan Patriotic Army, crossed the border into a national park in north-east Rwanda. They were well-drilled – in Uganda, many had helped Yoweri Museveni defeat President Milton Obote's dictatorship in 1985 – but at this stage they did not present a significant threat to the Rwandan government, which had been led since 1975 by Juvénal Habyarimana, a Hutu. Their actions were, nevertheless, an ideal pretext for Habyarimana and his party, the National Revolutionary Movement for Development (MRND), to do some housekeeping they had been in mind to do anyway. Lists of 'enemies' – prosperous Tutsis and sympathetic Hutus – had already been prepared and soon almost 10,000 Rwandans were arrested. In mid-October 1990, officials in a village near Gisenyi incited Hutus to attack their Tutsi neighbours by spreading a rumour that a local dignitary called Colonel Serubuga had been killed. The massacre in Kibilira, in which 350 died, was a low-level precursor of what was to come.

The conflict escalated in 1991, with a bolstered RPF making deeper incursions in northern Rwanda and Hutu leaders never missing an opportunity to drum up fear and insecurity among the mass population. Roadblocks clogged the country and travel was restricted. There would be no more Tours du Rwanda for a while. There was, however, an unexpected break in the growing tumult: Rwanda was asked to submit a team for the 1992 Olympics in Barcelona, including a complement for the men's cycling road race.

In recent years, Hutus had been favoured in the national

team; in fact, for the 1991 All-Africa Games in Egypt, two Tutsi riders were stripped of their places because of their ethnicity. That might have happened again had it not been for a surprising political development. Under pressure from aid donors in Europe and North America, who supplied more than half Rwanda's annual budget, Habyarimana announced in June 1990 that the country's totalitarian system – in the most recent election, in 1988, he had polled ninety-nine per cent – would now be open to other parties. The summer of 1991 saw the creation of more than ten new opposition parties, one of which, the Liberal Party, had a significant Tutsi membership.

Rwanda, suddenly in a brief window of democracy, would now send its best four riders to the Olympics. These were a Hutu, the two-time Tour winner Omar Masumbuko; and three Tutsis: Faustin Mparabanyi, a climber from Kigali; and a pair from Butare, all-rounder Emmanuel Nkurunziza and sprinter Alphonse Nshimiyiama, who was effectively paid to cycle by a French company that exported green beans. In the event only three of them made the selection, as it emerged that Omar had been born in Burundi. For Emmanuel and Alphonse, going to Spain was their first time out of the country; Faustin had previously been to Kenya. At the opening ceremony in Barcelona, they marched as part of Rwanda's largest-ever delegation – ten athletes – and watched slack-jawed as a disabled archer lit the cauldron with a flaming arrow. Everyone was talking about a group of Americans known as the Dream Team – the giants they called Jordan, Magic and Bird – but the Rwandans never fully understood the fuss.

The cyclists were all in their early twenties, young and single, but mostly they kept to themselves in the Olympic Village or went for walks along the beach, the first time they had seen the sea. On the middle Sunday of the Games, 2 August, they lined up with 151 other competitors, including a twenty-year-old American called Lance Armstrong, but they hadn't heard of him either. They looked at the machines around them and could hardly believe such technology existed: 'Our bikes must be twice as heavy!' they agreed. Still, they believed they had prepared well and were determined not to be intimidated. The Rwandans stayed with the main pack for the first hour, even the second, but they became tired and no one had thought to bring drinks or food to replace their energy. Everyone else had a support team to help them if they had mechanical glitches, but the three of them were on their own. After nine laps around the villages of Sant Sadurní d'Anoia, in Catalonia's cava district, they pulled out of the race.

It turned out, then, that Adrien was neither the first Rwandan cyclist to compete in the Olympics, nor even the first to ride alongside Lance Armstrong. 'We really thought it was the start of something,' said Faustin Mparabanyi. 'We would go home and come back for the next Olympics faster and better prepared.' They could not know that the three of them would never race together again.

2
ONE HUNDRED DAYS

On the evening of 6 April 1994, a Wednesday, just before 8.20 p.m., a Falcon 50 jet carrying President Habyarimana – and the new president of Burundi, Cyprien Ntaryamira, also a Hutu – was blasted out of the sky on approach to Kigali airport. A hot red flash clipped one of the wings, another spiralled into the tail, and the plane nosedived into Habyarimana's own back garden at the presidential palace, where it exploded. No one survived. It would be confirmed only in 2012 that the Russian-made surface-to-air missiles were launched from a nearby military barracks, which were manned by Habyarimana's forces, including the Presidential Guard, and were not fired by rebels from the Rwandan Patriotic Front, as was long claimed.

Even at the time, two things were clear to most Rwandans: first, if the president could be killed, no one was safe; and second, the darkest fears of Tutsis were set to be realised. The omens had been stacking up. The intensity of the attacks in 1959, 1962, 1964, 1973 and 1992 had steadily ratcheted up and with it the pliancy of the Hutu population to incendiary rhetoric. Hutu hardliners had been predicting an apocalypse for more than a year: not whispering it, but telling anyone who would listen. Armaments had been arriving from France; machetes – in extraordinary quantities, more than half a million – from China. Critics of Habyarimana had a nasty habit of slipping under the wheels of passing motor cars. Bands of youths and football thugs had been corralled into ramshackle militias, the most prominent of which was known as the *interahamwe*: 'those who attack together'. That there was a list of prominent Tutsis who were to be assassinated first was an open secret. When the radio stations announced on the evening of 6 April that everyone should stay in their homes, some Tutsis decided to do the exact opposite. They had to run.

Almost two decades on, Faustin Mparabanyi still had the indeterminate age of many Rwandans: there wasn't a line on his face or any trace of grey in his tidy buzzcut. He had the comfy paunch that many former cyclists develop when they are no longer burning many thousands of calories every day. It turned out he was born in 1968, so he was twenty-six at the beginning of the genocide and approaching his peak as a cyclist. He did not say that he was a Tutsi, just that he was 'among the side that was hunted'.

Faustin began moving the morning after Habyarimana's plane went down, grabbing his savings and whatever food he could stash in his pockets. It would be three months before he returned to his home in the south of Kigali. He had national renown because of his cycling – 'Everyone knew Mparabanyi,' he noted, not boastfully – and with his prize money, supplemented by work as a driver for the Ministry of Agriculture, he was by no means rich, but certainly comfortable. He did not yet have a wife or children to protect. No question, he would be a target. The killing started immediately, but initially, at least in Kigali, the victims were those who might be able to prevent it: the Hutu prime minister, Agathe Uwilingiyimana, was murdered on 7 April, followed by ten United Nations peacekeepers from Belgium. The attacks would then widen and deepen ominously. Two days later, *interahamwe* militia hacked down – they didn't want to waste bullets – more than a hundred Tutsis sheltering in a Polish Pallottine mission church in the district of Gikondo.

Faustin wondered if a Hutu friend might hide him for a few days and his first thought was his Ciné Elmay team-mate, Omar Masumbuko. The two of them were as close as brothers: they rode together most days and when they had to stay overnight they would often share a bed. Faustin travelled at night to Omar's house, but when he arrived it was obvious that he would not be safe. Omar's younger brother, also a cyclist, was determined to kill Faustin, who would have been a prominent Tutsi scalp. He was already stockpiling grenades for the job. When Omar showed Faustin the munitions stash, Faustin was shocked. Faustin and the brother had often ridden together – perhaps he'd just pushed him too hard, maybe he was jealous. Omar told Faustin what he knew about local roadblocks and they embraced affectionately. They would never see each other alive again.

The first wave of killings began to gain momentum. On the afternoon of 8 April, a gang of around fifty men, soldiers with guns and *interahamwe* twirling gleaming new machetes, arrived at the house of Anselme Sakumi in Nyamirambo, the Muslim district of Kigali. Sakumi's name was distinctive even to Rwandan ears – it actually means 'four o'clock' – and he was the vice-president of the cycling federation. He also owned the only factory in the country that made bicycles. He started selling imported Raleighs and distributing Singer sewing machines in the late seventies, but by the time of the genocide Sakumi was manufacturing the steel frames and wheels on site; everything in fact apart from the handlebars, chains and tyres. The factory employed fifty Rwandans and made around 5,000 bicycles a year in whatever colour the customer desired, echoing Henry Ford, so long as it was black. Sakumi was known for treating his employees well: at lunchtime every day, they would each be given a cup of milk. The family, which was Tutsi, was prosperous: the children went to good schools and they even went on vacations. 'By the time they killed him, he was a big man,' said Sakumi's son, Serge Rusagara.

Sakumi's death was brutal, if mercifully quick. A soldier ordered him out of his house with his wife, two daughters and four sons. There was a short conversation and at 4.10 p.m. the soldier shot him in the head. His family scrambled; the mother went in one direction, pursued by *interahamwe*, and the children ran the other way to escape into their neighbour's garden. 'It's a miracle,' said Serge, who was fourteen at the time, the oldest of the boys. 'People were shooting after us: guh-guh-guh-guh' – he mimes rifle fire, flicking up the grass around their feet – 'and you can't believe you were not caught by one of the bullets.' They returned to the house later that night, when they were sure their attackers would have disbanded. They found the house looted and their mother lying dead on the lawn, her body mangled with gunshots and machete blows. There was no time to bury her; they had to keep moving.

In Rwamagana, thirty miles east of Kigali, the violence was even more rampant. On 11 April, Adrien Niyonshuti's uncle Emmanuel Turatsinze left his home to seek out places to hide his wife and five children, plus assorted relatives, perhaps twenty family members. When he returned later that same day, he found them all murdered, brutally executed by their Hutu neighbours. Until this point, Emmanuel had imagined that only men would be targeted, but it was an early indication that this would be an extermination unlike anything seen in Rwanda. Tutsis were reviled simply as *inyenzi* or 'cockroaches' – a name, which as guerrilla fighters, they had appropriated to describe their resilience – and the Hutu Power leaders, who were now running the country, demanded they be stamped out. To Hutu citizens, these instructions were effectively the law of the land, their patriotic duty. Hutus who didn't comply were liable to be targeted themselves, but even with the risks some did refuse to obey and many 'moderate' Hutus died alongside the Tutsis.

Emmanuel, believing he might find protection from the Church, sought refuge in a compound for Roman Catholic priests called St Eloise, on Rwamagana's main street. That places of worship should be havens from attack was another principle that would be desecrated by the 1994 genocide. In many instances, the priests colluded with the *interahamwe* and their churches became rounding-up points for the death squads. But in Rwamagana there was no meek surrender, despite the Hutus' vast superiority in numbers and firepower. With only traditional weapons, such as spears and arrows, St Eloise became a pocket of fierce resistance. Battle raged for days, the building shelled with rifle fire and grenades. A key vantage point was a water tower, a hexagonal structure with a ladder up the side, maybe five metres off the ground; a soldier was stationed on the top permanently, shooting at anyone who tried to enter or leave St Eloise. Finally, according to legend, Emmanuel lost patience and broke cover. Moving swiftly, he took aim with a bow and arrow and picked off the soldier on the tower with one shot. It was a rare moment of empowerment for the Tutsis inside.

Outside of town, Adrien's parents had a choice to make. His father, a well-regarded tailor and Muslim *imam*, wanted them to leave their farm for Adrien's grandmother's house on the other side of Rwamagana. His mother, however, was determined to stay and protect their property. Business was good for her husband, his suits were much coveted in Kigali, and the farm had cows and goats, as well as banana trees and small plots of sweet potatoes and beans. The decision was taken for them when the *interahamwe* arrived, a week after Habyarimana's plane was shot down. One of Adrien's older brothers created a rudimentary firework from a canister, matches and some bicycle spokes. When the militia approached, he exploded it and the attackers fled, convinced that the family was armed. The stunt would not provide long-term relief, but it gave them a window to escape. To increase their chances of survival, Adrien's parents split the family up: Adrien, who had just turned seven, would stay with his parents, and try to find refuge in the town; the older children would travel through the bush to reach their grandmother's house.

Adrien's father decided to call in a favour. A couple of years before, when the rebel Rwandan Patriotic Front had raided north-east Rwanda, many Hutus in that area were forced to scatter and resettle. Among these new homeless was another family of Muslims, whom Adrien's parents had taken in until they had resettled in Rwamagana. Perhaps they would help? (Muslims, it is widely recognised, were alone among Rwanda's religious communities in not being swept along with the genocidal torrent for the most part.) Adrien followed his parents across the valley, picking their way through a rice plantation. At some point, he cut a deep gash in his leg, but he hardly even noticed until later. When they reached town they rapped on the door of their friends. The father, Segisekure, had recently died, but his wife ushered them briskly into the house. Even though one of her sons, Hassan, was a local *interahamwe* leader now, she assured them that he would not harm them. They were shown to a small room at the back of the house, where there were perhaps fifteen other Tutsis hiding. Adrien's parents knew most of them – they were neighbours mainly, including a well-to-do businessman called Modeste – but it was so packed in the room that it was hard to recognise everyone. They were scared but silent: no one left the room, no one spoke. All of them had surrendered the money they had to Segisekure's wife in return for protection.

Adrien, always an obedient child, knew he had to be quiet, but he wasn't exactly sure why. April is the middle of a wet season in in Rwanda and day after day they listened to rain rasping on the corrugated metal roof. Every so often, they would be brought a little water and perhaps some beans and bananas, but they were constantly hungry. Usually his parents would pray five times a day, but now their heads were bowed constantly, their lips moving soundlessly. There were no windows but they tried to construct narratives from the noises they heard outside. As the days went on, all they could hear was screaming, the sound of death. Finally, after almost a week in the room, the ruckus became closer and louder. Adrien's family suspected that the *interahamwe* had known their whereabouts all along, but wanted to see how much money they could extract first. It was just before noon on 19 April when they heard shouts, clearly audible in the room, 'Let's burn them alive!'

The Tutsis were called out to the street. They had not left the room for a week, so when they emerged it took a few seconds for their eyes to become accustomed to the glare. Slowly the baying mob was revealed in front of them, perhaps 200-strong. They carried jerry cans full of petrol and machetes stained with blood. They wanted Modeste first. But just at this moment, as if summoned by silent entreaty, rain began to fall. Within seconds it was a wild deluge, so hard that it felt like it must be coming from a special place. The *interahamwe* bolted for cover and when the storm eventually abated, news arrived that the RPF, sweeping in from the north-east, had reached the edge of Rwamagana. The *interahamwe* went off to investigate; they would return to Segisekure's house the next day.

Adrien and his parents went back to the windowless room; there was nowhere else to go. But, unbeknown to them, a defining swing was taking place. The RPF rebels – known as *Inkotanyi* or 'The Invincible' – numbered only 20,000 soldiers, but, led by their military commander Paul Kagame, they were scoring spectacular successes over a national army more than twice their size. Rwamagana was – in strictly relative terms – fortunate in its proximity to the Ugandan border. While the RPF would not stop the killing in Butare and Kigali until early July, Rwamagana was liberated on 20 April, just two weeks after Habyarimana's plane was shot down. The *interahamwe* did return to Segisekure's house the following day, but now they had a choice: stay and slaughter the *inyenzi* and probably die themselves, or take their extermination plans to the next district. They decided to run. They had killed 4,195 from the town's total population of 37,147.

Emmanuel had also survived. He had eventually been forced to leave St Eloise; the *interahamwe* couldn't break the resistance there, neither could the national army, but eventually the Presidential Guard arrived and the Tutsi stragglers were routed. Emmanuel escaped into the bush; he was followed and caught, his back and legs sliced open with machetes and battered with clubs. Somehow he didn't die, and he managed to crawl to the advancing RPF army. Almost everyone else in Adrien's immediate family was killed: he lost five brothers and a sister, all murdered at his grandmother's house. After the genocide, more than forty of his relatives were found on the land there, tossed in a pit that was used for fermenting bananas to make beer.

One of the other survivors in Adrien's family was his eldest sister, Jeanne Nyirantagorama, who was thirty-four when the genocide began. She lived in Kigali with her husband and two children, and was more than eight months pregnant with their third. In early April, already fearing the worst, Jeanne sent her elder daughter to stay with Emmanuel and she was slaughtered along with his family. When the attacks started in the capital, Jeanne was hunted down to an abandoned coffee plantation. She ran a small general store and her assailants included her Hutu employees and even a young man to whom she was godmother. They slashed at her with machetes and her godson attempted to pierce her womb with a spear. She felt the moment when her foetus died inside her. Jeanne's three-year-old son was strapped to her back and received a vicious crack to the skull. Eventually, they assumed Jeanne was dead and left her.

Hearing the details of Jeanne's story, which she told meticulously over the course of six hours one afternoon, it was almost impossible to believe that she could be sat in front of me. After eight months in a Red Cross hospital, she moved back to Rwamagana – her husband had been killed in a separate attack in Kigali – and she now ran a dairy store that sold hot and room-temperature milk and served the greasy, delicious beignets that Rwandans adore. Her hair covered the worst of her scars and a long dress hid most of the rest, although occasionally I caught a glimpse of a livid pink slash on the left side of her neck or her right arm. Her son Jean-Baptiste made it through the genocide, too; he was just about to finish high school.

Every time a customer entered the milk bar, Jeanne would stop and serve them. When they left, which might be half an hour later – it was a comfortable place to stick around – she would pick up her story exactly where she had left off. During one of these breaks a well-dressed man in his fifties walked in, ordered warm milk and a beignet. He ate slowly and they gossiped, in a jumble of Kinyarwanda and French, about local matters; in particular, a loan that shopkeepers had taken out to pay for a stretch of pavement outside the store. Wiping the crumbs from his beard, he stood up, '*Merci! Bonne journée!*' Only when he left did Jeanne's face drop.

'That man played a big role in the genocide in Rwamagana,' she said, betraying no emotion. 'He was a judge, so he might not have carried a machete or wielded a *masu*' – a studded club – 'but he knew everything that happened here. He was in prison for about seven years.'

My expression must have betrayed my shock. 'Are you surprised that someone could have played such a role and still buy something here?' Jeanne asked.

I nodded.

'What I need is money. How can I survive if I don't welcome any person to buy things? With time, we have managed to reconcile. We do not have any other choice. We've built a mechanism to cope with the situation.'

Such is the pragmatism that has become a fact of life for many Rwandans.

Back in Kigali, in late April of 1994, Faustin Mparabanyi, having failed to find sanctuary with his team-mate Omar Masumbuko, decided to flee the city for Butare. Again, the decision was really made for him: one day, he was hiding near his house when he saw a group of young Hutu men break in and loot his property. He had hidden his bicycle, the most valuable object he owned, under sackcloth in the kitchen, which, as in many Rwandan houses, was in a separate building. As the thieves wheeled it away, they laughed: 'I'd like to see Mparabanyi win races now.' Faustin believed that Butare might be safer: it was in the only province in Rwanda with a Tutsi governor and, because of the university and the Liberal Party, which was based there, the city had become the intellectual centre of the anti-Power movement. Besides, perhaps his friends from the Olympic team, Alphonse and Emmanuel, could look after him there.

Faustin was right about Butare, but only initially. For the first couple of weeks, reaction in the town had been measured and the violence sporadic. Then on 20 April the governor, Jean-Baptiste Habyarimana, who shared his second name with the former president, was deposed and murdered shortly afterwards. It was another landmark moment: Tutsis now understood that Hutus were truly intent on their complete annihilation. Jean-Baptiste Habyarimana was replaced with a hardliner from the army called Colonel Tharcisse Muvunyi; paramilitary units were sent from Kigali and they worked fast to make up for lost time. In the end, 220,000 Tutsis and sympathetic Hutus were killed in Butare, the most of any prefecture. Faustin, however, had no inkling of what was happening as he made his way there from Kigali.

Faustin travelled at night, under cover of darkness, dressed as a woman or a Muslim to avoid detection. All he had to eat now was sugar, which he would water down into a sludge. Sometimes he went four straight days without food. His weight crashed from sixty-four kilograms before the genocide to thirty-seven. 'But still I was strong,' he insisted. 'If you ran after me, I would run faster than you.'

From someone he met on his journey, Faustin had an update on his beloved bike. The thieves who took it offered it to a soldier, in return for easing their path through the roadblocks that restricted travel for Tutsi and Hutu alike. They put it in a Toyota Stout pick-up with looted goods, but they were stopped at Giticyinyoni on the southern fringes of Kigali and confronted by Omar Masumbuko, who happened to be manning the barrier. There were only six of these bicycles in the country, donated by a French cooperative to the 1992 Olympic cyclists. 'I know this bicycle,' Omar said. He confiscated it from the men and promised he would return it to Faustin if he was still alive.

Faustin, meanwhile, had reached the edges of Butare. Here, he was stopped by a roadblock. 'Are you a Tutsi?' the men guarding it demanded. He didn't answer, unprepared to lie and knowing that if he replied in the affirmative he would be killed. The soldiers pushed him around and it soon became violent. One, a dark-skinned Hutu from Gisenyi, knocked him to the ground with the butt of a rifle and pushed hard with his boot on the side of Faustin's head. Faustin felt his ear fill with blood – to this day, he is largely deaf on that side – and he thought his eyes might pop. Still, 'Are you a Tutsi?' A little louder, 'Are you a Tutsi?'

The soldier told Faustin that, as soon as his shift finished, he would take him to some nearby woods where they were collecting bodies and kill him there. But he did not want to leave his position just yet. At that moment, a young Hutu man passed by and recognised Faustin. The Hutu was a friend of Alphonse, Faustin's team-mate at the Olympics, and he had seen pictures of them together at Alphonse's house. The young man's father was a local Hutu Power leader and he decided to try to strike a deal with the soldier: how much for Faustin's life? They agreed on a sum – Faustin never found out how much – and the Hutu disappeared to find the money. When he returned the soldier put the cash in his pocket and said, 'It doesn't matter. Someone else will kill him anyway.'

Faustin had been planning to go to Alphonse's house, but the young Hutu man warned him of the chaos in Butare. If he'd not saved his life before, he surely did now. Faustin, who had false papers for Zaire, went instead to Gikongoro, fifteen miles outside Butare on the road to the border; there, he had a friend called Filogene who was a head teacher. He knew he could rest a little before going on to the border. He passed through acres of coffee trees, arriving the night of 24 May, but instead of continuing his journey, Filogene convinced him to stay. He cleared a room, telling his wife that he wanted to use it as a study and each night he would leave food outside the door. Faustin remained hidden until the RPF finally liberated the south of the country, more than a month later.

In Kigali, Anselme Sakumi's children had found their way to the Hôtel des Mille Collines, famously recreated in the 2004 film as Hôtel Rwanda. On screen, Paul Rusesabagina, a hotel manager, was portrayed by the American actor Don Cheadle. He was the good Hutu: the man who single-handedly saved 1,200 Tutsis with just a well-stocked bar and a fax machine (and was subsequently acclaimed with a clutch of humanitarian prizes). The story is a compelling one and it was certainly true that many Tutsis found protection in the hotel, which at the time was the most prestigious in Kigali, charging $125 a night. Hutu Power leaders were known to have dropped off their Tutsi wives and even their mothers with Rusesabagina, while army commanders were kept docile with cigars and whisky.

Serge, the oldest boy, remembered there were about twenty people crammed into each bedroom, easily a thousand refugees in all. His party was eleven – they had picked up some cousins along the way – ranging from teenagers to a three-year-old. They would collect water from the swimming pool and there was a small supply of sweet potatoes and rice. All phone lines had been severed, but a fax machine still worked and was being used to contact the United Nations, even President Bill Clinton in Washington, DC. Serge's family remained safe until they could be evacuated deep into an RPF-controlled zone and then on to Burundi. Still, he had mixed feelings about his stay at the hotel and disputed the idea that it was a haven of sanity in a crazy country. He claimed that all 'guests' at the hotel were expected to hand over whatever money and assets they had and, as these were the most prosperous Tutsis, this made Mille Collines a lucrative operation. Later, as the RPF laid siege to the capital, the hotel became a bargaining chip. The Tutsis detained there could have been killed in a moment, but it made sense to keep them alive while the rebels held Hutu hostages in a football stadium across town.

'Let me tell you, there's nothing true about that film,' Serge told me, as we walked around his father's abandoned bicycle factory one morning. The factory had been comprehensively ransacked during the genocide: every piece of stock taken – even machines that were bolted to the floor were somehow carried out. 'Making money is one thing, but making money from the death of people . . . . Every opportunity I have to say Paul Rusesabagina is not telling the truth, I'll say it – because he's not. When I look at that movie and remember what really happened, I feel a serious pain.'

Serge was now in his early thirties and worked part time with the national cycling federation – as did Faustin. In his bright purple polo shirt, designer shades and with his Mercedes parked outside, he was the picture of modern, affluent Rwanda. His day job was fixing computer systems, a booming profession in the country these days. No one made bicycles any more as his father once had; in fact, there was not a single bicycle shop in the whole of Rwanda. Serge did not ride himself, but he still felt an affinity for bicycles that many Rwandans had – and for him it was personal, too. 'The bike is what made our family: why should we abandon it?' he said. 'My father started something with his bikes and with the cycling federation, he wanted to succeed, even if he died without getting it to the level he wanted to. But he left me a task to finish, to accomplish for him. It's like a blood thing that still goes on.'

In the aftermath of the genocide, cycling was unsurprisingly not a priority. When representatives from the World Bank visited Rwanda in 1995, they declared it the poorest country on the globe; the word they used, clinically, was 'nonviable'. The population had been literally decimated in the course of three months: at least 800,000 killed from a population of eight million. That was five and a half deaths every minute for one hundred days. This did not take into account women who were raped or infected with HIV or those, like Adrien's sister Jeanne, who suffered devastating personal injuries.

The project to rebuild the country was immense. There was no infrastructure, few schools and barely any hospitals to start with. Rivers were clogged with bodies and the *génocidaires* – the French word, widely used in Rwanda, to describe the perpetrators – who remained in the country were either on the loose or held in prisons filled far beyond capacity. At one point 130,000 suspects were stuffed into institutions designed to incarcerate 12,000. Hundreds of thousands of Hutus had fled the country for Zaire, chased out by the arrival of the RPF and fearing reprisals. Even those who had not committed crimes left in swarms, convinced by the guilty that they would be blamed if they stuck around. A word often used to describe the country at this time was 'impossible'.

Every Rwandan needed to adapt to new personal

circumstances. Faustin returned to Kigali to find that his entire family had been killed, his mother and father, all his brothers and sisters. His friends had disappeared, either dead or in exile. Overnight, he went from being a bachelor to being the custodian of six children under the age of ten, four from an older brother and two from his sister. In 1996, he married, inheriting two nieces that his new wife was caring for; they would later have two children, bringing the total to ten. Many people in Rwanda have an equivalent genocide family of their own.

In Rwamagana, Adrien's parents decided they would move closer to town. They had returned to their farm and found it destroyed; it was in a remote spot and they feared for their safety if they stayed. 'Bad people lived in that area, wicked people,' said Jeanne. 'They could come and kill you and the first anyone would know about it was when it was too late. We don't trust them, we're afraid of them. They have missed the opportunity to kill you that time, but if they have another chance they will try to do it again.'

There was a psychological toll to deal with, too. When they had been evacuated to an RPF safe zone, Adrien and his parents had passed ten miles along the main road to Kayonza and seen scores of Tutsi bodies, lying mangled in heaps. Dirty red soil stained with dirty red blood. Adrien said little at the time, and he still does not say very much about it now, but it was clear that the memories remain. At the 2011 Tour of Rwanda, the race went past his grandmother's house and he admitted that he pedalled a little harder then, so he didn't have to think about it. On another day, I saw him after he had fallen off his bike; his shoulder was badly scuffed and he had abrasions all down his side. It was nasty, but fairly typical for a professional cyclist; riders couldn't last a day in the peloton if they were scared of crashing. Yet he looked badly shaken. 'When I saw the blood on the tarmac, it reminded me of the genocide and how I saw the blood in the water, in the rivers, on the roads,' he said. 'I don't like this stuff. I told my mind, "I don't have to think like that." Because if you think like that, you go crazy. You can't think like that every time you see blood.'

His uncle Emmanuel Turatsinze was particularly devastated. He had severe wounds from the genocide, but he refused to have them treated. He met a woman and remarried, but when their daughter was born disabled it seemed to plunge him even deeper into depression. He owned a cabaret: a one-room shop that during the day sold groceries, household and hardware items and at night became a casual drinking den. After 1994, he could often be found with a Primus beer or a cup of the Ugandan moonshine called *waragi* in his hand; 'getting drunk on painful memories', in Jeanne's words. His health deteriorated fast.

Towards the end of Emmanuel's life, the government, now led by the RPF general Paul Kagame, convened *gacaca* courts around the country. Faced with overflowing prisons and an absence of judges and lawyers, but no shortage of accused parties, these traditional courts were viewed as a fast way to administer rudimentary justice. Beginning in the spring of 2002, the citizens of a village or town would gather – *gacaca* means 'the flattened grass under the elders' tree' – and anyone suspected of crimes during the genocide could be tried. *Gacaca* could provide swift, uncompromising verdicts and, in many cases, the trials allowed Rwandans to fully understand what happened in 1994. But there were also frequent miscarriages of justice. Initially at least, genocide survivors were often afraid to speak out, and a disturbing number were intimidated or even murdered before they would testify. Emmanuel, however, was fearless. Perhaps because he lived in town, rather than on a remote farm, maybe because he felt he had nothing left to lose, he would stand up to anyone. It became widely believed that he had been bewitched, which only made him more intimidating.

Emmanuel had two more children, a boy and another girl, but died eventually in 2004. Some say that his wounds from the genocide killed him, others that his liver finally packed in. More than one person I spoke to said that he died of despair.

Rwandans did return to their bicycles. Not long after coming back to Kigali, Faustin was walking in the centre of town when he spotted his bike – the one that had been looted during the genocide – being worked on by a street mechanic. It was bashed and scraped, but it was unmistakably his. He tried to take it back, but the mechanic pleaded with him to speak with the RPF soldier who had brought it in. At the barracks down the road, Faustin pieced together the journey it had been on: Omar Masumbuko had fled with it to eastern Zaire, but at some point in the refugee camps the bike had been taken from him. When the Rwandan Hutus began to file back from exile, it was confiscated by the RPF and the soldier had bought it just a few days before. He was reluctant to hand his new bicycle over – property post-1994 was a somewhat nebulous concept – but Faustin produced a photograph of him riding it before the genocide, so that settled the matter. As he pedalled home, Faustin felt a preternatural calmness fall over him. 'I realised I'd forgiven all those people who killed because what they had done – their point, their goal – has never been attained,' he said. His eyes now glistened with tears. 'If this bicycle can go all that way and come back to me maybe even those people they killed are somewhere happy and not suffering.'

The return of Faustin's bike encouraged him to start racing again. Initially he didn't have much competition. Omar remained in Zaire; he would eventually return to Rwanda and was jailed as a *génocidaire*. He fell sick in an overcrowded prison and died in the Kigali Hospital Centre in 2001; Faustin took Omar's body to his home village for burial. Faustin's team-mate Alphonse had been killed in Butare and Emmanuel Nkurunziza, the other member of the Olympic trio, had survived the genocide by escaping to Zaire; he later moved to Kenya and then Saudi Arabia. The rest of the Rwandan cycling scene was obliterated. Ferdinand Sebera, another strong rider before 1994, had been a councillor for Habyarimana's MRND party and was now in jail. Celestin Ndengeyingoma, the winner of the forerunner for the Tour du Rwanda in 1988, had become an enthusiastic member of the *interahamwe*, but had died when he tossed a grenade at a group of Tutsis and it rebounded off a banana tree and detonated next to him. As Faustin related this information, he tried, and failed, to suppress the faintest smirk.

It is rarely straightforward finding out the fates of individuals during the genocide. With the veteran cyclist François Rudahunga, outside the primary school in Butare, I tried to discover exactly what happened to Alphonse, who had lived nearby. 'I last saw him in Butare at the beginning of 1994,' François replied. Was he killed during the genocide? 'I don't know exactly what happened to him.' Was he Hutu or Tutsi? 'I don't know.' François was not exactly the forgetful type. He could remember the position he finished in Kigali–Rusumo, his first long race, in 1979 (ninth); the exact price of his first bicycle (9,500 francs, paid in three, monthly instalments); and the date he raced in the All-Africa Games (2 August 1987). The truth had to emerge slowly. When I originally asked Adrien's mother of the name of the Muslim family that helped them, she said, 'I don't remember.' That was a response you heard often.

Led by Faustin, parts of bikes were slowly salvaged and

the materials were pooled to kit out about two-dozen racing bicycles. No one had the money to buy them, so they would just be handed out to any rider who showed promise. By 2001, there was enough enthusiasm to restart the Tour of Rwanda. Faustin recovered his form well enough and was selected for the All-Africa Games in Harare in 1995 and Johannesburg in 1999. His career ended shortly afterwards when a motorcycle outrider was clearing the course and managed to careen into him, smashing his ankle. It is a tradition in Rwandan cycling that when you finish racing you bequeath your bicycle to the next generation: Faustin honoured that and the bike that was taken from his home during the genocide and miraculously recovered had now been given to a talented young man from Kigali called Hassan Rukundo. He is Omar Masumbuko's son.

Before he died, Emmanuel passed on his steel Benotto frame to his nephew Adrien. It had old-fashioned shifters on the frame, rather than on the drop handlebars, but it was light and responsive. Adrien began to cycle seriously when he went to secondary school in Kigali; he wasn't particularly academic, but give him anything electronic and he could fix it or recondition it, so he was sent to a technical college in Nyarutarama. From his cousin's house in Kicukiro, it was a round-trip of ten miles every day, and at weekends he would cycle home to his parents in Rwamagana. He also played football – 'I was number two, sometimes number eight', meaning right-back or right midfield – and some of his friends now turn out in the top league in Rwanda. But Adrien preferred to cycle; when he was a teenager, he had headaches, but when he rode his bike they disappeared.

When Adrien was fourteen, he told his uncle that he wanted to be a cyclist, just like him. Emmanuel's advice was succinct: 'If you want to do cycling, don't waste your time. You have to focus your life on it completely. And don't drink beer.' He told him where to ride and how to build up his endurance. Before Emmanuel died, he saw Adrien compete against the best riders in Rwanda in the 100-mile, single-day Tour of Kigali in 2003. Adrien was sixteen and his training amounted mostly to his school run; still, he held his own for more than half the race before cramping up with dehydration. He practically fell off the bike while still pedalling. His older brother, Abdul-Wahab Twahirwa, one of three surviving siblings, took him to hospital and bought him an orange juice. 'He's going to be okay,' pronounced Emmanuel, and it was obvious that the verdict related to more than Adrien's immediate medical condition.

In 2004, now seventeen, Adrien signed up for the Tour of Rwanda. He told his parents only the day before, because they had been alarmed by his visit to the hospital. They were not happy. They thought he should wait until he was at least eighteen. He should concentrate on his studies, not go off riding his bike round the country for a week. Abdul-Wahab asked him if he had trained this time and Adrien admitted that no, he hadn't. Adrien asked if he could borrow his brother's bike, a smart aluminium Trek painted runny-egg yellow that Abdul-Wahab – a long-distance truck driver – had brought back from Tanzania, but its gears were set up for the flatlands of the Eastern Province, not the hills that Adrien would be racing over. So he would compete on his uncle's twenty-five-year-old Benotto.

After the first day of the Tour, it seemed that his parents, his brother, everyone was right. It was a long, punishing stage from Kigali to Gisenyi and Adrien was left, in his words, 'broken'. His fellow competitors were mostly gnarled bicycle-taxi riders a decade older than him who spent their days hauling hundreds of kilos of cargo and passengers up the same hills; it was not easy for them, but at least they knew what to expect. Adrien was skinny but not in a way that suggested prime condition, more that he might need a good meal. When he arrived in Gisenyi, he passed out for two hours flat on his back on a beach beside Lake Kivu, flies buzzing around him. But he raced again the next day, and felt stronger as the week progressed. When the race returned to Kigali he crossed the line sixth overall. 'Not bad,' his brother conceded. 'Not bad at all.'

Later that year, Abdul-Wahab died – probably tuberculosis, though no one knows for sure – and Adrien inherited his bike. He fixed the gears and rode the 2005 Tour of Rwanda, finishing seventh this time. His family were still not convinced. 'I used to see it as a waste of time,' said his mother. 'I'd say, "How's this going to benefit you?" I didn't approve really, but there was nothing I could do because he'd made up his mind.' The next year, he finished second in the race, but all the prize money went on replacing his balding tyres. Parts for racing bikes were impossible to find in Rwanda; he had to wait until a friend travelled to Europe. Many cyclists, bored and broke, just gave up.

Adrien began to imagine a life for himself after leaving school where he would open a shop fixing radios, computers and televisions during the week, then ride his bike at weekends. And that might have been what happened if an American millionaire, halfway round the world in California, had not been gripped by an almighty midlife crisis.

3
THE DOT CONNECTOR

Tom Ritchey had been cycling in Rwanda for a week when he came across the old man and his wife standing by the road. He had ventured all round the little country, pedalled up and over most of its 'thousand' hills. He never thought he'd go anywhere more spectacular than his backyard of northern California, but this place – with its mist-topped volcanoes, towering waterfalls, glassy lakes and monkeys hanging out like belligerent teenagers by the side of the road – certainly came close. He imagined that this was what the whole unspoilt planet looked like a few thousand years ago.

As he travelled round on his bike, he saw children, it felt like millions of them, most of them smiling, indomitably cheerful. They were entertained by nothing and everything; Tom wasn't sure which. They ran alongside him barefoot or in cheap rubber sandals until they collapsed in the dirt, breathless but gasping for air to keep laughing. Then, out of nowhere, another group of kids would appear, as if arriving for their designated spot in the relay, taking their turn to sprint up the track behind his back wheel screaming, '*Muzungu!*' White man! Relentlessly, '*Muzungu!*' Not a greeting as such, more an instinctual outburst of shock and curiosity.

Wherever Tom stopped, a crowd would form. What they made of him is anyone's guess. He stood a few inches over six foot and he wore skin-tight Lycra and reflective sunglasses. He had an impressive shock of black, backcombed hair and an exuberant moustache clipped somewhere between handlebar and Fu Manchu. Back home, he looked like someone whose fashion clock had stopped ticking in 1975, but in Rwanda they didn't have so many white men to compare him to. He could mangle a couple of words of Kinyarwanda and he spoke no French, the other useful language in the Rwandan countryside, but he chattered away obliviously in a mellifluous Californian drawl that no one even vaguely understood. He thought they might be interested in his bike, which he had designed and welded himself from aerospace titanium and should have looked like a rocket ship to them. But they couldn't care less. They just wanted to see him up close. The more adventurous ones would reach out to touch him. If he tossed down an empty bottle of water – '*Agacupa!*' – there would be a mad scrabble for the trophy.

On the bodies of some of the teenage children, Tom noticed deep, angry scars. But, as the days passed, it became obvious there was a lot he wasn't seeing, too. There were kids, there were their grandparents, but pretty much no one in their twenties and thirties; an entire generation had vanished. Tom realised how little he had really thought about this place before he arrived. He had expected to find a dangerous country, full of hatred and division. It was, after all, little more than a decade since one in ten Rwandans had been slaughtered by their friends and neighbours. Yet, here they were getting on with life. There was nothing even to distinguish one as Hutu or another as Tutsi. Eventually, he met an Anglican bishop, John Rucyahana, who had spent a year at a seminary in the United States, and asked him to explain. 'This is how we must live now,' Bishop John told him simply.

In his own small way, forgiveness was something that had been exercising Tom a lot recently. He arrived in Rwanda in December 2005, a few days before his forty-ninth birthday, in the midst of a spiralling midlife crisis. Nearly two years before, Tom's wife Katie had walked out on him without warning, ending more than twenty-five years of marriage. He came back one day to their home in Woodside, high in the Santa Cruz mountains, to find she had cleared it out. To say he was stunned would not come close; he was deeply committed to Katie and their relationship. She was, he always said, 'the love of my life'. When he eventually spoke to her and she told him she was unhappy and confused, he didn't have the first clue how to respond.

Tom was not accustomed to failure. In his teens he had been one of the most successful and ferociously competitive bike racers in the United States. Then in his early twenties, he was part of a crew in California that pioneered mountain biking. He didn't much like losing at that either. Over three decades he'd built a company, Ritchey Logic, which now had fifty employees and patented numerous innovations that had made him a millionaire many times over. It's a safe bet that any bike shop in the world will have components Tom has either designed or directly influenced. He still rode 10,000 miles on two wheels every year and had managed to organise an aspirational life round the catchphrase, 'My bike is my office.' He was respected by everyone in the industry, if not always loved.

But he was starting to realise that this had all come at a price. His wife had rejected him; they had a son, Jay, and two daughters, Sara and Annie, but they were either at college or about to go. He had status and money, but happiness remained elusive. 'It can be very lonely when you're just driving ahead, and you look behind you and there's no one there,' he said. Tom lived in a remote spot and, increasingly reclusive, he went days without any human contact. He was not a carouser or a sportscar guy, and he already had a shed full of high-end bicycles, that other refuge of the middle-aged man in crisis. He never quite found time to replace the furniture, so he rattled around the empty rooms, reading psychology books and Christian self-help texts. Sometimes he would head out on long rides in the hills to figure out what was happening, but the answers had stopped coming. For two years, he scarcely designed a new product.

Some friends did try to help; in fact, Tom had started to feel like a pinball being slapped around by well-meaning flippers. The idea to visit Rwanda came from Peb Jackson, an author and vice-president of Saddleback Church, Rick Warren's influential megachurch based in Orange County, California. Jackson had been introduced to the president of Rwanda, Paul Kagame, at the Hyatt Regency hotel in Denver in 2004, and their casual chat lasted two and a half hours. At the end of it, Jackson handed Kagame a copy of Warren's *The Purpose Driven Life*, a book that has sold more than thirty million copies since its publication in 2002. Kagame lit up. 'Purpose!' he said. 'If there's one word that describes me it's purpose.' The president, who is not openly religious himself, would subsequently declare his intention to make Rwanda the world's first 'purpose-driven nation'.

Jackson is a snowy-haired, avuncular figure in his sixties who looks like Santa Claus outfitted by Ralph Lauren. He has encouraged numerous influential Americans to visit Rwanda since meeting Kagame – 'maybe more than two hundred' – but Tom, a friend of more than twenty years, was one of the first to follow his recommendation. 'I knew he was going through difficult conflicts in his life and his marriage,' Jackson said over early-evening drinks at the Serena Hotel in Kigali. He was in the country introducing a delegation of American cook-stove entrepreneurs to President Kagame. 'Tom was at the top of his game in many ways and the mystifying nature of a failed relationship in the midst of success is a factor of bewilderment and stress for a lot of guys. So I thought he'd find something here.'

On autopilot, Tom agreed to go. Jackson hooked him up with an investment manager, Dan Cooper, who was going to the country on business, and both men took their bicycles. Word spread that a couple of Americans were looking for riding partners, and on the first morning in Kigali a handful of the country's best cyclists turned up at the Serena Hotel, where Tom and Dan were staying. Only one of them, a diminutive Rwandan with a cherubic face called Rafiki, knew any words of English, but they hatched out a route that would take them seventy miles north-west over four long climbs to Ruhengeri, in the foothills of the Virunga mountains. The ride lasted four hours and Tom realised he hadn't smiled this much in years. His was a slump that only privileged Westerners tend to endure, the kind he could not explain to Rwandans, however well he spoke their language.

The next day, the Rwandans went home, but Tom and Dan continued deeper into the country on unmade roads coloured the distinctive ochre of volcanic soil. The fact they were on bikes, rather than inside an NGO's air-conditioned 4x4, lifted one barrier between them and the local population. Early on, Tom spotted a boy pushing a strange prehistoric wooden scooter and pulled up. With its rickety handlebars and small wobbly wheels, it shouldn't work, but here was someone hauling probably fifty kilograms of firewood. Over the next few days, Tom saw dozens more and even commandeered one for a ride. As an engineer, he thought they were ingenious; as a bike racer, they were hysterical.

The Americans came across a number of traditional bicycles, too: hulking, decades-old Chinese behemoths that the locals had kept on the road using anything they could find – strips of car tyres for brake pads, tin cans for reflectors. They were battered, but their continued existence showed there was love there, too. It reminded Tom of the early days of the mountain bike when some like-minded friends in California took balloon-tyred Schwinn Excelsiors from the nineteen-thirties and patched them up with mongrel components they had scavenged. Seven thousand miles from home, Tom began to feel an unlikely affinity with the Rwandan people. He had always described himself as an 'evangelist for cycling', and here were people, a couple of worlds away from the United States, who shared his passion. Cycling was their national pastime, and they didn't even know it.

Then, as he came to the end of his trip, he saw the old man and his wife standing by the road. The gentleman, who wore a crumpled suit, came over and very deliberately offered a low bow. This was a greeting not of deference, but gratitude: it signified, to Tom, that they were pleased to welcome visitors. The Americans' presence in Rwanda meant that the country was no longer toxic. He realised how self-absorbed he'd become: the man was grateful *to him*. These people were dealing with incomprehensible amounts of pain, but with grace and forgiveness. Tears filled Tom's eyes.

Back in Kigali, as Tom boarded the plane, he realised he could go back to his life and continue as before, or he could make a radical change. Sat on the tarmac waiting for take-off, he determined, *What I do with my disappointments is going to define me for the rest of my life*. He had some time to think – travel between Rwanda and America's West Coast involves at least two changes and takes the better part of a day and a half. When Tom landed in San Francisco an outline for Project Rwanda had been sketched out.

In Silicon Valley in the nineteen-seventies, did anyone just keep, say, a car or a set of golf clubs in their garage? The first meeting of the Homebrew Computer Club was convened in Gordon French's garage in Menlo Park, California, in March 1975. Two early members, Steve Wozniak and a twenty-year-old Steve Jobs, then decamped a couple of miles across the valley, where over the next few months they would develop the first Apple home computer in Jobs's garage. Meanwhile, the original garage start-up Hewlett-Packard, founded in Dave Packard's one-car shed in Palo Alto in the thirties, was bringing compact technology into the home with the first scientific calculators that could fit in a (rather capacious) shirt pocket and wristwatch-calculators that cost $795. Add to that Vint Cerf, a young professor at nearby Stanford University, who was establishing the protocols that would become the building blocks for the world wide web and the mid-seventies was one of the outstanding periods of human creativity, all taking place in an area of just a few square miles.

Right in the middle of it was the Ritchey garage in downtown Palo Alto. Tom's father, also called Tom, was an R&D engineer at Ampex, an electronics company that pioneered eight-track (and subsequently sixteen- and twenty-four-track) musical recording, but the space had long been taken over by his son. Tom was a man's man, even as a boy. When he was five years old, he built a three-storey tree fort in the backyard. It was only when he fell to the ground from fifteen feet, attempting to construct a fourth level, that his father suggested he might want to scale it back. He was eleven when he made a small electric car and the following year he found plans for a sailboat and promptly built one. 'From the youngest age, my father didn't care if I cut my fingers off,' Tom recalled. 'Saws, power tools, I could punch holes in my body, and we'd go to the doctor's and he was okay with it.'

His real passion, though, was bicycles and this too he inherited from his father. Tom was born in December 1956 in New Jersey, and the family moved cross-country to northern California in the early sixties, when the job at Ampex came up. His father was a smoker and not much of an athlete when he arrived in the Bay Area, but he bought his daughter a three-speed Raleigh bicycle to ride to school and immediately stole it for his own seven-mile commute to work. Some of his colleagues raced small boats, so he started doing that as well, and he joined the Sierra Club, an early environmental group that encouraged its members (and their sometimes reluctant children) 'to explore, enjoy and protect the wild places of the earth'. Tom's father quickly upgraded his bike to a British-made Raleigh Carlton ten-speed racer, which cost around $100, and at weekends he would head into the hills around Palo Alto and Woodside with a local touring club for fifty-mile rides.

Tom would have been happy enough watching cartoons on Saturday mornings, but his father forced him to come out on one of these rides when he was eleven years old. Tom's father never made too many concessions for his son's age and pedalled off into the distance as soon as they started climbing into the foothills of the Santa Cruz mountains. This shouldn't have come as a surprise to young Tom, but he detested the experience and as he slogged away alone on his sister's bike he resolved he would not let it happen to him again.

He started going out on the bike for after-school excursions with his seventh-grade friend Donny McBride, whose father also happened to race bicycles, still an eccentric hobby in nineteen-sixties America. They made an odd couple: Tom was already tall and looked like a benign Gulliver next to geeky, bespectacled McBride. But they improved quickly and one afternoon they bumped into a group of older kids in matching blue-and-gold kit from the Belmont Bicycle Club. The club riders invited them to a local twilight event and Tom's racing career began. When he was fourteen, he upgraded to a Cinelli bicycle that he painted with high-quality English boat enamel. He went out with his father again and on Alpine Road, a rough, semi-paved track that rises 2,000 feet through dense trees out of Palo Alto, he left him trailing.

When Tom had a problem with his Cinelli, the nearest bike shop was a dozen miles away in Cupertino, so he took to fixing it himself. He even started to wonder if he could reverse-engineer a bicycle from scratch. When a friend of Tom's asked him to repair his Ron Cooper – one of Britain's most revered frame builders – he pulled it apart and thought, *This is made really poorly!* He was sure he could do better, so with the help of his father, he managed to track down a set of steel tubing made by the Italian company Falck and some lugs – the sockets that form the junction between two tubes – and crafted a primitive tool that held the parts in place. In 1972, aged fifteen, he built his first bicycle in the family garage, with his father looking over his shoulder. He followed it soon after with a second for Donny McBride. The next year, he bought a lathe and a Bridgefort milling machine: still a teenager, he had become one of just a handful of bespoke frame builders in the United States.

Meanwhile, Tom's father wasn't the only experienced cyclist who was discovering that his son was a formidable opponent, a rider who thrived in the hardest races. Now using his own hand-built bike, Tom was beating everyone his own age and some of the best racers in California, too. In May 1973, aged sixteen, he entered the prestigious Crockett–Martinez race, even though it was for over-eighteens only. One by one, he destroyed the field, including two members of the 1972 US Olympic team. He was subsequently disqualified for being underage, but the legend of the 'senior slayer' was gaining momentum. 'If he rode with the juniors, it wasn't even a bike race,' said Shawn Farrell, a contemporary who became the technical director of USA Cycling. 'He was the greatest natural talent we'd seen in the United States at that point.' Cycling legend Gary Fisher, who is six years older than Tom, recalled him with barely suppressed awe. 'He was a hot junior – oh my God, he was good. He was just this punk kid who was totally unbeatable.'

A key figure in Tom's development was Jobst Brandt, an engineer from Hewlett-Packard who was a friend of his father's. In West Germany, Brandt had been the designer of the Porsche 911 braking system and, later in his life, he would achieve renown on cycling websites as a cantankerous retrogrouch with purist views of the sport. When Tom met him, he was in his forties and famous for the sadistic rides that he led around the Bay Area. Brandt's routes would take the group on and off road – something unheard of at the time – and were equally punishing on their bodies and on the bicycles. In winter he would climb the highest peaks of the Sierra Nevada before the snow ploughs; in summer, he would ride through the heat until his young crew were pleading for a break. His unforgiving stance – he would not wait if anyone dropped behind for either mechanical or physical reasons – is one that Tom still subscribes to even now. The reason Brandt's acolytes put up with the strictures was that no one could find trails as stunning and untouched.

Brandt was also an inspiration to Tom in regard to his frame building. Before he had just been welding frames and fixing up wheels, now he started making his own seatposts, bottom brackets, hubs and dropouts. Most bike frames were fitted with lugs, but Tom began to pioneer a technique called fillet brazing that did without them. His goal was always to make a bicycle and its components lighter, faster and crucially 'Jobst-proof', so that they would not be destroyed however unforgiving the conditions.

Tom made his first lugless bike with oversized tubes in 1975 and gave it to Brandt. It was his final year of school and he struck a deal with Palo Alto High School that he would only have to attend classes from 8 a.m. to 11 a.m.; the principal agreed because of the rave notices and publicity Tom was attracting as a cyclist. In the afternoons, he would either go riding – he was now training with the US Olympic squad – or make bicycles. He recalled building up to a hundred frames that year. The business was profitable and he saved enough to buy a car to travel to cycle meets or sailboat races. Tom was a notorious 'straight edge': he didn't have time for drugs, or much socialising of any kind. He needed to graduate with 245 credits, and that's what he scored, exactly 245.

I met Tom at his house in Woodside, a town of 5,417 inhabitants, most of them well-known and at least millionaires: Oracle chief executive Larry Ellison, one of America's richest men, actress Michelle Pfeiffer and musician Neil Young among them. Steve Jobs had been building a house not far from here when he died in 2011. Tom had said that we could head out for a pedal around the hills he first explored with Brandt, but he'd been struck down by a mystery virus and was forced to rest up. I knew it must have been debilitating for him to turn down a ride. When he shattered his pelvis in 2010, he was off the bike for just four days. Around the time his wife left, he broke his ankle and couldn't cycle for two weeks, the longest he had not ridden since he was eleven. Eventually, he became so restless that he went out into his workshop, sawed away the upper part of the plaster from his calf and fixed Velcro straps and a cleat to the bottom half so that he could lock it directly into his pedal and head out on the road again.

Tom bought the plot of land, which overlooks San Francisco Bay, back in the late seventies, long before it became among the most desirable addresses in the United States. He had just turned twenty, was newly married to Katie and they had a baby on the way. His bicycle business was booming and he loved the fact that this place was on the edge of wilderness. It still is – at the end of his drive a sign offered advice on dealing with mountain lions: 'If attacked FIGHT BACK.' Tom started by building a workshop, so he could continue cranking out bikes, and only then turned his attention to the main domicile – perhaps an early indication to his wife of where his priorities lay. When their son Jay was born, there was still no heating.

The house was a deluxe cabin, really, as unfinicky, sparse and elegant as one of his frames. Inside there was a homely feel and it was once again fully furnished – thanks, perhaps, to Tom's second wife Martha, whom he married in 2009. But the real highlight was the workshop, a large wooden shed that housed a welding jig, metalworking machines and the scattered skeletons of frames past and present. It was here that many of the original mountain bikes took shape. After finishing high school, Tom had decided to concentrate on making bicycles and racing for fun rather than real competition. In January 1979, Joe Breeze, a fellow road racer and frame builder from forty miles up the coast in Marin County, came to the workshop with his friend Otis Guy to ask Tom to build them a bike for a transcontinental tandem record attempt. Breeze brought with him what he called a 'Breezer mountain bike', which he had made using lightweight tubing that had previously only been found on road bikes but combined it with cantilever brakes, Magura motorcycle brake levers and fat (2.125-inch) Uniroyal 'Knobby' tyres. Tom, a veteran of trail riding with Brandt, was intrigued and started to think how he could put his own spin on the design. He decided to make three 'mountain bikes' of his own: one for himself, one for a pal of Breeze's called Gary Fisher and a spare.

Breeze invited Tom to compete in his first and only Repack race. Repack was a two-mile off-road dash down Pine Mountain, a foothill of Mount Tamalpais in Marin, which dropped 1,300 feet with an average gradient of fourteen per cent. It has attained a posthumous infamy since it was last run in 1984 and is now widely regarded as the spot where the sport of mountain biking was born. The race, on Saturday 20 January 1979, was a salutary experience for Tom: he had to borrow photographer Wende Bragg's converted Schwinn 'clunker' – the best riders were mostly on Breezers – and after the first bump, the handlebars rotated round so they were facing the wrong direction. He ultimately stopped the watch at five minutes, seventeen seconds, which was more than forty-five seconds behind Fisher and Breeze in first and second place. Tom did have a light-bulb moment, though, and – just as when he first went riding with his father – he determined he would never endure such humiliation again; the fact that he was riding on a girls' bike on both occasions made it sting a little more. The following year he unveiled 'bull moose' handlebars, where the bar and stem formed a single unit and the stem split into two, making a triangle. It would now be impossible for the bars to spin round. Working without lugs, meanwhile, meant he could use stronger, oversized tubing. The final pieces of the mountain bike were in place.

Tom went into business with Fisher and Fisher's college room-mate Charlie Kelly, a writer and rock-band roadie, and they called the company MountainBikes. Their success was built on Fisher and Kelly's marketing and Tom's productivity. While Breeze might spend six months working on a bike, Tom could weld a frame in just an afternoon. His friends called him 'General Motors' because of his ferocious work rate. Fisher rode his first Repack race on a Ritchey MountainBike on Saturday 11 August 1979, and a month later their store opened in San Anselmo, Marin County. In 1980, with just the help of an unemployed eighteen-year-old neighbour, Tom built two hundred mountain bikes and around fifty road bikes. From 1981, he added an extra assistant and made four hundred bikes a year, all hand-finished and painted personally by Tom. They were the first mountain bikes available on the market and, even at a price of $1,300, demand swamped supply.

'If you couldn't do something in four hours back then it wasn't worth doing,' said Tom, as we sat at his kitchen table, while he sipped hot water with honey. 'To me, Silicon Valley is king. It's where inventive people live, they've always lived here. In the seventies and eighties, there was this "Think it, do it" bubble. No one stopped to ask, no one held anyone back from doing anything. There was no Internet to figure it out. It was just that creative environment at Apple and Hewlett-Packard and in bicycle design as well. There's a beehive of insanity when you're that driven: you just take eleven pieces of tubing and you don't take ten coffee breaks. I not only wanted to build a bike, I wanted to ride it that day, I wanted to test it, I wanted to be on it. I just didn't have any patience.'

Tom does everything fast, except perhaps talk. His speech quickened and rose only when I asked whom he credited with inventing the mountain bike. 'Jobst Brandt,' he replied definitively. 'He inspired most of the people who were involved in mountain bikes and he never gets any credit for it.' For Tom, there was a big distance – spiritually, if not geographically – between the innovation of Brandt, Steve Jobs and himself in the area around Palo Alto and the slacker counter-culture of Fisher and Kelly up the coast in Marin: what he called 'Haight-Ashbury north'. He paused for a short coughing fit, before gasping, like they were his final words: 'But it certainly didn't happen in Marin! That's just a smokescreen for a bunch of pot-smoking hippies that want to tell the story. The story gets told wonderfully well, but it's not real. It's just fun to say it.'

MountainBikes was dissolved not entirely amicably in 1983, when Kelly sold his share, and became Gary Fisher MountainBikes (as a result, it is Fisher who is now most likely to be hailed as 'the father of mountain biking'). Tom, despite 'a caveman approach to business', resuscitated his own operation, Ritchey Logic, making frames and components. Most of his innovations came when he was out on the trails – to this day, he has never had a desk at any of his offices or even a business card. The boom continued: mountain bike sales topped a million in 1984, beginning to outstrip road bike sales in the United States in the mid-eighties and in the United Kingdom in the nineties. In 1996, mountain biking became an Olympic event. Tom had certainly played his part in its ascent. One of his MountainBikes was taken by a new company Specialized

– based in San Jose, half an hour from Woodside – to Japan in 1980 and shamelessly copied. Five hundred of them came back the following year as the Specialized Stumpjumper, and that model has been in mass-production ever since; it was even added to the Smithsonian museum's permanent collection in 1994. 'There's no doubt that the first bike was definitely inspired by Tom,' Mike Sinyard, the founder of Specialized, admitted in the 2006 documentary *Klunkerz*. 'I would say to this day that Tom Ritchey is one of the very best craftsmen in the world. A true artist. The best of the best.'

Tom believes he just happened to be in the right place at the right time. 'I'm a dot connector, that's all I am,' he said. 'I just try to put two and two together and, you know, I'm good at it. I'm good at taking all kinds of ideas and creating something that makes people say, "Hey, that makes sense." And when it makes sense, they say, "I want one!"'

When Tom returned from Africa in December 2005, he started to wonder if he might be able to connect the dots once again. He investigated how the bicycle was used in Rwanda, tried to figure out how he could help. It did not look promising: a bike must be an attainable luxury in the West, but only one out of forty Rwandans could afford one. These basic single-speed bikes cost around 50,000 Rwandan francs – roughly £50 – but Tom discovered that before they were ever ridden, they had to be modified. The local dirt tracks were furrowed and unforgiving, which meant that the cranks and forks were going to bend, the bottom bracket would strip out and the racks would fall apart. These patch-ups, such as welding twirly steel rebars to reinforce key joints, might add another £20 to the price, pushing it far beyond the reach of most Rwandans. Despite dramatic improvements in the country's prosperity in recent years, the average income was still around a dollar a day. A third of the population did not have enough to eat.

A further conundrum for Tom was that, in this new century, did Rwandans still want bicycles? Two wheels beat travelling on foot, but now there were motorcycles or, for the really prosperous, cars. Status is keenly tracked in Rwanda, even though the differences might appear marginal to Westerners. In addition, not everyone shared Tom's belief that this relentlessly hilly country was a dream cycling destination. It did not help that most of the Chinese and Indian bikes had only one gear, which made it impossible to climb the steepest peaks and inefficient to ride down them.

'In their heads, there were only two bikes: the colonial bike and the wooden bike,' explained Tom. 'They didn't know there were a hundred different flavours of bicycle. I wanted to initiate the thought that the bike was incredibly developed and celebrated, not just as a utility tool for carrying hundreds of pounds of potatoes, but as recreation, transportation and sport. Rwanda is a small country and ideas travel quickly. So my hope was that if you could explode that idea, you could possibly – and it was just a thought – change the direction of the country.'

One area of potential, Tom thought, was Rwanda's coffee industry. Before the genocide, coffee – along with mountain gorillas – was one of the few natural resources that foreigners were interested in. The story started in the thirties, when the Belgians launched a series of 'coffee campaigns', which forced Rwandan farmers, most of whom were Hutus, to plant coffee trees. The quality of the coffee tended to be mediocre: with a standardised price set by the government, irrespective of the quality of the beans, there was little incentive to tend crops with too much love. There was also the fact that taxes were often collected by local Tutsi chiefs. Still, as world coffee prices rose through the nineteen-seventies and nineteen-eighties, coffee provided between sixty and eighty per cent of Rwanda's export revenue and President Habyarimana keenly scrutinised the returns. Each June, after the harvest, it was said that 'the aroma of coffee was in the air' – it sounds more poetic in Kinyarwanda – because the farmers, suddenly flush with their annual dividends, could now afford to buy clothes for their children, improve their houses or, if they had had an exceptional year, buy a cow.

Problems started around 1990. There was a global dip in coffee prices and Habyarimana needed all his resources to fight the incursions of the Rwandan Patriotic Front. Prices paid to farmers were slashed and all subsidies were terminated in 1992. The situation deteriorated radically during the genocide, as farmers were sometimes killed or fled their plots. Those smallholders who remained, or returned often years afterwards, were preoccupied with growing food that would keep them alive. Soil fertility declined, insects took over and trees withered and died. It takes three years for an Arabica coffee tree, the variety grown in Rwanda, to reach maturity: time that none of the farmers could now invest. Prices reached an all-time low in 1997 (around sixty francs – or six pence – per kilo), and in 2000, ninety per cent of Rwandan coffee was classified as low-grade or 'ordinary', unsuitable for export. It produced not a bean of top-quality, speciality coffee.

Tom, however, had found a different, more encouraging scene. The turnaround began in 2000, the year of the nadir for Rwandan coffee, as the government increased incentives for its half a million coffee farmers. Aid programmes from the United Kingdom and the United States were launched; one of the most effective was a US-backed NGO called Pearl, which helped organise the farmers into cooperatives and instructed them on how to produce high-end coffee for foreign markets. The improvements in quality were almost instantaneous: in 2002 a Pearl cooperative called Maraba in southern Rwanda, not far from Butare, was visited by two premium roasters, Community Coffee from New Orleans and Union Hard-Roasted Coffee from London, and both companies were impressed enough to place large orders. The price, $3 per kilo from Community, served notice to everyone – and crucially the farmers – that high standards could lead to high rewards. The following year, the British supermarket chain Sainsbury's sold Maraba coffee in all of its stores in the run-up to the annual poverty-awareness day, Comic Relief.

There was a recurring sticking point, though. The main complaint from foreign buyers was the speed at which the cherries were processed after being picked – a period that should not exceed eight hours and would ideally be much less. Coffee is different from other fruits in that it stops ripening immediately after it is harvested from the branch. The seed begins to ingest the moisture and sugar that is left inside, triggering fermentation. If the coffee bean is not removed from the fruity pulp with water at a specialised washing station and then processed very quickly it can develop rotten or overripe flavours. But in Rwanda, it was far from straightforward to satisfy these demands. A cooperative such as Maraba had 1,350 members dotted around the remote hillsides, around 2,000 metres above sea level, where the heirloom bourbon coffee they were growing is happiest. The nearest washing station, meanwhile, would typically be on a main road down in the valley. Some farmers, after picking the coffee in the morning, would have to walk up to fifteen miles in the sun, carrying hundreds of pounds of fast-fermenting cherries on a wooden bike or balanced in woven baskets on their heads.

After some conversations with Tim Schilling, the director of Pearl, Tom began to see his way in. A well-made bicycle could change the lives of the coffee farmers in Rwanda, enabling them to earn up to twenty-five per cent more by delivering the cherries within four hours of picking. Tom set some parameters. He needed to create a machine that was light enough to climb the country's formidable hills, but robust enough to survive the erratic trail surfaces. It had to be strong enough to carry up to 200 kilograms of produce, but also sleek and desirable so that a farmer might even prefer it to a motorised alternative. But most of all, it had to be cheap, not more than $100, practically the same cost as one of the bikes from India or China that had to be fixed out of the box. In early 2006, Tom took the short walk from his house to the workshop.

On 22 January 2007, almost a year after Tom created Project Rwanda, his first coffee bike prototype – the Ubike, a name soon abandoned, as was the tag 'Wheels of Mercy' – was ready to be shown at the Maraba cooperative. Tom's son, Jay Ritchey, a twenty-four-year-old graduate in global science and sociology from Azusa Pacific University, a Christian college in California, was in charge of the roll-out. He was like a missionary of old, only with two prototype bikes and a high-tech portable welder. The test rider was a farmer named Joseph, a man in his forties who lived with his wife and eight children in Cyendajuri zone. He owned 600 coffee trees, which the previous year had produced 800 kilograms of cherries and made him 96,000 francs, a little under £100. He already owned a standard *pneu ballon* bicycle, but on any significant incline he would be forced to climb off and push. The front wheel also tended to flip up in the air when he was riding it and carrying cherries, like a capsized boat, because all the weight was loaded behind the axle of the rear wheel.

The hillside beside the cooperative headquarters created an informal amphitheatre and about seventy farmers gathered round Jay. As the bike came on to the stage there were theatrical gasps and bemused tittering. Certainly it was *a different flavour of bicycle*. It was also unmistakably Jobst-proof: Tom had imagined it as a 'bicycle pick-up truck' and – with assistance from Tom Mount, head of product development at Schwinn – he had created a two-wheeled take on a stretched Hummer, a vehicle usually used to transport Saturday-night hen parties. It was normal enough at the front, but became weirder further back. The wheelbase had been radically elongated, by almost a metre, from a normal frame. There was a roll-cage structure for extra strength and a wooden rack, all of which could support at least 150 kilos – two bags of coffee cherries, two adult goats or three children – and probably much more. But there were quieter innovations too, such as powerful cable-drawn brakes, nine gears and a rear wheel that had forty-eight spokes so that it would not buckle on the difficult terrain. Amusingly, for the Rwandans, it wasn't black. It had a paint job of yellow, green and blue to match the national colours and 'Hope Bicycle' was written across the down tube. The price was 70,000 Rwandan francs, so $110 or £70.

A few days later, down the road at Koakaka Koperative y'Abanhinzi Ya Kawa Ya Karaba – a coffee cooperative better known as Karaba – a second bike was given to a farmer called Celestin Nemeyimana. He was younger than Joseph, in his mid-thirties, and he had been selected by his fellow members because he was already a regular rider, often travelling twenty miles from his farm to cooperative meetings on his Chinese-made Terex Speciale. His grandfather had been a coffee farmer, his father was a coffee farmer and now Celestin tended 300 plants himself. He was called an extension agent, because he informed Karaba's other remote farmers of the latest gossip from the cooperative. He was engaged and planned to marry after the next coffee harvest.

Karaba had a similar number of members as Maraba, and again a large crowd had turned up to watch the handover. Jay Ritchey was swamped with questions from the farmers, mostly relating to the cost of the new machines. Why should they buy one of these bikes when they could pick up a Chinese single-speed for half the price? Jay answered the queries patiently through his interpreter Isabella. The Hope Bicycles, he explained, cost $100 to produce and $20 each to ship to Rwanda, so they were not making any profit from the enterprise. In fact, if they sold them in Europe or the United States, they could easily charge five times as much. The bikes would be available through a micro-lending loan – Project Rwanda was explicitly interested in providing a 'hand up' rather than a 'hand out' – with very low interest rates. The bikes would be paid for by Spread, an NGO that had taken over from Pearl and was still run by Tim Schilling, and the farmers would reimburse them over three years. Part of their contract was a commitment to deliver their cherries by 3 p.m. every day during the harvest; cherries delivered before then would receive a premium price, but if they missed their deadline the amount would drop. The bikes would, Spread predicted, enable a farmer to boost his earnings by up to forty per cent each year, which would enable them to buy the bicycle and still turn a profit.

There were some wary nods, but the crowd had really come to see the bike in action. A group of thirty formed around Celestin and challenged him to ride up a steep hill across the valley. It was a nasty climb of a couple of miles that none of them had ever conquered on their *pneu ballon* roadsters. Celestin set off and a few minutes later a dot appeared on the hill opposite, making steady progress, slowing but never stopping. The group cheered so loud that he must almost have been able to hear them. Farmers who did not even grow coffee surrounded Jay to see if they could buy the bicycle, too. Eventually Celestin reappeared, out of breath, his shaven head dotted with perspiration. 'You could climb a wall on this bike,' he said. 'You could climb up a tree!' Cracking a huge smile, he predicted, 'This bicycle will make me a rich man!'

The bicycles appeared to be the final piece of the puzzle for Rwandan coffee. The country was beginning to hit the quality thresholds expected from it for export, and the infrastructure was now in place to support the end product. In 2002, there was just one washing station in all of Rwanda, at the Maraba cooperative; by 2007, as the bikes started to roll in, there were more than one hundred. From two foreign coffee buyers in 2002, there were now thirty. President Kagame, like the Belgians and Habyarimana before him, had little doubt of the importance of coffee – still Rwanda's number-one export – to the development of the country. After an introduction from Tom's cycling partner, Dan Cooper, Kagame flew to New York and had lunch with Jim Sinegal, the CEO of Costco, the world's seventh largest retailer. They hit it off and soon enough Sinegal took his family on a return trip to Rwanda – his grandchildren became penpals with Kagame's sons – and Costco was taking a quarter of Rwanda's best coffee. Sinegal then brokered a meeting between Kagame and Howard Schultz, CEO of Starbucks. They spent time at each other's homes, too. When asked what they had in common, Schultz replied, 'For a start, we both have an interest in coffee.'

What he did not say, of course, was that a little image

smoothing would not hurt either Starbucks or Rwanda. Starbucks had gone from one shop in Seattle to being the largest global coffee chain, but ubiquity had not come with universal popularity. It was trying to recast itself by becoming the biggest buyer of Fairtrade coffee in the world and if some of that came from Rwanda, so much the better. Kagame, meanwhile, was trying to shed the reputational taint of the genocide and to reposition Rwanda as a serious place to do business. Influential friends could only help.

Away from the mass market, Rwanda was also becoming a destination for an elite band of coffee hunters who travelled round the globe in search of the perfect cup. One of the most intrepid was a man who had been called coffee's 'Messiah', Duane Sorenson, the owner of Stumptown Coffee Roasters in Portland, Oregon. He visited the country in 2006 and prophesied, 'Rwanda appears to be on the cusp of becoming one of the foremost coffee producers in the world.' There was excited talk of flavours of Japanese plum, dark cherry, candied ginger and milk chocolate. The following year, after the country's best coffee producers battled it out in the first Rwanda Golden Cup 'cupping competition', Sorenson – and another small-batch roastery, Intelligensia Coffee Roasters and Tea Traders of Chicago – purchased the winner for a record price: $55 per kilo. Sorenson, after discussions with farmers, also decided that bicycles were the missing link and set up a charity called Bikes to Rwanda. Their first initiative was to buy 400 of Tom's bikes from Project Rwanda and supply them to their star farmers.

Citizens in Portland, Oregon, which considers itself both the cycling and the coffee capital of the United States, rejoiced. What could be more ethical than spending $5 on an artisanal Rwandan brew picked by genocide survivors? Bonus: the farmers got a cool new bike out of it, too. 'Coffee for these people is a way out of poverty,' Clare Seasholtz, the director of Bikes to Rwanda, explained to *GOOD* magazine in 2007. 'This was a way to extend that full-circle idea of connecting the consumer with the origin. We will be able to provide them with something they can use and appreciate, and they are providing us with some really fantastic coffee.'

In mid-February 2007, two weeks after he had first taken his father's bicycles to the coffee cooperatives, Jay Ritchey checked in again with Celestin and Joseph. Over goat brochettes and bananas, Celestin reported that he had cycled about 130 miles in the past fortnight and had saved himself up to an hour a day, which he'd used to tend his coffee trees more diligently and plant vegetables. He had carried three bags of cement, eight cases of soda and even the largest woman in his village, who announced she would never ride on his other bike again. His only criticism was that the tyres were susceptible to punctures and the brake pads had already worn down to the nub. Joseph had not cycled as much, but his main assessment was that he did not like the wooden rack on the back. It reminded him of the rickety wooden scooters, and he felt that a metal rack would be more prestigious.

Shortly afterwards, Cherie Blair happened to pass through Maraba – her husband, the British prime minister Tony Blair, was a long-standing supporter of Rwanda – and was given a demonstration of the coffee bike by Jay. He asked if she might like to ride on the back. 'Umm, no thanks,' she replied, flashing her particular half-smile, half-grimace.

Project Rwanda was taking shape. Tom would tinker with the design, including – to his bemusement – replacing the elegant wooden rack with an ugly steel one. They would supply

2,000 coffee bikes to Rwandan farmers in year one, built by the folding-bike company Dahon in China, and then a similar number in year two, scaling up production much like they had done with the mountain bike twenty-five years before. Ultimately, the hope was that any of the country's half-million coffee farmers who wanted a bike could have one. Beyond that, Tom mused that Africa needed millions, perhaps billions of bicycles. In line with the idea that this would be investment and not aid, they would also set up workshops at Maraba and Karaba, training up local mechanics, so the bikes could be fixed and the project would be sustainable. They would keep a supply of parts, such as serpentine two-metre-long chains that might not be so easy to procure in the local markets.

Alongside Project Rwanda, Tom felt there was potential for adventure travel and eco-tourism, building hotels and running cycle tours. And he wanted to roll the dice. There was cycling talent in the country, he had seen enough Rwandans climbing up hills on arthritic single-speeds to know that. They certainly looked like riders: athletic and rangy, with not a pinch of body fat. So, for a small investment of seed money, he set up Team Rwanda, a new national cycling outfit. It could be a 'marketing tool' for the coffee-bike programme, he thought. The goals for this arm would be more modest: initially, they would take a handful of riders, test them, train them, and see if they had the potential to be cycling's answer to Kenya's runners. All Tom needed now was someone to run the show.

4

COACH

Before I met Jock Boyer it was hard not to become fixated on every bizarre fact I'd heard and read about Jock Boyer. He is said to be a model of temperance: he has not touched alcohol for forty years, and he eschews processed food or snacks that are not dried fruit. He drinks only alkalised water that is zapped with ultraviolet light to remove microbes. He carries a Bible wherever he goes, and prays before every meal. He cares little for current affairs, avoiding all TV, radio and newspapers, though he is partial to the books of Christian evangelist Philip Yancey and the film *Gladiator*. His favourite way to relax is sitting in a sauna under ceramic infrared heaters and he swears by sleeping on an electromagnetic pulsating pad. He once spent $25,000 and physically ruined himself for a year to win a bet of $5,000. He doesn't take antimalarial drugs, despite living in a country where, only five years ago, malaria was the leading cause of death. His heart is almost a third larger than the average male's, and he is unusually cold blooded, like a reptile, with a core body temperature of 35.5°C, a degree and a half below normal. He was born Jonathan, but most people call him Jock, sometimes Jacques or, to his Rwandan charges, he is Coach.

Many of these eccentric details come from Steve Friedman's 2008 profile in *Bicycling* magazine, 'The Impossible Redemption of Jonathan Boyer'. The article covered his troubled childhood, pioneering professional career and his late-life do-gooding, but mostly it wrestled with the one aspect of his biography that has a tendency to overshadow all the others. Jock Boyer is a convicted sex offender, who admitted to his crime in 2002 and was sentenced to twenty years in prison, which was then reduced to five years, probation and a jail term of one year.

'Of course, a lot of people don't care about the different chapters in the child molester's life,' wrote Friedman. 'One chapter will do. That one chapter – the one titled "child molester" is enough for them. The child molester prays? Good for him. Let him pray. He wants to help poor Africans? Keep him supervised and far from minors. He was a great athlete and wants to be a good man? The first doesn't matter and he gave up rights to the second. That's what happens to child molesters. That's their fate.'

Can Jock ever make up for what he did? Is that what Team Rwanda is actually about: a mission to do penance? Those questions were on my mind when I first travelled to the country and then, one muggy November evening in Kigali, Jock was right in front of me. It was the pre-race briefing before the first stage of the 2010 Tour of Rwanda and he was the star attraction. He pumped my hand vigorously, and immediately looked over my shoulder for someone – anyone – to talk to. He was an inch under six foot and had a long, gaunt face with cold, sea-green eyes. He was in his mid-fifties, but looked a few years younger, and he was lean and sinewy. He was wearing jeans, adventure sandals and a Team Rwanda-issue T-shirt, which it turned out was what he wore most days. Jock could be charming, but he was no fan of small talk, and he moved on brusquely. His enforcer – a daunting American called Kimberly Coats who was in her early forties and wore her blonde hair in plaits – ensured he made a clean break.

The bland conference room bustled with organisers, team managers and one Italian photographer. We were at the Sportsview Hotel, a charmless new-build in the Remera district that was proud, perhaps overly so, of its unobstructed panoramic vista of the national football stadium. Outside, children learning to swim thrashed around noisily in the pool, while inside the lack of air-conditioning became even more noticeable as instructions for the Tour of Rwanda were translated between French and English, and sometimes for good measure into Swahili or Kinyarwanda.

This was the second year the ten-day event had been officially sanctioned by the International Cycling Union (UCI) and it had attracted national teams from across the continent, including South Africa, Eritrea and Morocco, as well as Seychelles and assorted commercial outfits from France, Belgium and the United States. The race was slowly building a reputation as the most demanding on the African calendar, although for some it still remained a punchline. 'I thought it was a joke,' admitted Simeon Green, a British rider on the semi-professional French team, CA Castelsarrasin. 'Like the Tour of Afghanistan.' The presence of these teams was testament to Jock, the first American to ride the Tour de France, single-handedly hounding every contact from his professional days and calling in a stack of favours. The scarcely credible fact that Team Rwanda was present with two strong squads of six riders and had an outside shout of taking the yellow jersey, that was down to Jock, too.

The emergence of a dynamic cycling team in a country that

is known to most outsiders as a killing field had also piqued the interest of broadcasters and journalists. BBC World Service had sent their man in Africa and there were crews from French television and radio, Belgium's most respected cycling magazine and the American author Philip Gourevitch, the defining voice on Rwanda since the genocide. In one sense, Jock needed the media here: they lent legitimacy to this improbable story and they let sponsors and benefactors, who had already handed over hundreds of thousands of pounds, know that their money was having an impact. And Jock, rightly, was proud of the team's achievements. He had always been drawn to different undertakings, but this was the most outlandish challenge he had ever attempted. Team Rwanda was the opportunity, he believed, to put to use every skill and experience that he had developed since he started cycling in the mid-seventies.

The attention was also inconvenient. It forced Jock to address publicly the exhausting rumours that followed him wherever he went. Coming to Africa, to a country ignorant of his past and frankly with its own problems to deal with, should have been the perfect escape. But the success and fame of the team meant that there was now an expectation for Jock to account, to explain, to repent. (At the end of an article about Adrien Niyonshuti's appearance at the 2012 Olympics in the *Wall Street Journal* one reader commented: 'From decorated bicycle racer to convicted child molester, Jack [sic] fell far and hard. I hope the victim is doing as well as he is . . .') Jock was aware that many people didn't like him; he once told me, wryly, that even insects steered clear of him. Yet, he had an unshakeable belief in every person's ability to create a new narrative, despite what had gone on before, and that was why Rwanda was such a neat fit for him now.

Maybe he was wrestling with this conundrum, maybe he was

late for dinner, but at the end of the press conference while the other team bosses scrabbled over meal vouchers and vehicle accreditation, Jock grabbed a crate of mineral water for his riders and ducked out of the conference room by a side door.

Jock Boyer did not want to come to Rwanda. Correction: he could not even fathom why anyone would want to go there. 'I didn't even know where Rwanda was,' he admitted. 'I'm such a media void that I didn't really know about the genocide when I came here. I never read the papers, I don't have a TV, I don't have radio – never have in my whole life – just no time for it, I'm always so occupied with what I'm doing.'

It was a week after our two-second handshake, halfway through the Tour of Rwanda. We were sitting in the dining area of the Bloom Hotel, the base for the home team in Kigali, an attractive spot with rear bedrooms overlooking a lush lawn. Despite the convivial surroundings, power cuts were a regular distraction, so much so that half the interview was conducted in darkness, the only light the red LED from my voice recorder. I didn't feel I was missing much. Jock's voice is flat and nasal, and he is not the most expressive of speakers. There is a saying among professional athletes: 'Do not stand when you can sit. Do not sit when you can lie down.' Jock, who made his living in the most punishing of endurance sports, seemed to have adopted this minimalist maxim for his facial expressions. Smiles are rare, laughter practically unheard of.

Jock was thinking back to 2006 and a conversation he had with Tom Ritchey, an acquaintance since their schooldays in northern California. Jock is a year older than Ritchey and as teenagers they were the fastest young road riders in the state, the swaggering 'senior slayers' written about in newspapers. They were not so close back then – they were rivals more than friends – but they met again in the mid-nineties at a surprise fortieth birthday party for Tom to which Jock showed up unexpectedly (Tom's first wife, Katie, scatter-bombed the invites). They had more in common now: they still liked to go out on their bikes – 'Very few people ride at the pace I do,' Tom said – and they were committed Christians.

When Tom came back from Rwanda at the end of 2005, he thought of Jock, not long released from prison. If the experience of visiting the country could have such a profound, restorative effect on him, Tom mused, perhaps it could do the same for his friend. Tom was already planning his next trip: he wanted to organise a race for those funny wooden bicycles. A date was set, September 2006, and he invited friends to join him. A Canadian former pro, Alex Steida, who wore the yellow jersey for one day at the Tour de France in 1986, becoming the first North American to do so, was the first to sign up. Jock was slower to commit, unsure even what Rwanda *was*. 'No idea. Had to look at a map,' he recalled. 'I said, "Where are we going, Tom?" "Rwanda." "Okay, what's so great about Rwanda?" "Well, it's a beautiful country, the president's great, and the potential for cycling is huge." "Okay, whatever. I'll go."'

The first Wooden Bike Classic was held in Kibuye, a picturesque town that sprawls around the edge of Lake Kivu, tucked in by ancient forests. Today it might just be the most tranquil spot in all of Rwanda, but it has a painful history, bleak even by Rwandan standards. Before the genocide, a third of the population in the district was Tutsi, more than twice the national average. Within a month most were dead, but the killing continued without respite until liberation, when it was estimated that nine out of every ten Tutsis had died. On the road to Kibuye from Kigali – a low priority for Hutu governments, it was the last province to be connected with the capital – Tom's party passed the Bisesero memorial. High in the hills above the town, more than 50,000 Tutsis escaped here, but they were hunted down and a little more than a thousand survived. Corpses were feasted on by cats and dogs or picked at by swarms of kites and buzzards. At the Kibuye stadium, where the racers convened, there was a simple plaque: *More than 10,000 people were inhumated here*.

Before the Wooden Bike Classic, President Kagame made announcements on the radio and television encouraging Rwandans to watch and participate. They would probably have come anyway – entertainment is thin on the ground in rural Rwanda, perhaps one reason why the birth rate is five or six children for a typical family. But at least 3,000 did and some competitors, such as Adrien Niyonshuti, had cycled two days just to reach the start line. As the riders gathered, they did not exactly scream: *the future stars of professional cycling*. They were dressed in a hotchpotch of found and donated clothing: an 'Aaron's Bar Mitzvah' T-shirt or the somehow ubiquitous red satin dress shirts; the lucky ones had matching sports shoes but more common were the green flip-flops that many Rwandan children wear because they cost less than a dollar. The bikes were cobbled together from any vaguely applicable parts their owners could find. They were in desperate need of attention but Tom's crew were worried that if they touched them they might disintegrate entirely.

The Americans, meanwhile, were kitted out in box-fresh Project Rwanda shirts in dazzling yellow, blue and green. As well as Alex Steida and Jock, Tom had begged and bullied a group of around ten, including a couple of mechanics from Scallyways Bike Shop in Minneapolis and a filmmaker from Austin, Texas, to make the trip. The link, for the most part, was curiosity and shared religious faith. Joseph Habineza, the ebullient minister for youth, sports and culture, attended on behalf of the government. Tom set out the rules to the crowd at the football stadium: in addition to a downhill race for wooden bikes, there would be an event on the road for single-speed roadsters and a mountain bike race. There being no mountain bikes in Rwanda, the visitors would loan what the visitors had. A Schwinn mountain bike would be awarded to the winner of each race.

The racing was chaotic, but out of the noise, crashes and bluster, the talent of the Rwandans was unmistakable. Riders pushed themselves as if it was the Tour de France – not that they would ever have heard of that event – and the prizes only partly explained their crazed determination. Spectators lined the route and cheered insatiably. The single-speed race was won by Daniel Ngendahayo, a twenty-five-year-old from a village outside Kigali. As a child, Daniel delivered milk churns to neighbours and was now a bicycle-taxi rider in the capital. Second place went to another bicycle-taxi rider, Nathan Byukusenge. On the mountain bikes, Adrien, wearing a grey T-shirt, Fila trainers and green do-rag, powered ahead of the field finishing first ahead of Nyandwi Uwase from Gisenyi. Jock was particularly impressed with Adrien's smooth pedalling style. They exchanged a few words – Adrien had picked up some French in school – and it was clear he had ambition, a trait not easy to sustain in luckless Rwanda.

Afterwards, Adrien found cameras and recorders shoved in his face by the Rwandan media. It was his first interview. 'I was surprised that I won,' he said in Kinyarwanda, looking stern. A reporter then asked, What's your hope for this sport? 'If we had more opportunities to compete with these *muzungus*, I think it would bring hope to our lives and our country. We might develop as cyclists.' No one can quite remember who won the wooden-bike race, mainly because they were laughing so hard, but it is said that at least one competitor had to be fished out of Lake Kivu.

Jock enjoyed the trip, but did not feel deeply changed as a person in the way that Tom had. 'Even when I was in Rwanda I wasn't particularly enthralled by it, to be honest,' Jock told me. 'Yeah, they had good riders; yeah, it's hilly – I was okay with just coming the one time.' So, what changed? 'Well, Dan Cooper and Tom said, "Let's do a team." We had no funding – Dan got funding. We needed a coach and they all looked at me. I didn't have a life, I was divorced and single, I had a shop selling bicycle parts but that was all. They all had lives and families and responsibilities. A couple of months later I said, "Okay, I guess, I'll go." Reluctantly.'

Tom was aware that Jock's conviction made him a high-risk appointment, one that could distract from or even derail the new team. But it was no easy task to find a cycling nut who would swap his life in America for an uncertain existence in one of the poorest countries on earth. More than that, Tom felt that Jock deserved an opportunity for a new beginning and nowhere in the world epitomised that more than Rwanda. 'They live side by side with murderers,' said Tom. 'People had scars all over them that were perpetrated by someone in their community and I realised that they were an example of living beyond their pain, beyond their hurt, beyond their disappointments and living with second chances. It was all a self-fulfilling thing that happens when people do forgive and when they do let down the walls of their hardness.'

Tom exhaled loudly, 'You know, you can either calculate the risk out of every decision so that you never do anything or you think, *Wouldn't it be interesting if you threw one mess at another mess and you ended up creating this beautiful mess?*'

Jock returned to Rwanda in February 2007, around the time that Project Rwanda was testing its prototype coffee bikes, saying that he would stay for three months maximum. He boarded with a French couple in Butare, and began scouting for potential riders. They came to him from every region of the country, both Hutu and Tutsi. Jock brought with him a CompuTrainer, which fixed to the back wheel of a bike and allowed him to test a rider's power output and his anaerobic threshold (AT), an essential marker for endurance athletes. He also measured the efficiency of each rider's pedal stroke on the SpinScan program. Riders who scored well on both were immediately fast-tracked. Jock maintained an online journal during these early phases and they read a little like an anthropologist's log from the nineteenth century, if that explorer had been particularly obsessed not by tribes and fauna but with wattage and maximum heart rates. Early on he gushed that he was uncovering some 'very unusual talent'. He was even struggling to keep pace on training rides: 'They dropped me on the long climb on our forty-mile ride, they had me at my AT for over thirty minutes before I finally blew!' he wrote, not long after he arrived. 'They did it again on the last hill coming into town. Those numbers would make them competitive in international competitions. I am relieved that what we all saw last September was not an illusion or over-optimistic zeal!'

More than the quality of the riders, however, Jock recognised an innate resilience. On any training ride, he would find that locals appeared on their bikes from nowhere to join the pack. One of the regulars was Alphonse Museruka, who was formerly a soldier in the Congolese army and was better known by his nickname 'Rambo'. Rambo wore size-twelve tennis pumps, a bandanna and what Jock called 'Mr Cool sunglasses'. He rode a pink seven-speed Bianchi that was at least three decades past its prime. Every day Rambo would be left behind by the best riders, but he would never stop smiling or riding to his limit and beyond. 'You have to love the guy,' wrote Jock. 'He is without a doubt a survivor. At twenty-eight, he is one of the older riders, but will make an incredibly loyal and valuable team-mate. He is the type of rider that you would tell to catch the breakaway ahead and he would not give up until it was caught.'

When three months were up, Jock found that he'd not quite scratched the itch. 'To this day, I'm just attracted to really hard things, adverse things,' he said, stretching out his legs at the Bloom Hotel. 'But I cannot think of anything, within my capabilities, that would have been harder. There might have been something – like teaching pool to pygmies, something like that, but I'm not a pool person.' Jock laughed; the first time I had seen him do so. 'No, I don't think there is. It was an impossibility to do what we were trying to do here.'

For proof that Jock is drawn to difficult experiences, speak to him about the Race Across America. RAAM, as it is known, is a test of masochism and sleep deprivation that is packaged as a non-stop cross-continental endurance bicycle race. In 1985, at the age of twenty-nine, Jock completed it in a then-record time of just over nine days. Even now, he has nerve damage on the pressure points of his hands and feet from spending up to twenty-two hours of each day in the saddle.

That was the first time. In June 2006, shortly before he left for Rwanda for the Wooden Bike Classic, a fifty-year-old Jock signed up again. On this occasion, within forty-eight hours his neck muscles were in such pain that he had to construct a pillar out of cardboard and tape it to his handlebars to offer head support while he pedalled; he later switched to a neck brace. Towards the end, he had to urinate on all fours, like a dog, because he was experiencing such extreme chafing. Again, he won the race.

During his first RAAM, a camera crew pulled up alongside Jock and he uttered a quote that could serve as a personal motto. 'If you have enough will-power,' he said, staring intensely down the lens, 'if you want something bad enough, you can get your body to do anything. Anything.'

Jonathan Swift Boyer was born on 8 October 1955 in Moab, Utah, the youngest of Josephine and Winston Boyer's three children. His mother was a teacher and his father, according to his obituary in 2000, 'was involved in mining, inventing, ranching and horse training'. Winston Boyer, never comfortable with responsibility, walked out on his family when Jock was five, and Josephine took the children across the country to California, settling first with her parents in Pebble Beach before moving to nearby Carmel. Jock, who owes his nickname to one of his mother's friends, took the separation particularly badly. Almost overnight he lost confidence, becoming shy and insular. Half a century on, he still recalled pulling away on the westbound California Zephyr train and said it was the saddest day of his life. He would not have meaningful contact with his father until the early nineties, when Winston fell ill and came to live with Jock for a year. Jock wondered if he'd know him, love him, even like him, but it all came back instantly.

As he spoke about his childhood, Jock didn't look for sympathy; his tone was neutral, like he was describing a disappointing meal at a restaurant he had heard good things about. He knew he had much to be grateful for. His mother's family, the Swifts, came from money – his great grandfather was Arthur Leonard, president of the Chicago Stockyards at the turn of the century – and his life was private schools and summers on the family estate in Massachusetts. But he was never particularly happy and always dreamed of escape. The children fought among themselves and his mother, who never remarried, had little idea how to control them. Like his father, Jock was turning out to be a loner, drawn to wild ideas and self-sufficiency.

He sipped a glass of South African white wine. I wasn't sure if he drank alcohol, I said. 'I started drinking a year ago, first time in my life,' said Jock. 'I like wine, I knew I'd like wine, I just wanted to wait until I was over fifty and could enjoy it. Both sides of my family are alcoholic, serious problems, and I've just seen too much ugliness that I never wanted to be even remotely prone to that, so . . . I think at this point, I'm safe.'

Jock always had formidable will-power. At fourteen, a neighbour in Carmel introduced him to cycling and he realised immediately that it was a sport in which he could excel. He liked the pain of riding for hours and he had no problem making the sacrifices off the bike needed to succeed. His first bicycle was a black ten-speed Raleigh Competition and, when that was stolen, he traded up to a $180 blue LeJeune. He entered races and his plans for escape took shape. Remo d'Agliano, the owner of a local Italian restaurant who had competed in Europe himself, gave Jock training advice.

After high school, Jock was offered a place at the University of Colorado in Boulder to study veterinary science; he thought one day he might work in a game park in Africa. But he was winning more and more events, and had qualified to ride in the 1973 Junior World Championships in West Germany. He spent the summer taking a nine-week crash course in French at the Monterey Institute of Foreign Studies, where he was tutored for six hours a day by a Parisian, a Belgian, a Canadian and a Tahitian. In the autumn, aged seventeen, he asked the university if he could defer until further notice, and prepared to move to France. He had saved $350 from working as a waiter in d'Agliano's restaurant to buy his plane ticket to Paris and with the name of a friend of a friend – 'an address really, not even a contact' – he set out to do what no American had ever done before him: make a living as an elite professional cyclist in Europe.

France had dominated competitive cycling since the sport's inception in the 1890s. The rules and conventions were strict and hierarchical, and many remain in place to this day. All teams had a lead rider and everyone else on the squad rode in his service; they were his *domestiques* or 'servants', fetching him drinks and food when he needed them, and protecting him from the elements. In return, they received a share of the pot if he won. When Jock arrived, drug use was institutionalised, often facilitated by a *soigneur*, literally a 'healer' but in practice an assistant who would do odd jobs for the team and provide post-race massages. Riders still believed that alcohol could have performance-enhancing qualities and the approach to nutrition was best summed up by their preferred post-race sustenance: a prime cut of steak, chewed to extract all the nutrients before being spat out to avoid ingesting unnecessary calories. The possibly apocryphal bonus of this approach was that the fillet could then be popped down a rider's shorts the next day to provide extra cushioning on the saddle.

Jock did not set out to change these methods, but he made it clear that he was going to approach the sport his own way. At the peak of his professional career in 1983, the year he finished twelfth in the Tour de France, the American would arrive at races with a personal acupuncturist and insist that his massages be administered with his own brand of liniment,

Sweet Almond. Alcohol was off-limits, of course; so were soft drinks and caffeine. He would eat small amounts of chicken and fish – disdainfully tossing ham sandwiches passed to him during a race into the bushes – supplemented by industrial quantities of fruit, nuts and vegetables. 'He knows a lot about nutrition,' Jock's nutritionist Dr Gerard McLane told *The New York Times* in 1982, 'and mixes his own "smoothies", which are a paste of fruit, nuts and grains. He takes them from a tube while he's riding.' Jacques Anquetil, who won the Tour five times, famously said, 'Only a fool would imagine it was possible to win the Tour de France on mineral water.' Jock Boyer was the first to attempt it on tahini.

Jock's progressive attitudes to nutrition can be traced to two events in the late seventies. At the 1977 World Championships in San Cristóbal, Venezuela, his career almost ended when he contracted a virulent intestinal bug. He shrank from his racing weight of sixty-three kilograms to fifty-six kilograms and would take almost two years to fully recover. Around this time, he also became a committed Seventh-Day Adventist. One of Adventists' core tenets, from the era of cereal man John Harvey Kellogg in the late nineteenth century, is a wholesome, low-fat diet very similar to the one that Jock ended up adopting in his racing career. He remained a picky eater in Rwanda, perhaps mindful of the 2005 research that suggested the average Adventist in California lived four to ten years longer than the average Californian.

His religion was a mild curiosity on the cycling circuit; during his first Tour de France in 1981, the story goes that British journalists were worried he might be lonely and offered him some porn magazines, but Jock declined, saying he was happy reading the Bible. Adventist beliefs strictly forbade him from work or play from Friday sunset to Saturday sunset, but, as he said at the time, 'I must justify with myself for riding on the Sabbath. I just ask for forgiveness.'

Jock is often characterised as an outsider during this period, but that ignores some of the subtleties, according to those who were around him at the time. He was popular with fans, becoming known as 'Cowboy' for the trademark ten-gallon hat he wore off the bike (he was also saluted as 'Jacques' and 'Boy-AY' by the French or just *'L'Américain'* since he was the only one in the peloton in those days). He was a novelty for race organisers, too: riding for the Renault-Gitane team in 1981, he wore a stars-and-stripes jersey for the duration of the Tour de France, as though he somehow represented the whole country. 'He was an iconoclast,' the legendary American sportswriter George Vecsey, who shadowed Jock during the 1982 Tour, told me. 'He spoke French perfectly, so well that French people did not make their characteristic grimace when he spoke to them. But Jonathan just saw things more from an American perspective. He was going to do things his way, he didn't accept the rote behaviour of the Tour. American athletes always ask, "Why?" and that is not how those European teams were set up.'

Bernard Hinault, for whom Jock served as a *domestique* at the 1981 Tour de France, the third of five victories for the indomitable 'Badger', remembered him with great affection. 'As a team-mate he was golden,' he said. 'He was one of us. We didn't treat him any better or worse because he was American. He spoke French fluently and he had already raced in France for some time, so that helped his integration into the team. I have nothing but good memories of him.'

Jock was at his most idiosyncratic when insisting that his wife be allowed to follow the Tour. In 1980, he married a Stanford University student and aspiring writer called Elizabeth Underwood. French cycling teams had a draconian policy on wives and girlfriends, considering them an unwanted distraction for serious racers. This led to the curious situation in 1982 where Elizabeth, informed by Tour officials that women were not allowed to follow the race in support cars, chose to roll her hair up under a cap and wear a loose sweater and do it anyway. (For the record, Jock agreed with the tradition of sexual abstinence during the three-week Tour de France: 'They can trust us,' said Elizabeth. 'We just want to spend some time together.') The couple lived happily enough in Annecy's old town for a while, but when Elizabeth returned home to resume her studies, the strain of living on two continents eventually showed and they separated in the mid-eighties.

Jock was not a cyclist with supreme natural gifts – neither what the Italians call *fuoriclasse*, meaning 'of superlative quality', nor what the French describe as *surdoué* or 'exceptionally gifted' – but there was no doubting his fortitude. When he arrived in France, he survived for years with no money before a professional team would take a chance on him, staying in hotels that smelled of urine and left him infested with fleas and lice. What he lacked in intrinsic class, he made up for in hard work and an obsessive observance of his body and its conditioning. 'I wasn't a Bernard Hinault,' Jock said, 'but I did my utmost to get the most out of what I had.'

At a certain point, however, Jock realised that he had hit a ceiling in professional cycling, one that had both physiological and pharmacological explanations. 'I'm not getting any better,' he admitted in a candid interview after he had finished in twenty-third place in the 1982 Tour de France. 'I'm starting to wonder if I'll ever do better than this without them [drugs]. I'd guess that eighty per cent of the riders use something, even if it's not detectable. Maybe it's ninety-nine per cent. I won't take anything.'

It was partly his disenchantment with the world of professional cycling that led Jock to forego the Tour de France in 1985 and enter the Race Across America instead. 'Actually, I did it because of a bet,' he clarified. Today, RAAM is perhaps the world's most famous ultra-marathon race contested by nearly 200 of the hardiest athletes from around the globe, but in the early eighties it was a novelty. For the first cross-continental in 1982, then called the Great American Bike Race, there were just four competitors and almost no dramatic tension, since the riders were often hundreds of miles apart. Race Across America was launched the next year, but the racing cycling scene, of which Jock was a star member, remained dismissive of its participants. They called them 'Freds', a pejorative term that implied they were middle-aged and dowdy, and sniped that their only talent was staying awake for long periods. After it had been running for a couple of years, one of Jock's friends challenged him to put the Freds in their place. Jock, his competitive spirit pricked, agreed.

Jock could have been excused for feeling confident in 1985. Few of the twenty-five men and women on the start line in Huntingdon Beach, California, were full-time athletes and they included Jim Penseyres, a Vietnam veteran who lost his left leg after stepping on a mine. Jock's strongest competition was expected to come from Michael Secrest, a one-time truck driver from Flint, Michigan. Jock publicly declared that he would avoid traditional ultra-marathon techniques, which would see them ride all day and grab one or two hours' sleep a night in their motorhome. He would push a bigger gear and ride faster, enabling him to make more civilised prearranged stops at motels.

In the event, Secrest, whose tenacity in two previous RAAMs had earned him the sobriquet 'Bulldog', turned out to be a tougher competitor than Jock had anticipated. They exchanged the lead early on in Arizona, but then Secrest was out of sight through New Mexico, over the Rockies, Texas, Oklahoma and halfway through Arkansas. After 45°C heat in the Mojave Desert, the racers were persistently battered by thunderstorms so severe that the television helicopter following the race was repeatedly forced to land. Jock realised that he needed to change his strategy if he was to overhaul Secrest and he had to spend less time off the bike; one eyewitness, charged with escorting him around detours on the route, reported how he pedalled alongside Jock at twenty-two miles per hour with him 'calmly eating a plate of spaghetti'. Jock ultimately prevailed, but only by four hours, and when he arrived in Atlantic City, he commented, 'I just gotta learn how to walk again.'

The bet had spectacularly backfired on Jock. He had just started to make good money in France, but passed it up for ten days of unrelenting hell. His prize was $5,000 but this was a fraction of the amount he had invested in a motorhome and crew, plus a motorbike, pick-up truck and rented sedan to support the effort; Jock spent at least $25,000, he estimated. Moreover, having set out to discredit endurance athletes, Jock had given them crucial legitimacy, as television audiences were enthralled by his duel with the former trucker. RAAM founder John Marino even credited Jock and Secrest with saving the race from extinction.

Worse was to come when he returned to Europe. Still recovering from his efforts, Jock missed the 1986 Tour de France, a race won with flair and aggression by a twenty-five-year-old from Nevada, Greg LeMond. With a shock of blond hair and a dashing riding style, LeMond became the first non-European to win the race and was an instant global superstar, even back home. His achievements would spark a massive cycling boom in the United States, the beginning of a two-decade dominance of the sport. Jock's dream of an American racing team had been realised with the formation of the 7-Eleven squad, but now he was only strong enough to be a '*super-domestique*' to another flamboyant young compatriot, Andy Hampsten. Jock had his worst-ever Tour de France in 1987, finishing ninety-eighth, and retired soon afterwards.

How must Jock have felt? While it would be an exaggeration to say that he was a model and inspiration for LeMond and later Lance Armstrong, he certainly proved to a generation of American cyclists that it was possible to integrate and thrive within the European system. He learned the language, stayed in parasite-infested hotels and fought for credibility so they didn't have to. (A professional rider from Britain at the Tour of Rwanda said, almost reverentially, of Jock: 'You actually had to be mad to make it in those days.') Yet he was forgotten almost the moment he stopped riding. He had won eighty-seven races as an amateur and forty-four as a professional. He had competed in five Tours de France, three editions of the Giro d'Italia and nine world championships. He might even have won the 1982 World Championships in Goodwood, Sussex, when he sprinted clear of the field on the final lap only to be chased down by his team-mate LeMond, an act of treachery that Jock could recall three decades on as if it was yesterday.

'Oddly enough,' said Jock, 'while I'm in Rwanda I get emails from random people that encourage me with the team and in parentheses say, "You have always been a real pioneer" or "You affected my life". I get more of that now than ever before, probably because I'm more visible now. Up until three years ago, I had a really bad time in my life, then I was pretty much inaccessible or people didn't know what I was doing.'

He stopped and scratched his jaw. 'You never know how many people you can affect. It's good we don't know.'

This was Jock's first mention of a 'bad time'. We were sitting in the late-afternoon sun on the lawn of the Bloom Hotel, while in the background a Rwandan team rider walked chastely across the grass with his girlfriend, not even holding hands, like the leads in an English period drama. It was not so far from Jock and Elizabeth three decades before. A menagerie of birds belted out their enthusiastic if limited repertoire. Our conversation was briefly interrupted by the arrival of an Eritrean rider who wanted to speak with Jock privately. The speed of the Eritreans on the bike was rumoured to be second only to how quickly team members would defect when racing abroad. From what I could glean, he raised the possibility of becoming involved in the Rwanda set-up, but Jock, mindful of diplomatic repercussions, suggested that he would be wiser to stay where he was, at least for now.

Jock's problems started almost immediately on retirement. He had been cycling since the age of seventeen and had not looked up for fifteen years; now thirty-two, neither too young nor too old, he had precisely no idea what to do with his life. With hindsight, he thinks he should have competed in mountain biking – or even gone in to business with those 'smoothies' – but back then he fell into what he categorised as a serious depression. 'Lasted about six months, I think every cyclist goes through it,' he said matter-of-factly. Ever the Adventist, the only blessing was a physical one. Many riders when they stop racing put on enormous amounts of weight, eating the same quantities as before but no longer burning up to 8,000 calories a day. But when Jock stopped he immediately lost his appetite – he was not certain why.

He moved to the Netherlands and set up a company exporting high-end bicycle parts to the United States. Greg LeMond, recently recovered from a freak shotgun accident on a turkey hunt, won the closest and most exciting Tour de France in history in 1989 and was named 'Sportsman of the Year' by the American magazine *Sports Illustrated*, the first cyclist to receive the honour. He claimed his third win in the race the following year. Jock's business, meanwhile, collapsed after a disagreement with his Dutch partner and in 1992 he moved back to California. Here, he sold bicycle parts on a smaller scale out of a shop on a disused airfield in Marina. He became more involved with the church again and was baptised. In 1994, he met a local woman called Kim at the Seventh-Day Adventist Church in Monterey and three years later he married for the second time.

Around this time, Jock began a sexual relationship with a twelve-year-old girl, reported only as a friend of the family to protect her identity, which continued for three years until 2000. Jock and Kim separated that year, and in October 2001 the girl, then sixteen years old, brought charges against him. He was arrested the following May, and in September, he pleaded guilty to ten felony counts. The maximum penalty was twenty-two years, but state superior judge Gary E. Meyer decided that Jock did not present a significant threat to the victim or to anyone else and he was sentenced to one year at Monterey County Jail. His term began on 31 October 2002, and ended a little over eight months later on 7 July 2003.

A surprising thing happened when I raised the subject of his child abuse with Jock. We had moved inside to evade the mosquitoes that were ignoring him but amassed in hordes around my head. Jock had been his usual self, which was to say intense, prickly and evasive when it came to personal matters, much happier to talk about Rwanda and the riders, and mostly acting as if he would have been happy to swat me away like one of those flying bugs. But when his conviction came up, he softened instantly, physically he seemed to unclench; he appeared almost relieved. *It* had been acknowledged openly, not just whispered behind his back.

Those hoping for Jock to break down in contrition, however, would be disappointed. During the court case, he expressed remorse and, a decade on, he maintained the same line. But in an Oprah Winfrey era, where there is an established pattern for a public confession, his response was troubling and unsympathetic. There were no tears, no pleas for forgiveness, no outpouring of sympathy for his victim. There was scarcely any empathy, either; he had no contact with the girl and had only cursory interest in her life now. Jock could not control how she responded to the events, so he had chosen – at least publicly – not to engage with that aspect. 'If you let something destroy you, whose fault is that?' he told Steve Friedman in *Bicycling*. 'God doesn't want you to be destroyed. We all have an opportunity to choose a path that will make us stronger. I just hope she's making the right choices in her life despite her past. We are all responsible for our choices. I was responsible for my choices and I take full responsibility.'

One of Jock's favourite sayings, often used as a compliment to his Team Rwanda protégés, was, 'Tragedies will either make you a better person or a bitter person,' and he made it clear to me that he believed that maxim applied equally to himself and the girl.

Jock's response was at best pragmatic, at worst heartless and emotionally stunted. He believes that his crime should be given context: he is not a predator or a pervert, the kind who spend time around school playgrounds or commit repeat offences; he makes a point of stating that both he and the girl remained clothed during their encounters. He is a man who overstepped certain boundaries and has been punished. 'I can go through the sequence of events in my mind,' he said, 'see where I took the wrong path, probably not something I really want to talk about in-depth, but yes, it's a very clear sequence of just really stupid mistakes. Some things I might not completely understand and nor do I really have to. I just know that the past is the past. I'm okay with people not liking me, I've had that all my life, so it's not new.' He paused and, as he had done many times before, shifted the conversation back to Rwanda. 'From a certain point on, people can judge me by what's happening now, what's happening in my life. Time really tells the character of a person, whether good or bad, and I feel good about what I'm doing, I'm really in my element here . . .'

At this point, his mobile phone trilled. It was Kimberly, the enforcer, Team Rwanda's director of marketing and logistics since 2009 and now Jock's girlfriend. (Jock tended to call her 'Moki' – which means 'enthusiastic' in Swahili – a nickname partly used, she suspected, because she shared her first name with his second wife.) He had been missing for too long and their group of American expatriates was keen to go out for food. 'Yes, almost,' he said into the receiver. Pause. 'Okay, I'm in – maybe Tim will want to come.' To me, 'Do you want to have dinner with us at Sol e Luna? It's a pizza place.'

To say I was taken aback would come nowhere close; Jock had spent days avoiding my gaze and suddenly looking very busy every time I came close. But it turned out that this was typical Jock: having spent his life as a bike racer, a profession where any sign of emotion or weakness is ruthlessly set upon, he had conditioned himself to become almost unreadable. I was reminded of Michael Secrest. The pair spent the entire

1985 Race Across America as sworn enemies, Jock scarcely able to conceal his contempt for his rival every time the TV cameras interviewed him. But when I spoke to Secrest on the phone, he had nothing but affection for Jock. The autumn after RAAM, Jock invited him to California and they took extended rides with Chris Carmichael, who would go on to become Lance Armstrong's coach. During the visit Secrest mentioned a long-held ambition to ride the 350-mile Bordeaux–Paris race and Jock hooked him up with his professional team in France and found him a spot the next year.

Jock was clearly capable of acts of great kindness and inspired unswerving loyalty from his friends. Dan Cooper, for example, described him as 'as close to a walking angel as I have ever met', while Tom Ritchey called him 'faithful, reliable, uniquely gifted'. When Jock began his relationship with Kimberly, who had volunteered for more than a decade with abused and neglected children in the United States, he asked her why, knowing his history, she had volunteered for Team Rwanda. According to Philip Gourevitch's report in *The New Yorker*, she replied, 'You know what I think? I think you were really stupid, you put yourself in a bad situation, and you didn't think. That's what it was.'

For Tom, it was not even personal. However low anyone sinks, they should be allowed an opportunity to turn their life around. It was a simple matter of mercy and forgiveness. 'We all need second chances,' he told me, sitting in his kitchen in California. 'Everybody. Doesn't matter. That's a universal agreement. Everyone needs to be cut slack. I don't know anyone who wouldn't agree with that.'

If only the matter offered such simple resolution. On the evidence of the online discussion following the *Bicycling* article on Jock, the audience was split almost down the middle: 'I can't imagine a crime more detestable than child molestation, so for me his crime will always overshadow whatever "good" that he does in his life,' was one of the more measured criticisms; 'He's served his time and is clearly making the best of his second chance,' wrote another. One reader announced he would be cancelling his subscription because of the 'misguided' story: 'Why do I have to read about this in my cycling magazine?' he asked. Having sat across from Jock, as he talked about – but usually around – his crimes, I have no difficulty understanding any of these responses.

Indisputably, there was a group of riders on Team Rwanda whose lives had been changed far beyond their dreams by Coach, plus many others he had helped besides; Rambo never made the grade as a cyclist but was employed as a security guard at the team compound. Jock regarded how he ended up in Rwanda as nothing less than 'a divine appointment'. After his cycling career had wound down, he had become isolated from reality. He had a talent and a knowledge that was unique, but no one in the United States was interested. He was looking for an outlet to use everything he had learned in his life and finally it was presented to him. He was initially resistant to go, but it had wound up being his proudest achievement.

Nevertheless, even if one accepted Jock's version of events, the question remained: whatever he did in Rwanda, however many people he helped, could he ever truly make amends? 'I think God is not as interested in our mistakes, because we all make mistakes,' said Jock. 'He's more interested in what we do after we've realised that we've made them. How we change our direction in life or if we change it. Or if we dig in and continue to make the same mistakes over and over again. I made a choice to let the past be the past.'

Again his phone rang, the car was waiting. 'All of us are

capable of doing anything, given the right or wrong situation,' he said. 'And a lot of the times we get into situations so unawares because it's just a slow consequence of little things and all of a sudden we find ourselves not knowing where we are, what we are doing or who we are. With my past mistakes, I'm able now to see the red flags, I can avoid going down the wrong road. So, it's been good, I'm in a really healthy place right now.'

There was not much left to say. I turned off the voice recorder and we went for pizza.

5

THE FIVE

Many Rwandans thought they would never see Jock Boyer again after the Wooden Bike Classic in 2006. They were used to *muzungus* turning up, putting on a show that didn't make much sense to them and then disappearing home to feel pleased with themselves. Rwanda was fast becoming the land of a thousand NGOs; actually, there were closer to 300 non-governmental organisations in the country but it always seemed like more, particularly at the fussier restaurants in Kigali or the better hotels in Butare. The Americans and the British, in particular, were regular visitors during the first decade of the new century. This was partly guilt at the West having spent the genocide 'stood around with its hands in its pockets', in President Paul Kagame's lacerating put-down, but an added factor was that Rwanda was a comfortable place to do work: an Africa that was welcoming and palatable. The crime was petty, the traffic was mostly solicitous and there was even a growing number of coffee shops with reassuringly expensive lattes and Wi-Fi.

Whatever his reasons, Jock did return in February 2007, six months after his original visit, and he brought with him a clutch of gadgets and testing equipment. Ten of the best riders in the country were invited to Butare, where Jock rigged up a CompuTrainer to his laptop in the porch of the house where Tim Schilling, the director of the Spread coffee NGO, was staying. They arrived in a bundle on a Friday, all on two wheels of various gradations; the better bicycles reminded Jock of what he rode in the seventies, the worst of a garage sale. They had come from Kigali, a tough haul of nearly eighty miles with more than 2,000 metres of climbing, but they wore old football boots or tennis shoes. He put them up in the Centre Sainte-Jean-Baptiste, near the Roman Catholic church. The lodging was around £15 a night for room and full board, not cheap for Rwanda, but, when he saw how much the riders ate, it became rather good value. As they piled their plates high with food one night, the Rwandans began to realise this was serious: if the white coach was prepared to lavish three meals a day on them for a full weekend, then it might be worth sticking around.

Jock had a back-of-a-napkin budget for a team of four or five riders. Over the weekend, he took the group out riding, first to the border with Burundi and then west, along the road to the Democratic Republic of Congo. He chivvied them to string out in a line, each man's front wheel so close to the rear tyre of the rider in front that it was almost touching, searching for that sweet spot where he was shielded from the wind. When the gusts came from the side, Jock gesticulated at them to fan out across the road, rotating the lead riders, so that everyone had some respite. They didn't know it, but the Rwandans had formed their first single- and double-pace lines and an echelon. Stranger still, they stopped for ride food: they found a farmer on the road and cleared him out of bananas; a crowd formed – always a crowd formed – and cheered. Like Tom Ritchey, Jock noticed scars on almost all of them.

On Sunday morning they each did a test, riding a bicycle with its back wheel locked into a stand and hooked up to a power meter. Adrien Niyonshuti went early and posted an impressive wattage, particularly for his weight and build. When he finished, despite being one of the youngest riders, only just twenty, he stood by each of the riders as they were tested, urged them on, advised them on cadence and pacing. He was the first name on Jock's list. A natural-born leader: The Chosen One.

Not far behind was Nyandwi Uwase, who finished second to Adrien in the Wooden Bike mountain bike event. As characters, they were opposites: Nyandwi was more combustible than Adrien and less eager to please. He was ten when the genocide began, was forced to leave school and he never returned. He lived in Gisenyi on Lake Kivu with his mother and grandmother, five brothers and two sisters. Straight away, he had to become the main earner in his family. By the age of thirteen he had saved enough to buy an old single-speed and he started as a bicycle-taxi rider, one of the fastest in town. Each year, there was a race among bicycle-taxis in Gisenyi for bragging rights and a little prize money, and Nyandwi won it five years in succession. He was earning well – that is to say, maybe £10 in a good week – mostly taking goods and passengers across the Congo border to Goma, and he even had enough spare to buy a racing bike: a 1985 Eddy Merckx. Only two out of five gears actually worked, but he began entering the Tour of Rwanda and placed third the year that Jock returned. Jock suspected he might be trouble down the line, but his brute power was indisputable. He was The Flash One.

A counterbalance for Nyandwi was Nathan Byukusenge, The Dependable One. A Tutsi, he had grown up on a farm with cows, chickens and goats on a small rise about twenty miles south of Kigali. He had disappeared into the hills when the attacks started in 1994 and when Rwandan Patriotic Front soldiers eventually liberated his area, they spread the word that it was safe to return home. Nathan was convinced it must be a trap, but finally he was so hungry that he decided to take a chance. 'Life in the mountains was so difficult that I was ready to die,' he admitted. Four years older than Nyandwi, Nathan had also been at school in 1994 and only returned for one term afterwards. His father had been killed and as the eldest child he needed to earn for his three brothers and two sisters. He became a barber, but graduated to bicycle-taxis when he had saved enough for a basic *pneu ballon*. Just before the Americans arrived, he had decided to give up racing, so – at the age of twenty-six – this was his final throw. He had the maturity of someone who had already been providing for his family for more than a decade. Jock knew he was not an explosive talent, but he could ride all day, every day, and would never let him down.

Then there was The Smiley One, Jean de Dieu Uwimana, whom everyone called Rafiki, Swahili for 'friend'. He was the youngest cyclist in the group, but he had also been cycling competitively for the longest. His first memory was of being strapped to his mother's back, aged perhaps two or three, and her walking down from where they lived, near the top of Mount Kigali, to watch the finale of the 1990 Tour du Rwanda. The racers arrived at Nyamirambo stadium, spraying up dust and heat, and there was a magnificent scene as the top riders were given cows and goats as prizes. By the age of five, he was doodling bicycles in his school books and after the genocide – during which he was separated from his parents for five years, neither side of the family knowing if the other had survived – he would sneak money from his mother to rent a bike to ride. Not long after, Emmanuel Mayaka, the boss of the Ciné Elmay club in Kigali, gave him a racer to compete on.

Rafiki had chubby cheeks, saucer eyes and a few sparse strands of goatee hanging off his chin that only made him look younger than he was: nineteen. After Adrien, he was the most educated of the Rwandans – he had made it to the third year of secondary school – and with his snatches of English, Adrien's French, some hand signals and a lot of laughing, they had become the main liaisons between the riders and Jock. Rafiki's numbers on the CompuTrainer were fine, not off the charts, but the Coach recognised that if Team Rwanda was going to succeed, they would need to travel and it had to become a media story. Someone with Rafiki's charisma could easily become its star.

On Monday, Jock cycled halfway back to Kigali with the riders, bought some more bananas and said that he would call a select group back for further training the next weekend. Team Rwanda was taking shape.

While the testing was taking place, one word kept coming up: *Ruhumuriza, Ruhumuriza, Ruhumuriza*. Jock thought it might be a local word for 'bicycle' and it was a mistake that even Rwandans made. At that time – and years later, in fact – one name was synonymous with the sport in the country and that was Abraham Ruhumuriza.

Eventually the Coach worked this out, and discovered that Abraham lived just outside Butare, where Jock was staying. He even used a bike that belonged to Tim Schilling. Since the Tour of Rwanda had restarted in 2001, Abraham had dominated it, winning four years in succession from 2002. No one since Adrien's uncle Emmanuel Turatsinze had been so invincible. For forty-nine weeks a year, he was Butare's speediest bicycle-taxi. He would then take a fortnight's break before the Tour of Rwanda, do some cursory training and show up at the week-long race to thrash the field. On the Monday afterwards, he would be back at work. His hours were 6 a.m. to 5 p.m., seven days a week and usually there would be a queue for his services. 'It was prestigious to ride with me,' he told me. 'None of the other bicycle-taxis would get a passenger if I was there.' I suggested that he could have charged extra for his services, but he looked horrified. His customers were his friends.

No one becomes rich riding a bicycle-taxi, however fast they are, and Abraham had a wife and three children to support. The most he ever earned in one day was 4,500 Rwandan francs, around £4.50: 'That was fantastic!' he exclaimed, his face exploding into a broad smile. How far would he ride on a busy day as a bicycle-taxi: maybe twenty, thirty miles? More like eighty or a hundred, he thought. His earnings would be bolstered by his annual Tour of Rwanda winnings, perhaps £50. What would he do with the prize money? 'I'd buy a goat and eat it!' He laughed a joyous gargle.

Abraham was short, but his legs were real kegs, with calves that appeared to have been inflated by a bicycle pump. He was charming, but people often described him as the most stubborn man they had ever met. This partly explained why he was such a powerful cyclist and certainly contributed to the fact that he could be a nightmare to manage. When the Americans arrived, Abraham was not particularly intrigued. He didn't attend the Wooden Bike Classic in Kibuye, because he would miss out on the taxi fares that he could collect in Butare. When Jock returned, word again reached Abraham from the Coach's driver Saidi. Would he like to come and test? 'Ruhumuriza does not need to be tested. He is the best,' came the reply, dictated to Saidi. Jock asked him to come out for a bike ride. Abraham sent back a message that his bike was 'broken'. He might as well have added that he was washing his hair and alphabetising his CD collection, too.

But almost a month passed and Abraham saw that Jock was not leaving. More than that, he was still paying for meals and accommodation and handing out kit and free shoes to the riders. He begrudgingly accepted that this might be worth investigating after all. He agreed to go for a ride with Jock: while the American stuck to the right side of the road, as the law of the land dictated, Abraham determinedly stayed on the left, staring down the oncoming traffic. They returned to Tim Schilling's house and Abraham scored disdainfully well on the CompuTrainer, even though he insisted on a bike set-up that Jock knew was clearly not maximising his power. Jock asked him to cycle with the four new members of Team Rwanda, and Abraham showed up hours late, despite being the only one who lived locally.

Alarm bells were ringing, but for some reason Jock chose to ignore them: he asked Abraham to join the team. Abraham took a moment to think – there was talk of a monthly salary of $100 in the future, which was a lot of bicycle-taxi trips – and accepted. The Belligerent One was in, and now they were five.

For the first team ride, Abraham and Jock pedalled up to Kigali, this time on the same side of the road, to meet the others. They stayed at the Presbyterian Centre and the next morning headed forty miles east to Rwamagana to visit Adrien's home. Rwamagana had a quiet sleepiness that reminded Jock of old Western towns, the kind where saloon doors swing and creak. At Adrien's family home, Jock found they had no electricity or running water and just the most basic furniture. He felt chastened for having handed each of the riders new Polar CS600 heart-rate monitors the previous week and suggesting they download the files onto their laptops. It was a similar tale when they returned to Kigali and stopped at Rafiki's house, except he didn't even have cement floors, just freshly swept dirt. His mother, who introduced him to cycling, served the energetically boiled cassava dish *sombe*, which Jock described later as like 'green Play-Doh'. The riders ate it wearing their new Oakley M-Frame glasses, a gift from one of the team's new sponsors, which the Rwandans had taken to wearing indoors and out.

The five riders were cycling more than they had ever done in their lives, more than they imagined possible. There is always a moment in a professional's life when this pastime crosses from fun to job: their body changes, hardens, behaves differently; it becomes a machine. For Jock, that happened in May 1977, when he joined his first serious team in France, Lejeune BP. He suddenly realised how deep tiredness could go. 'Think of being completely exhausted, then train and ride as much as when you're fresh,' he remembered. Now he was inflicting similar punishment on his Rwandan charges. He made them cycle at least thirty miles even on rest days. Later Adrien looked back on all the training he had done before Coach had arrived and thought: *Until now, I was just joking*. But the spirit in the group remained strong. Jock, the cod-anthropologist, noted in his journal, 'I am also struck that there are seemingly no animosities or fights amongst them or, if they are, they are very passive ones.'

Entirely unwittingly, he had selected a group of five individuals who were both Hutu and Tutsi – though, of course, no one used those distinctions anyone – and from a mix of the country's regions, classes and religions. It was, in its way, a perfect representation of President Kagame's new Rwanda. And it was sort of working.

*

Over dinner one night, Jock asked the riders, 'Right, which of you has got a passport?' Each of them in turn slowly shook his head. After the laptops, Jock was prepared for this answer, but it needed to be rectified. Tom Ritchey had signed up Team Rwanda for its first race, the Cape Epic, the biggest and rowdiest mountain bike event in the world, which was taking place in South Africa at the end of March 2007. The good news was that Kagame was on side, thanks in part to Tom's friend Peb Jackson, and the torturous passport-application process was expedited by the minister of the interior. Entry into the Cape Epic hinted at a difference in opinion between Tom and Jock. Tom, whose mountain bike squads in the eighties were packed with Olympians and world champions, had an original concept that the team should concentrate on off-road competitions. Jock, because of his experience as a road racer, leaned in that direction. Initially, at least, they compromised by doing both.

The two riders selected for the Cape Epic were Adrien and Rafiki; Abraham would have taken Rafiki's spot, but he had not yet come out of his sulk. For both riders, the only time they had ever sat on a mountain bike was the previous year's Wooden Bike Classic, but that was only the start of the new experiences. Adrien had never left Rwanda before and it was the first time he had flown on an aeroplane. When they arrived in Cape Town, it was the first time he had eaten salmon, the first time he had seen a chandelier. For someone whose idea of prosperity was a concrete floor, it could have been a sensory overload.

But then there was the race to think about. Jock did not know too much about it; he had been sent a DVD but never quite got round to watching it. Afterwards he admitted that was probably for the best because, if he had seen it, he would never have allowed Adrien and Rafiki to ride. There were more than 1,200 competitors, including seven of the top ten cross-country riders in the world. They rode in pairs, so Adrien teamed up with Jock, and Rafiki partnered with another American, Doug Andrews. The race lasted eight days and covered 550 miles around the Western Cape, climbing almost twice the height of Mount Everest; the longest stage was almost ninety miles, which is monstrous on a mountain bike. Each morning, they were woken by an earth-shuddering horn at 4.50 a.m. and then faced with a day of battling technical downhills, river traverses and 'hike a bike' sections where they had to clamber on foot across miles of rocks. On one day, Jock and Adrien had a combined total of fifteen flat tyres. At night they bunked down in a field of a thousand one-man tents and waited for daybreak, the horn, and a new episode of misery to start.

After the first day, Adrien was wrecked; he collapsed at the finish line and begged Jock to let them quit the race. Jock laughed him off and said they had done well. Only later did he find out how well: they had finished in twenty-fourth place on the stage. The days became tougher after that, but – just as had happened during his Tour of Rwanda debut in 2004 – Adrien seemed to become stronger, find inner reserves. On the sixth day, they stayed with the front group – the best cross-country mountain bikers in the world – for the whole day through the lush farmland of Robertson Valley and finished thirteenth. By the end, it was obvious that the potential of the Rwandan riders was more than just numbers and lines on graphs. In the event that has been called 'the Tour de France of mountain biking', Adrien and Jock had finished in thirty-third place out of 607 teams; they had been on their bikes for more than forty hours, a full working week. Rafiki spent much of the race in the bushes – 'In my life I thought I had seen scarier things,' he said, incredulous. 'People would come on big motorcycles to see if I was dead' – but he and Doug Andrews came a creditable sixty-third.

Jock tried not to let on quite how excited he was. The talent was there, their capacity for suffering was certainly there. What are the best cyclists if not a combination of these traits? When they returned to Rwanda, President Kagame asked to meet the riders and their team-mates on Team Rwanda. They had dinner and he explained to them that they were now ambassadors for the country. Kagame knew something the cyclists did not: Jock's foreign ambitions were only just beginning. And this time the whole squad would be going.

'America! Am-er-eeeca!' One of the Rwandans would say it, shaking his head, and the other four would howl with glee.

The first time they screamed was when they entered the 101 Freeway, all six lanes of it, just outside San Francisco airport. There are no motorways in Rwanda, all the roads are two-lane highways. Outside Rwamagana, there's a loop road that could probably be described as a bypass, but that's about as complicated as road layouts get. Now, after thirty-six hours in airports, planes and immigration, thousands of cars were swirling around them. Jock was driving his crew-cab pick-up truck and the Rwandans were lined up on the rear bench seat, climbing over each other to look out of the windows. At one point, they drew alongside a Hummer with twenty-inch chrome wheels driven by a petite woman, and Rafiki announced, 'This will be my car in Kigali!' The rest of the group fell off their seats in hysterics.

'America! Am-er-eeeca!'

The Rwandans left Kigali on 24 April 2007, a little more than two months after the creation of the team, and stayed in the United States until the end of June. The aim of the trip was to expose the five riders to an intensity of racing that they would never find on the African continent. It was also to introduce them to their new backers. Team Rwanda was run on donations and they needed to raise at least £100,000 a year from companies and private individuals. The project always wanted to give 'eyeball to eyeball': donors would invest in a small group of people who would then influence hundreds, thousands, perhaps millions of their compatriots. In both these respects, the American trip was a conspicuous success: the money rolled in and the Rwandans sucked up race experience.

I always enjoyed talking to the Rwandans about visiting America. It was not so much that they fell in love with the country, but they found it confusing and eccentric. Its excesses had hardened into anecdotes that they obviously revelled in telling. Our conversations could take a surreal turn. They would describe something and, like a Christmas party game, I would have to decipher what they meant. A motorbike on water? Easy, a jetski. Abraham talked about 'salads that looked like flowers' and 'grapes with seeds that I thought was meat', neither of which I satisfactorily resolved. I spent five minutes talking with Nathan about one particularly memorable meal and only realised in the car on the way home that he had been describing his first burrito.

We talked for hours, but still I never came close to working out how they processed what they saw, as they ventured up and down America's West Coast and headed across into Utah and Nevada. With the exception of three sprawling, Kenyan-owned Nakumatt supermarkets in Kigali, where *muzungus* far outnumber locals, food shops in Rwanda are simple affairs. They are pretty well stocked, the fruits are extraordinary, but there are often large gaps between different items and exaggerated prominence is given to products an outsider might take for granted, such as drinking straws. Now, for two months, the Rwandans' local grocery store was the Whole Foods Market in Monterey and they were staying down the road in Carmel, the seaside resort where not so long ago the actor Clint Eastwood was mayor. How could they make sense of that?

There were wondrous moments, certainly. On a training ride, high in the La Sal Mountains above Moab in Utah, they found a patch of snow no larger than a blanket and all the riders stopped and rubbed the white powder on their heads, arms and legs. Adrien removed his shoes and squealed as he padded round on it. The five of them were struck dumb as they drove down The Strip in Las Vegas at 1 a.m. in a 1972 Blue Bird Wanderlodge, their rented motorhome that was originally customised for John Wayne. The Rwandans rode horses, they saw a train for the first time, they learned to make pizzas. Jock wondered if they might be able to take the experience back, but then he remembered that none of them had anything close to an oven at home. In Foot Locker, two supporters of the team said they could each pick out one outfit they liked and a pair of sneakers. Faced with hundreds of pairs of shoes and racks of clothing, the choice was paralysing. More than an hour later – they would still have been there now, if they had not been set a deadline – they were ready to buy an identical line-up of pristine white sweats. The Americans intervened and Abraham swapped his for black and Adrien, daringly, went with grey. 'They didn't seem to like varying much from what the others got,' Jock noted. 'Odd.'

'America! Am-er-eeeca!'

What the Rwandans returned to again and again in our conversations, though, was the space. In densely packed

Rwanda, only the very wealthy would have any. Families lived together, while siblings and friends shared beds; privacy did not exist. It was more ingrained than that, too. In Tucson, Arizona, Jock picked up a new eighteen-seater Ford Econoline van. There was plenty of room to spread out, the Rwandans could have had a bench each practically, but they crowded together in one row. This was common across Rwanda: people sat vacuum-packed in the local buses; in fact, these vehicles are known colloquially as *twegerane* or 'let's stick together'. One day, I tried to explain to my interpreter, Liberal, that it was a deeply instilled desire of all British people not to sit next to anyone on public transport. He laughed, and said a version of something that I heard many times in Rwanda: 'That individual life – as you have in Europe – we don't have that here.'

One manifestation of this communal ethos is *Umuganda*. Since colonial times, citizens have engaged in mandatory community service on the last Saturday of each month. On those mornings, the roads clear, public transport stops. If a neighbour's house, say, has been damaged by a landslide, a crew might be organised to fix it up. Doctors – or anyone with a special skill – are expected to offer their services for free on *Umuganda* days. Everyone between the ages of eighteen and sixty-five is obliged to contribute – including the new stars of Team Rwanda. So when Jock instructed his recruits to work together to improve their lots it was really a message that had been drilled into them throughout their lives.

When they left California for their road trips through the desert, the Rwandans drove fifty miles without seeing a soul. Or, stranger still, there would be one house standing on its own. 'In our culture, when you don't have salt you just go to your neighbour and get some salt or some oil,' Rafiki explained. 'In America, you have to have your own salt and your own oil

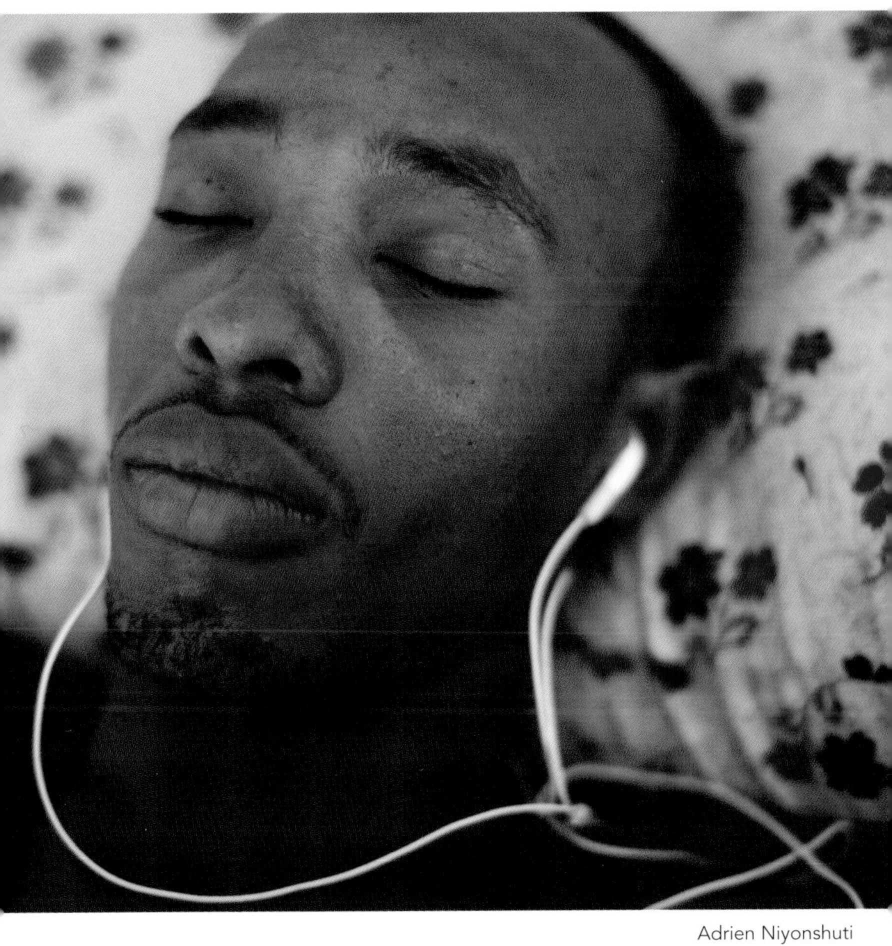

Adrien Niyonshuti

14

Tour of Rwanda

96
96

NDA

Gasore Hategeka at home in Sashwara, Western Province

16
PROJECT RWANDA
RWANDA
16
12
RWANDA
12

Emmanuel Rudahunga (No. 16) and Gasore Hategeka (No. 12) at the Tour of Rwanda, 2010

Left: President Paul Kagame;
Right: Adrien Niyonshuti and Jock Boyer

– you have to be completely self-sufficient – because otherwise you will have to drive a hundred kilometres to get it.'

The racing, which no one worried too much about, was equally discombobulating. The five Rwandans had arrived in America in the best shape of their lives and they now had gleaming fluorescent kit and a new Schwinn road bike and Scott mountain bike each waiting for them. Their first competition was the five-day Tour of the Gila road race through the New Mexico desert. From the first stage, the Team Rwanda riders were badly off the pace; they would finish each day exhausted, complaining of 'piri piri' lungs, a neologism they created for the feeling of hyperventilating in the hot, dry air. On day two, Abraham announced that he had malaria, but would continue the race with medication. The competition was fierce – Levi Leipheimer, a podium finisher in the Tour de France, has been a recent two-time Gila champion – and the mild-mannered Rwandans shrunk away from confrontation and were comprehensively out-muscled by their race-hardened competitors.

The worst stage was actually the shortest, a manic one-hour criterium around the streets of Silver City. Rafiki was popped out of the bunch after just one lap, Nyandwi lasted a few laps more and Nathan followed shortly afterwards. Abraham and Adrien hung in longest, but both were eventually lapped by the main field. Back in John Wayne's Blue Bird Wanderlodge, Jock was surprised to find the Rwandans laughing. Abraham said it was like a 'genocide' and that they had been 'slaughtered'. They had not been able to drink because they had been too scared to remove their hands from the handlebars. They were still carrying armfuls of energy bars in their shirt pockets. As they dumped them in a pile on the table, even Jock cracked a smile. But, at the final reckoning, Team Rwanda had finished dead last of the thirteen squads.

The rest of the racing followed a similar pattern: no lack of effort, but a profound absence of experience and ruthlessness. At the Mount Hood Cycling Classic in Oregon, Nyandwi and Abraham were involved in a pile-up and withdrew. Jock tracked them down to the local hospital's emergency room, but Nyandwi had only a few minor scratches, while Abraham had a pain in his side and nothing showed up on X-ray. It occurred to Jock that the issue was simple naivety: they had always been used to leading races, avoiding the worst crashes; they had simply never had to deal with such high speeds and complicated tactics before.

Before they left America, Jock organised full medical check-ups for the five Rwandans, including dental work. It was an act of thoughtfulness for which they would not thank him. Over the course of two days in Montery, Dr Steve Chang administered eighteen fillings for Nathan, a root canal for Adrien and doped them all up on novocaine. Rafiki's wisdom teeth were so mangled that Dr Chang broke his instruments trying to extract them. When each of them emerged shakily from the consulting room, the other riders stood up and consoled him like they were grieving. They were packed off with armfuls of toothpaste and mouthwash, but sadly, these were all confiscated from their hand luggage by a security official at San Francisco airport as they went to board the flight home.

'America! Am-er-eeeca!'

The most enduring legacy of the American adventure was that Team Rwanda was now just that: a team. They had been used to racing back home as loners; each position in any race there was contested tooth-and-nail for the extra francs it would yield. But cycling, at any serious level, is a collective endeavour. The most celebrated example is the Tour de France where the winner does not take a cent of the victory cheque, instead splitting it between his eight team-mates. This is not altruism, rather an acceptance that it is a feat that can only be achieved collectively.

When the Rwandans landed at Kigali airport, their bags stripped of dental-hygiene products, they were swamped by family, friends, newspaper and radio reporters and a crew from the one television station. Rafiki had bought a stack of postcards to give away, but he was quickly cleaned out. Everyone wanted to hear about their experiences, but where could they start? The fact that the Americans kept animals in their homes? The time they ate four chickens, vegetables, salad and two loaves of wholegrain bread – and then had dessert? The night they went to the multiplex and watched *Spider-Man* 3, stuffing their faces with popcorn? Or perhaps when they drove 800 miles overnight and arrived in the little town of Hood River (population: 7,214) in Oregon to find an entire street swishing with Rwandan flags?

The five were back training soon enough, and that was somehow easier. They were the only ones who really understood what they had been through. Rafiki told me once that they felt like a hand and, if any of the others was absent, it was like missing a finger.

Jock was moved by how close they were becoming. They had given each other nicknames: Abraham was *punda*, the donkey; Nathan was *icyugu*, a lizard with a big head; Adrien, just Dri Dri. Jock had noticed that if he gave them a hotel room each, the Rwandans hated it. They much preferred to sleep together, throwing the mattresses on the floor, as if it was a children's sleepover. And the bond was reinforced every time they climbed on the bike. 'It is a harmonious team, it definitely is,' Jock told me at the 2010 Tour of Rwanda. 'They are a team out there suffering together and when you suffer together it puts a whole different dynamic on the relationship you have with the other person.

'I saw it in the pro peloton,' he went on. 'Very few people understand what you are going through except those that are going through it, too. It's like being in the trench with somebody. When you share pain with somebody and you are on the same side, it puts a bond there that you can't really describe.'

I asked Rafiki if they talked about the genocide, and he replied that they did, but not so often. They knew each other's stories but it was not something that they brought up much. It was too raw, it didn't serve any purpose. It was impossible that they had not been affected by it – a Unicef study estimated that five out of six children who had been in Rwanda during the genocide had, at the very least, witnessed bloodshed – but it made little sense to dwell on it. The five were an intriguing cross-section of what Philip Gourevitch has called 'the interim generation'. Each of them had a vivid personal experience of the terror and they were not so young that it was purely a historical event. But equally, because they were still children when the killing was taking place – Abraham, the oldest, was fourteen, Nathan thirteen – they were not implicated in the slaughter.

The distinction remained an important one. While there is widespread acceptance of President Kagame's tenet that it is no longer helpful to think of Hutu and Tutsi, those labels have not been entirely abandoned, particularly by the older generation. I noticed it creeping in when I spoke with Adrien's sister, Jeanne, at the milk bar in Rwamagana. She laughed bitterly and said, 'It's better to keep quiet instead of talking about delicate issues, because in the long run, I would only end up getting very angry.' The feeling was even more evident with Serge Rusagara, Anselme Sakumi's son, who had to watch his parents being killed. 'The thing is: they wanted us to die,' he said. 'I'm still alive and I will not say that I'm richer than them, but I live a better life than what they have at the moment. God will punish them, I will not spend my time running after them. If they come back to disturb me that will be an issue, but they live their life, I live mine.'

This interim generation, however, appeared to have found it easier to move on. All of the riders had lost loved ones. Some in the first wave of attacks in April 1994, while others were killed in the government reprisals that followed the genocide – the 'War of Infiltration', as Hutu Power forces in exile waged a guerrilla campaign against the Rwandan mainland throughout the nineties. All of the members of Team Rwanda had suffered deeply, and that was enough. When Adrien snapped his chain trying to qualify for the Olympic road race, much was made of the fact that the rider who selflessly gave up his bicycle was a Hutu, Gasore Hategeka. 'In the past that could have been a totally different situation,' Kimberly Coats told Clive Owen in ominous tones at the Criterion Theatre in London before the Olympics. In practice, Team Rwanda seemed to have resolved many of those deep-seated issues within months of formation, back in 2007.

Still, it was hard not to become swept along with the narrative of redemption. At the 2010 Tour of Rwanda, Adrien took the yellow jersey after a spectacular solo effort over the mountains and a bird-like descent into Gisenyi. There had been thrashing rain for more than an hour, but when finally it became evident that he had done enough mathematically to secure a lead in the race, the clouds dramatically cleared and sunshine burst through. The sound system pumped out 'Intsinzi bana b'u Rwanda', a patriotic anthem written by a schoolteacher in 1992 while in exile in Uganda that was played after the liberation in 1994 and had accompanied each of President Kagame's election victories. Podium girls in the traditional wrap dresses, *imishanana*, sashayed to the music, thousands in the crowd screamed and it felt like all of Rwanda joined them in their celebration.

Later that evening, I caught up with Joseph Habineza, the minister for youth, sport and culture. He was having an aperitif on the patio of the Lake Kiva Serena Hotel. The hotel, the smartest in Rwanda, had been ransacked by fleeing *génocidaires* in 1994 and he pointed out bullet holes in the wall. Did Adrien's personal history, I wondered, the death of so many family members, make this a particularly symbolic moment for Rwandans? 'Minister Joe', a true silverback of a man, looked confused. 'That doesn't make sense for many Rwandans, because many have the same story,' he replied. 'But for people like you – outsiders – the story gives them more emotions. For Rwandans, it's part of society; many people have tragic stories like that. What you saw today was our resilience: we had a bad experience, but now is our time. Let's move, let's win, let's conquer the world!'

Jock was never particularly interested in the life experiences of his riders – even after years in the country his knowledge of the genocide was cursory – but he was fascinated by their ability to suffer. He talked about pain a lot and he had a weakness for those motivational aphorisms that one imagines are pinned up in the weights rooms of American high schools. Pain was Jock's leitmotif, the ink lines that joined the dots in his life. After his father left their family when he was a child, he was never particularly happy. He discovered cycling at an impressionable age and it allowed him to channel his negative emotions into something he could control. A suffering that had purpose. In his career, he sought out the most difficult challenges: first the Tour de France and then the Race Across America. He discovered that as much as pain really hurt – obviously – the feeling of dominating it was transcendent.

Among people who cycle for a living, Jock is not the exception, he's the rule. The greatest racers have always loved going beyond their threshold. Since the nineteen-nineties, the dominant theory in endurance sport has been that our bodies are regulated by a mechanism in our brains called 'the central governor'. This stops us harming ourselves before things get really serious – the originator of the concept, Professor Tim Noakes from the University of Cape Town, compared it to the reflex that stops us holding our breath until we die. The central governor theory explained why doping could be so dangerous; drugs such as amphetamines artificially jeopardise the connections between our brains and the muscles they control. That was why Tom Simpson, the greatest British cyclist before Bradley Wiggins, died on Mount Ventoux in the 1967 Tour de France on a day when – the story goes – a thermometer in a café exploded when showing 54°C. The drugs did not kill him, but the fact that they could override the central governor, which would have been screaming at him to stop, did.

All professional cyclists have a complicated relationship with their central governor. The German cult hero Jens Voigt frequently shouted at his to 'Shut up!' Many riders, too, appear to find the sport helpful for exorcising personal demons. Greg LeMond was abused as a twelve-year-old and struggled for years with undiagnosed attention-deficit disorder: 'a fog' in his brain. 'I'm kind of a survivor,' he once said. 'In cycling, you can't really give up in races, even when you're really dying. And I've won races because I don't give up.' The first line of Tyler Hamilton's autobiography *The Secret Race* is, 'I'm good at pain.'

Hamilton fractured his shoulder at the 2002 Giro d'Italia and kept riding, but ground down eleven of his teeth to the roots.

Lance Armstrong's mother gave birth to him when she was seventeen, two years later his father disappeared and he never saw him again. A cancer survivor, he often compared the rigours of chemotherapy with the demands of hard riding. But Armstrong – sometimes with chemical help, it turned out – went on to bully his central governor around, just like he did everyone else. 'Cycling is so hard, the suffering is so intense, that it's absolutely cleansing,' he wrote in his book, *It's Not About the Bike*, in 2000. 'The pain is so deep and strong that a curtain descends over your brain . . . Once, someone asked me what pleasure I took in riding for so long. "Pleasure?" I said. "I don't understand the question." I didn't do it for pleasure, I did it for pain.'

With his Rwandan riders, Jock liked the fact that they did not complain. Even Abraham eventually started to toe the line. They would set out on a training ride, no food in their pockets, no idea how long they would be out on the road, and just put their heads down and spin. If he bought them some bananas – a bunch of ten pudgy fingers costs around seventy pence – they were embarrassingly grateful. 'These riders start empty, ride empty and finish empty,' Jock marvelled. At one stop, deep in the primal Nyungwe Forest National Park, near the Congo border, the guesthouse only had ice-cold water for their showers. Jock ducked his head under and then jumped into bed for half an hour to warm up. The Rwandans took their leisurely time, savouring their first running water for weeks. 'Just more evidence that I'm not as tough as these guys,' Jock noted that day in his journal.

Pain on the bike is only alleviated by the belief – often misguided – that others are suffering as much or even more.

This perception existed in Team Rwanda, too. Adrien told me that he couldn't even conceive how hard it must be to work as a bicycle-taxi. 'My luck I didn't do that job,' he said, shaking his head in disbelief. 'Those guys are very, very strong. I can't imagine how someone would ride for three years or five years on a single-speed taxi . . . Oof! They have power. More power than me.' Nathan, who did the job for almost a decade, brushed off the compliment. 'When I was doing taxi, I could go slowly and when I was really tired I could stop. In racing, you can only carry on.'

It was tempting to see these Rwandans as riding their bikes out of poverty. Turning the emotional and mental torment of the genocide in an empowering and cleansing new direction. Tempting but probably simplistic. There is a deep-rooted culture of work in Rwanda, and any nation with so few natural resources and so many people is sure to have competitiveness as one of its national traits. The country always produced skilled and determined cyclists, long before the events of 1994, whether it was Emmanuel Turatsinze or a farmer who had to haul eighty kilograms of bananas over four hills on an ancient bike to reach the local market. The five riders whom Jock selected were exceptional mostly in their good fortune to be at the peak of their powers when he arrived in Rwanda and to have quickly recognised the golden ticket he was offering them.

The paradox of cycling, of course, is that the rider who does best often suffers the least, or certainly for the shortest period of time. This meant that the summer of 2007, after Team Rwanda returned from the United States, must have been unrelenting torture for the five riders. Their tour of Africa stopped first in Cape Town for the 'B' World Championship, a second-tier road race that was still strong enough to include competitors from

China, Egypt, Namibia and Azerbaijan. Adrien, Abraham and Nyandwi were sent for that, and their best placing was Adrien in seventy-first. At the All-Africa Games in Algeria, they did not fare any better. There were crashes, mechanical issues and they were simply way off the pace: Adrien again led them in, this time in thirty-eighth position.

In July 2007, the riders had their first opportunity to qualify for the Olympics at the African Mountain Bike Championships in Namibia. This was the event that, four years later, Adrien would complete in fourth place to secure his passage to London. From the start their quest appeared doomed. At Windhoek airport, only one of the ten bags they had checked in arrived, and none of the bikes. Rafiki came down with malaria. The race field was desperately weak: twenty-two riders in total, five of whom were Rwandan, and they just had to finish among the first three nations. But the riders could not practise on the course, because their bikes arrived late, and they had five flat tyres in the race. Adrien finished ninth, outside the Olympic qualification.

The Rwandan riders took these failures badly. At nights, they talked in their rooms about how they were letting down Coach. After the progress they had made in America, they all realised that they had stalled. Surely Jock would leave them and go home now. Finally, Rafiki and Adrien were pushed by the others to ask: *Is this the end?*

Jock was taken aback: the thought hadn't crossed his mind. He had, in fact, been stunned by their progress. He had actually been about to tell them that they would now be on a salary of $100 a week. They had gone from riding 120 miles a week to upwards of 400 miles and they were only becoming fitter and more powerful. They had participated in more races in six months than they had in the rest of their lives. It could take one or two years for their bodies to adapt to the increased workload. This did not even take into account the cultural challenges, exotic foods and endless hours spent in airports. Jock did not say it, but his instincts were particularly strong with Adrien. He recognised the same drive and single-minded focus that he had once had.

'We're only just starting,' he promised them.

6
IKINAMICO

Modern Rwanda can, at times, feel like an unprecedented, high-stakes sociological experiment. Never before has any nation tried to integrate the victims of a genocide with the perpetrators of the crimes on such an epic scale. People who for decades defined themselves as Hutu or Tutsi really do live side by side in the same villages, towns and cities where the attacks were unleashed less than two decades ago. With such a dysfunctional core premise, the country should be a wild, anarchic place. But that is exactly what it is not, for the most part. At the end of one stage of the Tour of Rwanda, I met an American who had lived in the country for about a year. He was still dripping with sweat from a morning's mountain biking. 'The country is incredibly safe; it's very clean,' he explained. 'It's actually quite boring, to be honest.'

Boring in Africa, though, is a badge of honour. It means stability, an inconceivable dream for most countries in the continent. Boring means that motorcycle riders all wear helmets and passengers in cars are legally obliged to wear seatbelts (albeit a law enforced by policemen toting machine guns). It means national health insurance and ambitious schools where attendance at primary level has trebled and where the One Laptop Per Child programme is making a visible difference. Boring means working with health agencies to counteract epidemics of AIDS, malaria and tuberculosis and a reduction of child mortality, in recent years, by seventy per cent. It means not having to routinely pay bribes. Boring is President Paul Kagame's signature achievement.

In 1994, Rwanda was a broken, blood-drenched country with seemingly insurmountable problems – not least that as many as one million of its citizens were implicated in the violence and hatred of the genocide. Even years later, its recovery remained almost unfathomable. Kagame's core strategy was risky, even antithetical: he believed that to rebuild Rwanda in a time span of decades, not centuries, the country needed to concentrate on reconciliation not revenge. He abolished the death penalty. He was so convinced by the plan that he offered extraordinary incentives for Hutus who had fled the country to return. *Génocidaires* were sent to demobilisation camps, where they were lectured on the new tenets of Rwandan life. Somehow, Kagame convinced a grieving and embittered population – enough of them, anyway – that his hunch was the right one.

Kagame himself was a man so unlike other rapacious African kleptocrats that it was said that his sister once worked a nine-to-five job in a kiosk in Kigali airport. Here was a leader who had outlawed plastic bags in the whole country for environmental reasons. He spent hundreds of millions of dollars on an infrastructure for fibre-optic cables that he believed would rival any in the developed world. He sunk an eight-figure investment into an American biotech company. Yet his only personal extravagances were regular games of tennis at the capital's Cercle Sportif club and a reputation for changing his shirt three times a day. His house in Kigali was modest, certainly not a palace, though it did emerge that when he went to New York in 2011 he booked the Mandarin Oriental's Presidential Suite at a cost of more than $15,000 a night.

The president was not charming so much as formidable, and he approached his job not with the wonkiness of a politician but with the directness of a brilliant military general – which everyone agrees he was. This meant that, with his blessing, major change could be effected with impressive haste. Bill Clinton called Kagame, 'One of the greatest leaders of our time.' To Tony Blair, he was no less than 'a visionary leader'; in 2008, Blair set up a foundation, the Africa Governance Initiative, that placed around a dozen advisers from the UK in the president's policy unit and the prime minister's office. (Kagame's friends were overwhelmingly Anglophone and he showed where his priorities lay in 2008 when he announced that Rwanda's entire education system was switching from French to English-language. The following year, Rwanda joined the Commonwealth, becoming only the second member – the other is Mozambique – not to have been part of the British Empire.)

So it may have been boring, but it was not as if nothing ever happened in Rwanda. Construction in Kigali appeared to be booming: a skyline of five-star hotels and convention centres was rising, and there are advanced plans for a new international airport and a national museum of Rwanda. Children are everywhere – over half the population is under eighteen, and have no direct memory of the genocide – and rural areas, in particular, often exude a joyous atmosphere. History, which takes place over decades or even centuries in the Old World, happens here in fast-forward.

At the same time, it is undeniable that the magic of Rwanda can sometimes feel buried. In a society that prizes order, no one wants to stand out for being too different. It is a country that desperately needs to loosen its tie a little. On a recent New Year's Eve, the police announced a curfew for midnight. 'It defeats the whole thing,' spluttered Albert Rudatsimburwa, the head of Contact FM, Rwanda's most popular radio station. 'That's when it starts!'

Rwanda had not always been so strait-laced, Albert claimed. In the immediate aftermath of the genocide, in fact, there was a burst of creativity; live bands played every night all over Kigali. But around the turn of the millennium, a conservative mayor began to enforce stricter rules and the scene died out. 'The president lives in town, not far from the city centre, so the guys are always freaking out that it's too loud. Hell, we're in Africa! You want to be loud in the open air. So everything is clean but flavourless.' Albert paused, trying to encapsulate Kigali's problems: 'It doesn't smell of funk any more.'

What did Rwandans feel about the eerie calm that engulfed much of their country? The first person I felt comfortable asking this question to was Claude, the night porter in my hotel in Kigali on my first visit. Thanks to irregular sleep patterns, I ended up spending a lot of time with Claude. He was young and smart; a university student who worked nights to pay his fees – I never established when he actually slept. Our conversations started safely enough: Premier League football, the unshowy beauty of Rwanda. But quickly they became more interesting. Claude was born a Tutsi, but was one of the seven per cent who didn't vote at the last election for President Kagame ('Mister K' he called him, because he was worried that our conversations were being listened to by the military intelligence unit known as J2). He was no fan of the *gacaca* community courts that dispensed justice to the perpetrators of the genocide and he said that any Hutus in the government were basically tokenistic. 'The fight', he predicted, would return in ten to fifteen years.

Claude said there was one thing I had to know about his compatriots. 'All Rwandans are hypocrites,' he hissed, whispering but jabbing the counter with his index finger. 'They tell you lies, lies, lies.' I told him this didn't square with what I had experienced so far: I'd never met such unfailingly polite and amenable people. 'Acting,' he explained. I laughed; he had the wild eyes and urgent delivery of a conspiracy theorist. Claude shook his head. Rwandans would never speak to a *muzungu* like they would speak to each other. An outsider could never penetrate that core unknowability. 'Trust me, my friend Lewis, we are hypocrites – maybe God created us like that.'

Jock Boyer was starting to realise that there was much he needed to learn about Rwandans, too. No question, the riders were improving and growing stronger. Not long after coming back from the African Mountain Bike Championships in Namibia, Abraham Ruhumuriza won the 2007 Tour of Rwanda, his fifth career overall victory. Team Rwanda's five riders won every stage. The second Wooden Bike Classic was held shortly afterwards in Butare; in the blue-riband event, Adrien Niyonshuti pipped his team-mates in a bunch sprint at the end of a road race from Kigali. The pace was too hot for the visitors who included Marion Clignet, a world champion track cyclist, and Kelly Crowley, a Paralympian; Tom Ritchey crashed into a ditch after a high-speed front-wheel flat, but groggily finished the course. Off the bikes, a new set of potential benefactors was introduced to the country, including Dick DeVos, part of the dynasty that owns Amway, one of the United States' largest direct-selling companies (DeVos was escorted by an incongruous posse of bodyguards: 'like toting a bazooka to a baby shower,' one obsever noted). It was gratifying for Jock to see how much fitter his five men were than other

Rwandan competitors and some strong American riders. But their performances were still patchy: to make a real difference in Rwanda, he needed new riders pushing through.

But, as Jock widened the team, his frustrations grew. Most of these niggles, he knew, were cultural. It often came back to time-keeping. Everyone had warned him about the fluidity of 'African time': they would arrange to meet at 8 a.m. and the riders might, if he was lucky, roll in at 10 a.m. Abraham was particularly unreliable, even though he lived nearby. Jock bought them watches, but it did not make any difference. His journal from the time became increasingly consumed with details of airports, lost bags and missed or narrowly caught aeroplanes. An hour before one flight departed for Algeria, the riders were sat eating a relaxed lunch, not even at the airport. Jock tracked them down: their bags were packed, right? No. Their bikes broken down? Not all of them. A car booked to pick them up? He didn't even need to ask.

The scale of the challenge facing Jock was starting to hit home. During training camps, the riders had purified water, but as soon as they went home, they would drink from contaminated local supplies. They were regularly struck down with malaria. On the bikes, Jock noticed that every time one of the Rwandans took a sip from his water bottle, he would lose ground on the pack by a few metres. So, after stowing his bidon, he wasted energy catching up. It took more than a year of coaching to teach them to drink and keep pedalling. In America, Jock's spies in the peloton told him that they were also spending too long sitting in the full force of the wind. He had tried to explain slipstreaming to them – the idea that the rider at the front of a group expends about a third more energy than those who are sheltering behind him; the fact that the benefits of drafting disappear when a rider falls more than one bicycle-length behind – but he started to wonder if they understood what he was talking about.

The list went on: they would apply their brakes at the bottom of a descent, losing all their momentum for the climb up the other side. If he didn't make them, they would not think to eat during a race. Jock adjusted each rider's saddle so that it was in the most efficient position but the next time he looked it would be three inches higher. Abraham, again, was particularly infuriating, as he would carry his bike on the public buses and remove his saddle to stow it. Jock estimated that in the first two years of Team Rwanda he adjusted Abraham's seat fifty times; some days he would be losing five to six per cent of his potential power with each pedal stroke.

Jock knew that these complaints were petty, but as the team added new members, the problems became more serious. 'Lying is endemic in this country,' Jock told me. It might have seemed a lazy generalisation if I hadn't heard Claude – and, by this point, other Rwandans – tell me the same thing. 'A lot of times they will say what you want to hear,' he went on. 'Even about silly things. You'll ask, "Did you have breakfast this morning?" If they think I want to hear yes, they'll say yes, even if they haven't eaten in two days. It's really strange; they will lie about anything.' (He sounded like Pippi Longstocking, the precocious heroine of Astrid Lindgren's 1945 children's book: 'I can tell you that in the Belgian Congo there isn't a single person who tells the truth,' she told her friends Tommy and Annika. 'They tell fibs all day and every day, begin at seven in the morning and keep it up till sunset. So if I should happen to tell a fib sometimes you must try to forgive me and remember that it's only because I've been a little too long in the Belgian Congo.')

Jock became infuriated by the inability of his riders to accept responsibility for their mistakes. There would be a touch of wheels, two of them would crash, and both riders would swear blind that it was not their fault. Rwandans call it *ikinamico*: a word that covers everything from little white lies to larger, more ambitious duplicity. But it is used in a way that suggested it is institutionalised, almost part of a dance between two people. 'It often refers to soap operas,' my interpreter Liberal explained. 'It has a few connotations: acting, simulation, pretence. Trying to present an image that is purposefully deceitful either to hide one's motives or identity or to seek favours.'

I didn't want to accept Jock's version of events blindly, so I asked Abraham about equipment. (Team Rwanda's mechanic, a young Parisian called Maxime Darcel, had been, if anything, even more scathing, ranting about how Abraham looked after his bike, how quickly he ruined the team-issue gear, how his children would mess around with the brake cables, yanking this and that.) But Abraham looked at me solemnly. 'The bike is precious to me,' he said. 'I'll not even allow it to go in the mud, so when I leave my house to train, I carry it to the tarmac.' They couldn't both be right: was it *ikinamico* or a cultural misunderstanding? It was hard to say.

Mild insubordination was creeping in, too. After winning the 2007 Tour of Rwanda, Abraham publicly criticised his prize: £100 in cash and a £400 racing bike. It didn't make sense, he flounced; the money was less than previous years and the bike was worse than the one he had competed on. The president of the cycling federation, Charles Kamanda, reacted angrily. 'In future, our cyclists should focus on the race rather than diverting all their attention and worries on cash prizes,' he said. 'In fact, for international races, top cyclists are only rewarded with medals. No cash is involved.'

Jock introduced a zero-tolerance policy on stealing. The first test was when his razor went missing from the house one day;

it took triple-A batteries, which are almost impossible to find in Rwanda. Jock had his suspicions: one of the newer riders. He asked him once, the rider denied it. He asked again, still a resolute 'No'. Finally Jock went through his bag and found it. The rider was immediately expelled from the team, his gear and bike detained. The uncompromising discipline was, Jock felt, endorsed by Kagame. A quote was posted on the Team Rwanda website and it took a moment to realise that they were the president's words, not the Coach's: 'People have to be pushed hard, until it hurts,' it read. 'I push myself, many days until I almost drop dead. There is nothing to be complacent about. We are poor, and being poor is bad. If being pushed hurts, it cannot hurt as much as poverty, as much as being hungry and sick. I make no apologies about pushing people hard. I wish I had even more energy than I have to push them. It hurts them, but they come up in the end as winners.'

Jock should have been an appalling coach, by rights; one of those kick-every-ball types who found it impossible to empathise with anyone who did not share his commitment. Early on, he decided not to learn Kinyarwanda, because his riders would need to speak another language if they moved abroad anyway. This led to some misunderstandings, though it also simplified their relationship in a way: Jock was strict but he was consistent. 'I listen to *everything*,' he told them one time. 'I see *everything*.' Even if the riders did not exactly understand the words, the sentiment registered loud and clear.

In the summer of 2008, Team Rwanda moved to a permanent address. After a little more than a year of couch-surfing in Butare and Kigali, Jock settled on the city of Ruhengeri (now also known as Musanze) in the volcanic north-west of the country. It is not exactly a metropolis – just a main road with a bustling covered market running down one side – but thanks to the area's indecently fertile soil, it has become the most densely populated region of the most densely populated country in all of Africa. It is also the last pit-stop for travellers passing through on the way to commune with the mountain gorillas in the Volcanoes National Park. It should have been a strange fit for a loner whose favourite spot on earth was the wide-open plains of Wyoming. But the riding was probably the most testing in all of Rwanda and, looking ahead, it would be an ideal base for mountain-bike tourism. It turned out many of the new riders coming into Team Rwanda were from that area, too.

The house was a four-bedroom brick bungalow dating from colonial times that sat at the dead end of a dirt road. By Rwandan standards it was palatial: there was a bath, a shower, a four-burner stove hooked up to a natural-gas canister and red-painted, concrete floors. Outside was a neat lawn and the house was shaded by two giant trees that dropped a regular supply of Hass avocados, the colour of a deep bruise. A smaller building that had once sheltered rescued gorillas would be a perfect mechanic's shed. There was a blue steel gate, an eight-foot wall that surrounded the compound and a cosy brick guard's hut that would be manned round the clock. Jock immediately offered one of the two jobs to Rambo, the ex-soldier who had failed to make the grade as a cyclist. He accepted and, even though his responsibilities mainly consisted of opening the gates for drivers and riders, he still wore combat fatigues to work. When he was relieved, he would jump on his mountain bike, slip on those Mr Cool sunglasses and ride with the team until he could not keep up.

The house had a warm, noisy ambience. There were Team Rwanda camps for around thirty weeks of each year and the format was well-established. Riders started trickling in on

Monday – depending on where they lived, their commute could be anywhere between a few miles and more than a hundred – and they stayed until Friday. Breakfast was at seven, then a morning ride, lunch, perhaps another spin in the afternoon, English lessons or a yoga class. They ate again at seven-thirty, had some downtime and then bed at nine. A cook, Célestin, prepared feasts of porridge, eggs, rice, beans and bananas, often all tossed in a bowl together. Before the evening meal, everyone – riders, staff, volunteers – held hands, bowed heads and listened to grace in Kinyarwanda. With up to eighteen riders at some camps, the team had grown so large that they now slept in another building nearby. But they still came to the Coach's House for meals, to check Facebook on Jock's computer and to watch his library of cycling DVDs. Kimberly Coats arrived in 2009 to look after logistics and imposed her formidable personality on all aspects of team life. Mechanic Maxime Darcel's garage throbbed at all hours with French hip-hop blasted from an iPod speaker dock.

Back in the beginning, though, Jock was rattling around the house alone. To keep him company, he acquired a jowly South African Boerboel named Zulu, a cat, Kongo, and a pied crow called Jambo. He took a picture of the original five riders, framed it and put it above the mantelpiece in the living room. Alongside it, he hung a snap of Rambo, posing with an AK-47 in his hands and a bullet belt draped over his shoulder. He bought a map of Rwanda and another of the whole of Africa and tacked them up. Seeing the size of the country, practically a speck on the continent, was a perpetual reminder of the scale of the challenge they faced.

The race results were, at least, slowly improving. Abraham finished seventh against Africa's elite riders at the 2007 Continental Championships road race in Yaoundé, Cameroon.

Then, competing against three of the best professional squads in Europe, Adrien finished fifteenth at the five-day Intaka Tech World's View Challenge in South Africa in February 2008. A couple of months later he switched back to his mountain bike and returned to the Cape Epic; this time, partnered with Nathan, they finished twenty-sixth overall out of more than 600 teams. In their colourful uniforms, it would have been easy to dismiss the Rwandans as a media-friendly novelty, but the team had stuck around and they were only getting better. 'There's a huge bank of talent in this country that is still untapped,' Jock told officials from the International Cycling Union. 'There might be a thousand cyclists even better than the ones we have.'

Their globetrotting agenda was, however, catching up with them. In May 2008, stretched by the move into new premises and their exotic itinerary, Team Rwanda ran out of money. President Kagame had been a vocal supporter of the team, but so far the government-backed Rwandan cycling federation had only paid for the occasional airfare. Plenty of companies were willing to supply kit – Schwinn and Scott bikes, Lake Shoes, Louis Garneau helmets and accessories, Oakley sunglasses – but the coffers were empty. Jock had to tell the five riders that their monthly stipend of $100 was being suspended. This went on for a couple of months until a South African businessman, Michael Spicer, came to Rwanda to meet Kagame and track gorillas. He stopped by the house in Ruhengeri and went for a ride with Jock and Nyandwi and, before they got back, he had pledged $6,000, enough to pay the wages for ten months. Dick DeVos came through with an Amway donation not long afterwards.

If it all sounds a little haphazard, that's because it was. Jock was a one-man team coach, head mechanic, director of logistics, *soigneur*, driver, travel agent and publicist. His commitment wavered at times, but, when he was low, he realised that what kept him there was Adrien. Of all the Rwandans, Jock felt he had the best chance to succeed. More than that, he wanted to demonstrate his commitment to him. Jock's life had been defined by the disappearance of his father when he was five years old. Now he was in a similar position of responsibility, he couldn't let it happen again. 'Back then, I told Adrien, no matter what, I'd be there, I'd continue,' Jock remembered. 'Even if we'd run out of funds, I'd get him on a team. I couldn't let him down. I needed to be a solid figure in his life and that's what I really wanted to be.'

Jock decided that Adrien needed to follow the same path he had taken: leave home, go in search of harder riding. (This would relieve some of the pressure on Team Rwanda's finances, too.) For Jock it had been France, for Adrien it would be South Africa. So, after winning the 2008 Tour of Rwanda, Adrien was packed off with Nathan Byukusenge for a training stint at the UCI-funded African Continental Cycling Centre in Potchefstroom, a pleasant-enough college town seventy-five miles outside Johannesburg. Jock then began pleading with Douglas Ryder, the owner of MTN Cycling, the top professional cycling team in Africa, to take him on. Douglas, it turned out, did not take much convincing.

Like Jock, Douglas was a flinty ex-professional, although he is more than a decade younger. For much of the nineties, he was the top rider in South Africa on the road, but his only experience in Europe was a few weeks with a Belgian professional team, which he described as 'eye-opening in terms of substance abuse by riders'. He competed at the Olympics and world championships but found that, because of his country's backward preparations, 'It was like racing against motorbikes.' Now, as a team principal, he wanted to level the playing field for all Africans and he had the backing of MTN, the continent's ubiquitous telecommunications giant. Jock thought Rwandans could hold their own in professional cycling; Douglas, a more extroverted showman, saw no reason why black Africans should not dominate the sport, much as Kenyans and Ethiopians did with distance running.

Douglas organised physiological tests for Adrien and then packed him off to Crater Cruise, the hardest single-day mountain bike race in South Africa. It was a hot, dusty day, and the seventy-mile course over the rim of the Vredefort Crater was a test of endurance and courage. Two of Douglas's MTN riders, Melt Swanepoel and Kevin Evans, finished first and second, but in a classy field Adrien placed seventh. Douglas immediately offered him a contract to race mountain bikes for MTN Cycling in the 2009 season. He also took on Nathan and a pair of Zambian riders, Jupiter Nameembo and Trust Munangandu. They would live in Potchefstroom, take English courses at the nearby North-West University and their goal would be a top-ten finish at the Cape Epic. Rwanda had its first professional cyclists.

At home, all of Team Rwanda had become well known: 'I'm a star!' Rafiki liked to exclaim. They had met the president and had extravagant tales of visiting foreign lands – most recently, Namibia's airless Skeleton Coast, an inhospitable place that's known in local legend as 'the land that God made in anger'. They were clearly going up in the world. Rafiki got his driving licence, an arduous and expensive process – around £200 – that ensured he would never want for a job in Rwanda. They became a common sight on the roads, as their training rides took them to all parts of the country, and many thousands watched their races. They were certainly hard to miss: in their Lycra, on

£2,500 road bikes, they would blast past women carrying huge stacks of banana leaves, prisoners in their brilliant jumpsuits – orange for the short-term inmates, pink for more serious offenders – and children in matching uniforms walking miles to and from school. If they came up alongside anyone on a bike, the race would be on. Their $100-a-month salary – more than twice the average national income – inspired some envy but anyone could see how hard they worked: training every day, in the rain and the heat, sweat running down their faces, salt streaked into their shirts and shorts. Most Rwandans were not so knowledgeable about bikes, but there was nothing they didn't know about suffering.

Making the team would change a young man's life, and there were always contenders turning up in Ruhengeri asking Jock to test them. In the Rwandan tradition, when a rider had finished with a bike, he donated it to a cyclist coming through. Nathan's was handed down to Nicodem Habiyambere, his younger brother; Nyandwi gave his battered Eddy Merckx to Innocent Sibomana, a bicycle-taxi rider whom he used to pass on the road to the Coach's House. Both of them would graduate to Team Rwanda. Adrien was particularly close to a teenager from his hometown of Rwamagana called Godfrey Gahemba; in fact they were distantly related – their grandmothers were sisters. Godfrey was an orphan: his father was killed in the genocide and his mother fell ill and passed away not long after. He was raised, along with his younger sister, by their grandmother. Godfrey became a bicycle-taxi rider, but Adrien gave him his brother's yellow Trek and encouraged him to start racing. Soon, Godfrey was the most promising young rider in Rwanda.

Jock decided to send Godfrey to the African Continental Cycling Centre in South Africa in mid-2008, so he needed to apply for a passport. All of Godfrey's papers had been lost in the genocide and Jock assigned him the birth date of 8 April 1991: 'April signifying the rain that fills the earth and germinates the flowers in spring and the eighth signifying the first day after creation week, a new beginning, a new life,' he explained. Everyone called him *Cho*, French argot for 'little one'. After two months in Potchefstroom, he raced the Junior World Championships with Innocent Sibomana in Cape Town. He then returned home and finished third overall in the 2008 Tour of Rwanda, behind Adrien and Nathan, at the age of just eighteen (or thereabouts). He was tiny, with skinny legs and a shy, wonky smile, but there was already excitement that he could be a star performer at the 2012 Olympics.

Not long afterwards, Adrien was in South Africa, confirming his new deal with MTN Cycling. Word reached him that his father was sick, but before Adrien could make it home he died. Adrien had a few weeks before his contract started, so after the funeral he stayed in Rwamagana with his mother and trained with Godfrey. On Sunday 14 December 2008, they were both riding in a race to promote 'good governance', a nebulous phrase from international-develoment literature that Kagame had enthusiastically appropriated. It was a short event contested by local riders on old-fashioned single-speed bikes, but all of the regions were invited to submit teams – so civic pride was at stake and there were prizes for the winners. The Team Rwanda stars were celebrity cheerleaders, offering advice to competitors from their region, which in Adrien and Godfrey's case was Eastern Province. Towards the end of the course, one of the Eastern Province riders could not match the pace of his team-mates, so dropped off the back of the group. Adrien stayed with the front riders, and Godfrey held back to encourage the rider. As he was handing him a water bottle, their handlebars locked and they tumbled into road. The car following behind them was too close and ended up driving over Godfrey. He died before he even made it to hospital.

In Rwamagana, they still talk about the requiem mass at the town's cathedral. Some people say there were many hundreds of mourners, others thousands. The ceremony lasted five hours and a family friend of Godfrey's told me that the ground must still be wet from all the tears. The members of the team, including Adrien, took shovels to bury him.

'Godfrey was super-talented,' said Jean-Pierre 'JP' Van Zyl, a track cyclist who was his coach at the African Continental Cycling Centre in Potchefstroom. 'You kind of know when you see a rider: "Okay, this one's special." He was a climber, he was just built for road cycling. He had the shape to become one of those riders who would have excelled in the hard European road stages. I get tears in my eyes just thinking about him.'

It was a terrible story but, like many in Rwanda, it also turned out to be a complicated one. I met with Jean Baptiste Rugambwa, the president of Rwamagana's cycling club Les Amis Sportifs, and his grief gave way quickly to suspicion. 'I feel it may have been a conspiracy,' he said, as we sat in his living room on sofas adorned with doilies. 'It makes no sense to me that this could have just happened when Godfrey was passing a drink of water. And even if the car hit him, I do not understand how the car could have run straight over him. I find that,' he chose his word carefully, 'awkward.'

The car following Godfrey was from Gisenyi, a cycling heartland in the north-west of Rwanda, and Jean had found out that, before the incident, the passengers in the car had been arguing with Godfrey. 'They were actually spitting at each other,' he said. 'So it was quite violent.' There is certainly a surprisingly fierce rivalry between cycling clubs in Rwanda, and Godfrey's recent success might only have made that envy more pointed. 'Maybe they were not intending to kill him, just make him a little uncomfortable,' Jean said. 'Just like in football, you would foul a player to stop them from scoring.' The police became involved and the passengers of the car were detained overnight for questioning, but not charged. The driver was sent to Kigali Central Prison for three months.

The resignation with which Jean told this story was heartbreaking. Did he feel that Godfrey's death had been properly investigated? He shrugged, it didn't really matter and, considering the number of *génocidaires* walking the streets, perhaps he had a point. Jean was a Tutsi and in April 1994 he had hidden for days in a latrine pit to avoid being killed: 'It felt like you were losing your brains,' he said. Perhaps that informed his response now, maybe it didn't. It was revealing, too, that this version of events had taken so long to come out. I had spoken to most of the riders and the management about Godfrey, but this was the first time there had been a suggestion that his death had been anything other than a horrible accident. It was another reminder that there were some stories that Rwandans did not care to share.

Adrien had lost his father and his best friend within a few weeks. For many people, these events would be the defining moments of their life. When talking about the genocide, Adrien's mother quoted a Swahili saying: 'The death of many is like a wedding.' It's a pessimistic sentiment suggesting that multiple deaths made one not more despondent but more resigned. It became fate, an inevitability. But somehow Adrien managed to resist this negativity. His family was almost extinct, friends who were younger than him had followed them, but he decided that this did not have to be his own destiny. Two weeks after Godfrey's death, Adrien flew from Kigali to Johannesburg to join the MTN Cycling team, determined that this was his shot at a new life.

7

BLACK MAGIC

The men came on a Sunday evening – 31 May 2009 – a little after six. They knew to come then. The coach, JP Van Zyl, had stopped by the apartment in Potchefstroom a few minutes before to drop off training programmes for the next week and the MTN Cycling riders would be alone in the house, relaxing before dinner. JP always told them to lock the gates, but they were forever zipping in and out with their bicycles, so they did not always remember. Tonight the gates were wide open.

When the four men came in, Adrien Niyonshuti was in his bedroom; the sun was beginning to dip, so he had laid his mat down and he was preparing for *maghrib*, the fourth of his five daily prayers. When he heard raised voices in the living area, he didn't investigate. He locked his room and climbed inside his cupboard, balled up like a foetus. The Zambians, Jupiter Nameembo and Trust Munangandu, were in their shared room. Nathan Byukusenge, the other Rwandan, was chatting with his Algerian team-mate, Hichem Chabane; Hichem spoke Arabic, Berber and French, Nathan had Kinyarwanda and a little English, but somehow they muddled through. Hichem was young, only twenty years old, but the most senior rider in the house, the only full member of MTN Cycling. He had finished fifth in the 2008 African Continental Championships and had represented Algeria the same year at the Olympic Games in Beijing. A spirited climber, he had been identified as one of the best young talents on the continent.

He had also just been fired. Since arriving in South Africa, perhaps enjoying a freedom he didn't have in Blida, the affluent colonial-era city where he lived with his parents, he had taken to spending his evenings in Potchefstroom's bars with other Algerian expatriates. His form dropped off alarmingly and the team boss Douglas Ryder had told him that they were sending him home on Tuesday.

Suddenly four men stood in front of Hichem and Nathan; they wore balaclavas and gloves and carried knives. For a moment, Nathan wasn't scared, he thought it must be a prank. He could only see their eyes and in their black outfits they reminded him of ninjas from kung-fu movies. But the men spoke with an easy but menacing familiarity to Hichem and, though Nathan could not understand the words, he knew that something was wrong. Jupiter and Trust were rounded up and dragged into the living room, but the men never found Adrien or couldn't be bothered to break down the door to get to him.

The men, it turned out, were impressively briefed on the riders. They knew that they didn't have work permits and that they didn't have bank accounts. They knew they were paid in cash and, what they didn't send home, they kept in their rooms. Each rider had been given a laptop and a mobile phone by the team. Hichem, because of his greater experience, earned more than the others and had just bought his own computer to take home to Algeria. The men knew all this because Hichem had been bragging in a bar the night before.

Hichem's room was locked; the men wanted the key. Hichem

refused, so one of the men took the butt of his knife and thumped him fiercely in the face. Hichem dropped to the ground and blood spurted from his nose. His face immediately ballooned. Still he refused to hand over the key. None of the other cyclists could understand what was being said, but the robbers were growing more and more agitated. They were screaming at Hichem now. Then suddenly, one of them lurched for Hichem and the blade sliced his arm as he tried to defend himself, then his chest. It sounded like a knife piercing fruit. Hichem rolled over on the floor and the man stabbed him again, this time puncturing the back of his thigh. The room went quiet; evidently no one expected this to happen. Blood pooled around Hichem's thin body, but with his undamaged arm he reached into the pocket of his tracksuit trousers and dropped the key beside him.

Still it wasn't over. The men went through the rooms, hastily collecting up laptops and cash, but they couldn't find where Hichem had stashed his savings. He was dipping in and out of consciousness, so the men grabbed Nathan and dragged him to Hichem's room. 'Where's the money?' they screamed in thickly accented English. Nathan had no idea, so one of them punched him in the side of the head. He felt his teeth crush together, an instant headache erupted. As he bent down, they struck him again. Finally, one of the men found a thick brick of South African rand. They bundled Nathan back to the living room, bound him up along with the Zambians, duct tape covering their eyes and mouths, and hurried out carrying their haul. Nathan heard a set of keys fall to the ground outside the door and, a few seconds later, a car revving its engine.

Nathan didn't want to move, he just wanted to lie on the ground and cry. He never thought he'd see anything like 1994 again. But he could feel the men had tied his hands sloppily, so he slipped free, removed the tape from his face and did the same for the Zambians. There was an alarm by the front door of the apartment and he pressed it. He didn't know where to start with Hichem: the Algerian was changing colour in front of his eyes, blood seeping out of his body and leaving his pale skin almost translucent. Nathan slumped on the floor; he had been in South Africa for almost five months and he was earning well, but really what was he doing here? This wasn't his country, these were not his people. He was grateful for the opportunity he had been given, but he was suddenly exhausted and he missed his family. As the sky darkened outside, a single thought played on a loop in his throbbing head: *I need to go home*.

Armed robberies were disturbingly common in South Africa, a country where 15,000 people were murdered every year. But such assaults did not happen in Potchefstroom, a genteel and mild-mannered place; particularly not in the smart part of the city where the riders were staying. The police were confused: for one thing, who uses knives? Guns are easy enough to come by and ubiquitous among South Africa's criminal classes. It had to be an opportunist attack. As Hichem was stabilised in the Mediclinic private hospital, the National Intelligence Agency dispatched a unit to investigate. It didn't take too long for the full story – the bar, the boasting – to emerge and for the four robbers to be rounded up. The ringleader was sentenced to a few years in jail, his accomplices deported to Algeria. Hichem had been sent home, too, as soon as he was fit enough to travel.

There were longer-term repercussions, too. JP Van Zyl thought that his African Continental Cycling Centre might be forced to close. 'It was survival time,' he remembered. 'The whole town was like, "Maybe it's not a good idea to bring your athletes to this town, because it brings danger."' JP had been one of the first to arrive on the scene and in the days afterwards he worked to make sure that media coverage was restrained. But the aftershocks kept rumbling. Not long afterwards, he separated from his wife, who worked with him at the centre: she didn't feel safe in South Africa any more; he didn't want to leave the project. 'So I've invested my life into this thing,' he said. 'And I've paid the price in many ways.'

It became a turning point for the riders, as well. Hichem didn't ride much for a couple of years, but eventually returned to cycling and won a stage of the 2012 Tour du Faso riding for an Algerian team. The Zambians did not have their contracts renewed at the end of the season. Adrien and Nathan were given two weeks' leave to go back to Rwanda. They talked about what happened a lot while they were home, and at the end of the fortnight Adrien boarded the plane to Johannesburg and Nathan did not. 'He couldn't hold that pain,' Adrien told me. 'To be outside of your country is to hold a pain – and if you don't have the heart and mind to hold it, you can't. It's so difficult.'

Adrien obviously felt different – why was that? It was true that he had not witnessed the attack on Hichem first-hand, but it had been a terrifying ordeal nevertheless. Like Nathan, as he cowered in his closet fearing discovery, he had been transported back to 1994, hiding in that airless room in Rwamagana. Now he would return to South Africa on his own. 'I said just to myself, *When I was seven years old I saw what happened in genocide, I saw a lot of stuff, a lot of experiences I will never forget. But if I came back to Rwanda, what am I going to be?* If I came back, there wouldn't be anyone to give money to my mum, or the 500,000 or 600,000 francs' – around £500 – 'to pay for school fees for one year for my nieces and nephews. My family is not very rich, it's not very poor, and I knew if I came to stay with them I would have nothing to do. So I say, "No, I'm not going back home."'

I asked JP why he thought that Adrien stayed and Nathan didn't. 'He's obviously got a drive for a better life,' he said. 'That's what has made him successful. He wants to get away from the past.' For Douglas Ryder it was even simpler: 'I just think he's smarter.'

There is an enduring perception that road cycling is a working man's sport. Tom Simpson, Britain's first world champion, was the sixth and youngest child of a coal miner from County Durham. Bradley Wiggins grew up on the Dibdin House council estate in Maida Vale, north London. None of the great European champions came from landed backgrounds; Fausto Coppi's family were Italian peasant farmers, Jacques Anquetil's grew strawberries in Normandy. Why would they? There are many easier ways to make a living than racing a bike for 200-plus days a year. Much as we expect the most fearsome boxers to have fought their way out of the barrios of Mexico or Puerto Rico, so we like to believe that cyclists somehow embody a deeper and often all-consuming drive for self-improvement.

I often wondered why Adrien had succeeded where other Rwandans had not. Some of the explanation had to be physiological: he was just naturally a superior athlete. But all of his coaches downplayed that idea. His results in tests were unexceptional, certainly in the beginning; some of his compatriots were similar or better. When the Rwandans first visited the United States in 2007, Adrien submitted to an extensive range of prodding and poking in a high-performance lab at the University of California in Davis. One test was for VO_2 Max: essentially the subject pedals on a stationary bike until they are almost sick, which then produces a number showing the maximum amount of oxygen their lungs can consume during exercise. VO_2 Max results are of debatable value, but that has not stopped some becoming legend: Miguel Indurain, the Spanish five-time Tour de France winner, registered eighty-eight millilitres per kilogram of body weight; Greg LeMond has implied that his score of ninety-two was one reason why he did not need to dope. Adrien scored seventy-two, which was respectable – forty is typical for a healthy adult – but would hardly strike fear into the professional peloton.

It is certainly true that plenty of cyclists with a VO_2 Max of seventy-two have raced and beaten riders with a score in the eighties, because they are tactically more astute or just have a greater desire to win. Equally, the ability of African riders – experience was now starting to show – was not always best reflected in their performances on stationary bikes. 'Indoors they just can't get motivated – it's not life or death. They don't feel the heat of the road,' said Douglas Ryder. 'But you see them sprint for even the lower places in a race, where there's a few bucks at stake, and they'll kill themselves.'

The distinction is an integral one. In the West, there are many reasons people might ride a bike: for fitness, enjoyment, self-improvement or just to experience temporary discomfort in an otherwise comfortable, modern life. But when I asked any Rwandan cyclist why he rode, he gave the same reply: to provide for his family. All of the members of Team Rwanda had become the highest earners in their communities; some of the senior racers made £4,000 a year, and Adrien earned significantly more. These funds had a remarkable, trickle-down impact: the riders were expected to provide for family – near, extended and long-lost – and friends, too. There were medical bills, school fees, food and clothes. Abraham quoted to me from

Luke's gospel: 'Give to everyone who asks you, and if anyone takes what belongs to you, do not demand it back.'

Jock tried to make sure his riders were not taken advantage of. He encouraged them to save money or invest it in property or an alternative income stream; perhaps buying a motorbike and loaning it to a moto-taxi rider. In the early days of the team, Rafiki got together with a sixteen-year-old girlfriend. She became pregnant and they had a boy they called Jonathan, named after Jock. It was an endearing story that appeared to offer hope that this impossible mangling of nations and cultures could actually work. But the relationship quickly turned sour, and Rafiki's girlfriend asked for money. Rafiki's cycling began to deteriorate rapidly, his potential was leaking away. Eventually he took full custody of Jonathan, though mostly the child stayed with his parents, and he effectively retired from racing, working for the team as a mechanic. In Team Rwanda there was talk of 'a pay-off' for the girl.

The most complicated character within the set-up was Abraham. He was an exceptional athlete: he would annoy his team-mates no end by scarcely training, then turning up at a race and easily beating them. That irritated Jock, too. In one of his updates for financial donors, he gave a savage appraisal of the experience of managing him since 2007: 'Abraham Ruhumuriza has been the most difficult member of Team Rwanda since its inception,' he wrote. 'He is the nightmare team member, a waste of incredible talent, a toxic influence to new members and veterans, young and old. A young man who clings to abhorrent behaviour with the tenacity of an octopus, clinging to it not really knowing why, just knowing he does not want to let go.'

I met Abraham at his house in Butare. It was not hard to find: well, it was, my interpreter Liberal and I had to navigate some heavy-going roads to reach it, but there was no shortage of locals to give us directions. Everyone knew where Ruhumuriza lived; he was the local celebrity, mobbed by children whenever he walked to the shops. At times, he must have felt what it was like to be a *muzungu* in this country.

In many ways, Abraham had followed Jock's instructions to the letter. He had bought the house, a simple, two-bedroom bungalow, in late 2008, the first of the Team Rwanda riders to do so. It cost around £5,000, which he cobbled together from a combination of race winnings, a large donation from Jock's Seventh-Day Adventist church in Monterey and an advance on his Team Rwanda salary. As I walked in, my eyes were drawn to a plasticky trophy that he won at the 2010 Tour of Cameroon. Then they lingered on a high-rise bank of maybe a dozen video recorders and a stack of VHS tapes that was easily the height of a man. This was his sideline. He would borrow a film in Kigali, copy it and then hire a room to screen it in Butare. 'A lot of people look down on it, but it's quite a lucrative business,' he explained. 'The entry fee is fifty francs' – around five pence – 'but you can get around fifty people into one showing and you can screen five films a week. It's much better than a motorcycle where you have to pay a lot up front and the returns are not so good.'

Abraham was partial to romantic comedies, though he also liked Sylvester Stallone in *Rambo*. He had recently started bootlegging live stages of the Tour de France. 'Man, those guys don't ride bicycles, they fly; I don't think I could keep up with them,' he said, shaking his head. 'But I don't think I'd be last either.'

Abraham was always laughing, but the tale he told was, for the most part, a tragic one. In November 2007, his mother, whom he lived with and cared for, died in unexplained circumstances. Abraham left Rwanda shortly afterwards to race in Cameroon, and when he came back he found that his sister and brother-in-law had moved into the house that his mother had left to him. Then, just after Christmas, Abraham's wife woke up with a fever and severe nausea. He took her to the hospital, but by the evening she, too, was dead. They had had five children: the first two had died as infants; two boys had survived, aged six and four, and they also had a nine-month-old daughter who was still breastfeeding. Abraham felt he had no choice but to put the baby up for adoption.

These deaths were, to Abraham, difficult to fathom. His wife had not even been sick the night before she fell ill. Before she died, their first-born had developed a disease that rotted his flesh; no one in their community had ever seen the like of it before. The elders in his village advised him that witchcraft was the only explanation for such an unusual condition. 'Some of the deaths might have been natural causes,' Abraham accepted, 'but I'm more inclined to believe that they had been bewitched, someone had put a spell on them.' After his wife's death, he called upon a local healer, an old man whom he had met through the Seventh-Day Adventist church to which his wife belonged. Abraham asked him to produce a potion that he could give to his surviving children, and the man disappeared into the bush to collect grasses and plants. When they fed the concoction to the children, they each vomited profusely. Abraham took this as a sign that the sickness was leaving their bodies.

Did he have any clue who was responsible for the curse? 'These things often relate to land rights,' he said. 'There's a Rwandan saying: "You may not know where a thief has hidden your possessions, but that doesn't mean you don't know who stole."'

Witchcraft is alive and well in Africa, particularly in rural areas. Marc Vincent, a Belgian paediatrician, visited Rwanda in the early nineteen-fifties, the last days of colonialism, and was taken aback by how often the children he treated referred to poison or sorcery as the cause of their ailments and the deaths of others. He wrote a report that concluded, 'The natives see poisoners everywhere.' It was not just the locals either. When the American research student Dian Fossey landed in Rwanda in 1967 to track mountain gorillas, having been run out of Congo by the civil war, it did not take long for her to realise the potency of *sumu*, a Swahili word for 'poison'. Poachers particularly prized the primates, believing that if they consumed their flesh they would inherit their strength and vitality. Over the three decades that she lived in the country, Fossey learned to cultivate the power of the dark arts to protect her gorillas – who numbered just 480 when she arrived and were fast disappearing – and to manipulate the local population. Some of them called her *Nyiramacibili*, the Woman Who Lives Alone in the Forest, but to others she was regarded warily as 'the sorceress'.

Fossey developed a reputation for being merciless with any poachers that the park guards apprehended. In a letter to a friend she described a rehabilitation session on a Twa pygmy from an 'ordinary day' in 1976: 'We stripped him and spreadeagled him outside my cabin and lashed the holy blue sweat out of him with [stinging] nettle stalks and leaves, concentrating on the areas where it might hurt a mite. Wow, I never knew such little fellows had such big things . . .' As mountain gorilla numbers dipped, by her estimation, into the two hundreds, her methods became more extreme: she painted hexes and spat out curses. She spent a fortune on painted masks, staged mock hangings and force-fed her captives mind-altering drugs. She was so paranoid about a revenge attack that she would burn any loose strands of hair after brushing each day, convinced that it could be collected and used in spells against her. She was right to be worried: during the night of Boxing Day 1985, she was slaughtered in her bed, her skull cracked open with a *panga*, a heavy-bladed machete. The chief suspect was a man called Yavani Hategeka: he was an old-school poacher whom Fossey had detained one time. She had done a search and found a pouch of what she said looked like 'vacuum cleaner debris', flakes of skin and vegetation; it was his *impigi*, his talisman, and she confiscated it. No one thought it far-fetched that Hategeka would have killed to secure its return.

There was no direct comparison, but I sometimes thought that Jock could have had a therapeutic debrief with Fossey, if they had ever crossed paths. They would have been near-neighbours, in fact. Fossey set up camp at 10,000 feet in the clammy, inhospitable Volcanoes National Park; she picked a saddle of land between two mountains, Karisimbi and Visoke, and called it Karisoke. Jock could pretty well see the spot – the famous mist permitting – when he sat on his porch. Both Jock and Fossey had to deal with frustrations, loneliness and sporadic shafts of vindication in pursuit of what must have often felt like insurmountable odds. They shared a zero-tolerance, neo-colonial approach to dealing with Rwandans. Fossey was much stricter even than Jock: she felt that by nature Rwandans were lazy, incompetent and deceitful; she called them 'woggiepoos'. There was no shortage of suspects when she was killed. She made scant attempt to speak Kinyarwanda (one of the few snatches she learned was, 'I am the Goddess of the Mountain and I will avenge you for killing my children'), but paradoxically, in her pragmatism, ruthlessness and lack of sentiment, she adopted some very African traits. The same could be said for Jock as he prepared his riders for the selfish, cut-throat world of professional cycling.

Rafiki laughed when I asked if he believed in black magic.

He was a city boy; he wore camouflage cargo shorts, Adidas sneakers with Rastafarian detailing and his sunglasses were perched on the top of his head. 'You hear of that in the villages,' he said, 'but people in town don't have time for that.'

That was only partly true. When a drink is served in Rwanda – from the most upmarket hotel in Kigali to a rough little cabaret in the country – the bottle will be opened in front of the customer's eyes, often with an ostentatious flourish. The clientele want assurance that it has not been tampered with. When locals drink banana beer from a communal jug, the server makes a point of tasting it first, to prove that it has not been spiked. Doctors have no qualms about referring their patients to traditional healers and witchcraft is written about with authority and respect in the *New Times*, Rwanda's English-language newspaper. In 2008, the paper reported that, during an international football match between Rwanda and Morocco, the North Africans checked the goalposts because they were convinced their shots were being kept out by black magic. 'People were surprised to see Arabs behaving the way they did,' the article read, 'but forgot that their colour did not stop them from being Africans.' Suspected 'witches' are still burned alive in Africa – sometimes these are simply elderly women suffering from Alzheimer's disease or dementia.

After Abraham's house was taken over by his sister and her husband, he decided to move closer to Butare. He made little attempt to hide his suspicion that they were responsible for his recent misfortune, probably because of jealousy. But even in the city, he didn't feel secure. 'You see the wall?' he said, gesturing outside. It was eight foot tall, made from bricks and topped with spikes, surrounding the property. 'That was the first thing I had built when I moved in, before I even looked at the house.' Now, at family gatherings, Abraham would not touch either food or drink. He did not spit on the ground, in case someone collected his saliva. If he went out to a public place, he never drank from a communal pot. He had remarried and he and his new wife had another boy; they had also reclaimed the girl that Abraham gave up for adoption after his first wife's death. His immediate family were the only people with whom he shared meals.

Even the video machines in Abraham's front room told a tale of woe. While he was away training with the team, his manager had run off with all the movies and the takings. The video machines sat unused while Abraham decided whether it was worth starting again from scratch. It had been a difficult couple of years, all told. Jock's patience had worn out; Abraham's fate was sealed at the 2010 African Continental Championships: in the team time trial, Abraham was stronger than his Rwandan team-mates, but instead of measuring his efforts he obliterated his own team in the opening miles. Afterwards, he complained to journalists that the real problem was Rwanda's substandard bikes and equipment. Jock was enraged and kicked him off Team Rwanda for insubordination and attempting to incite rider boycotts. Abraham used his savings to have motorbike lessons; he thought he could become a moto-taxi rider. But, when the money ran out, he went to Jock to beg for another chance. Eventually he was allowed to rejoin the team. He struck me, as we sat in his living room, not as a reformed character but as a broken man.

Abraham seemed to be aware of his reputation for causing trouble. 'My father called me Ruhumuriza: the word means "comforter",' he explained; he was smiling but his eyes were downcast. 'When I was a child and I fooled around, he would shout at me, "Look, I called you Ruhumuriza, so that you would provide comfort for me. Now you're adding trouble to my life!"'

I had arrived to meet Abraham wondering why it was Adrien, not him, who had become Team Rwanda's star rider. None of the Rwandans had it easy, but if you were looking for someone who could really have used cycling to provide escape and absolution, Abraham was a perfect candidate. Part of the explanation, clearly, was age. His 'official' birth date was 28 July 1979, but it was possible that he was even older; one of his rivals thought he could be forty-five. His intransigent personality was undoubtedly a factor, too. He lacked Adrien's education and his ability to see the bigger picture. More than that, though, his life was a mess.

Adrien's existence was all rather straightforward in comparison. At the 2011 Tour of Rwanda, I asked one of his team-mates, the South African rider James Tennent, what it was like to live with Adrien – at the time, they shared a house in Pretoria. 'We never really see him,' he replied. 'All Adrien does is eat, sleep and train. I've never come across anyone as focused as him. I'd actually describe him as the perfect athlete.'

Jock liked to tell a story about the team travelling to a race in Cameroon, before Adrien left for South Africa to join MTN Cycling. Jock was teasing the riders, asking if there was anyone special in their lives. He went round each of the team and eventually he reached Adrien: 'No, Coach,' he said shyly. 'For now, girlfriend is bike.'

At the first Wooden Bike Classic in 2007, the mountain bike race was won by Adrien; in the companion event, for single-speed bikes, the winner was a strapping young man called Daniel Ngendahayo. He was obviously a talented rider – he had beaten Nathan into second place – but by the time I arrived in Rwanda in 2010, he was nowhere to be seen. 'He was very good, tall and very strong, maybe even the best in Rwanda,' remembered Rafiki. 'But he lacked the passion. He didn't have it in his heart. When we went to Gabon for the Tour of Amissa Bongo, he said, "If this is what it's like, I can't handle it." Then we raced in Egypt and he took his clothes and his bike and he said to Coach: "That's it, finished. Here's your clothes, here's your bike, goodbye! I can't take it any more. It's just pain."'

Faustin Mparabanyi, the old-time star of Rwandan cycling who still travelled with the team on foreign assignments, told a different story. 'No, no, no, Daniel had a terrible phobia of aeroplanes,' he explained. 'He was so scared that he had to leave cycling entirely. I remember when we were in Gabon, he pleaded with me to find any other way to come back apart from on the plane. He'd go on the road, anything. He was seriously traumatised.' Daniel, the non-flying Rwandan, sounded intriguing; what was he doing now? No one exactly knew. He lived somewhere on the road between Kigali and Gitarama, the second largest city in Rwanda, and one person thought Daniel might make a living from charging mobile phones for a fee – the World Bank found in 2011 that nearly half of Rwandans owned a mobile phone, but not so many people have electricity. It was enough to go on.

It wasn't too hard to track down Daniel in the end. We stopped in a couple of places on the road to Gitarama and my interpreter Liberal asked for 'Ngendahayo, the one who used to ride bicycles'. It was the middle of the rainy season, and just climbing out of the car and running for cover left us soaked through. But outside a market in a village called Ruhunga, we found a child in pristine white overalls – white would seem to be a high-risk colour in a country of dirt floors and no washing machines, but Rwandans are, almost without exception, fastidious about their clothes. He said he knew Daniel and would bring him to us if we bought him a soda. Deal!

The lost hope of Rwandan cycling arrived a couple of minutes later, cruising on the padded seat of a bicycle-taxi. Daniel wore ratty jeans, an olive hooded sweatshirt and flip-flops; he was average height, medium build, but his jersey swelled with a little pot belly. We chatted a little and he explained he ran a barber shop now, we could speak to him there. We piled into the car just as the rain crashed down even harder and the streets turned molten. Outside the shop was a vibrant hand-painted sign; inside, there were two ancient leather chairs in front of a pair of mirrors. If Daniel and his colleague used scissors, I didn't see them; it was clippers or nothing. On the wall, one laminated poster suggested 'Powerful Hair Kuts', a scrapbook of flat-tops, sculpted sideburns and braids, modelled by hip-hop stars Warren G, Jay-Z and Usher. Alongside it was a display of fifty-five 'Everlasting Cuts' that the customer could select, like ordering off the menu at a Chinese restaurant. People will always need haircuts, it is said, and the wooden benches round the perimeter of the small concrete room were full.

At last, I had someone to ask a question that had intrigued me since I arrived in Rwanda: why did all Rwandan men – and many of the women – have a grade-one crop? What about the fifty-four other 'everlasting cuts'? 'That's fashion,' said Daniel. 'People tell you what they want and you do it. Rwandans don't like to look so different from each other.' That was surely too simple, I insisted: was there something in the fact that hair had been used in the past to differentiate Hutu and Tutsi? Tutsis were said to have straighter hair, and now that Rwanda no longer used those markers, maybe it was helpful that everyone's hair was shaved close. 'Perhaps,' he said. But Daniel was uneasy talking about such matters in a crowd: 'Shall we go to a bar for a drink?'

We crossed the road to the Umucyo Saloon and ordered

Cokes. Daniel was born in 1982, the last of fourteen children, twelve of whom had survived. His father died when he was one and he was raised by his mother on a typical beans-and-maize farm, just up a hill from his barber shop. He first rode a bike when he was fifteen, borrowing it from his brother to pick up and deliver churns of milk half his size and twice his weight. A few years later, he became a bicycle-taxi rider and not long after that he was spotted by Emmanuel Mayaka and fast-tracked to the Ciné Elmay team. He was given a wage by Mayaka of 5,000 francs a week – around £5 – plus meals and drinks when he turned up for training on Wednesdays and Sundays. His first racing bike was an Eddy Merckx and once he mastered the gears he held his own, and often a little better. He entered his first Tour of Rwanda in 2004. On the first stage of the race he finished second, just behind Abraham, and it continued that way for the first four days of the week-long event. Abraham led, Daniel was his shadow.

On the fifth day the race headed east to Nyagatare, through Rwamagana and towards the border with Tanzania. Daniel was out front with Abraham, but as Abraham swept smoothly round a corner, Daniel ditched his Eddy Merckx into a pothole and he flew over the handlebars. He was badly bashed up; his knees and hands were bruised and bloodied, and he had a deep cut under his eye that would require stitches. A car, part of the eclectic, semi-authorised crew that followed cycling races in Rwanda, pulled up and bundled him in the back to take him to hospital. But as they sped away, the driver said something that disturbed Daniel. He was going to have to abandon the race: even though he had been in second place, he would not earn any prize money.

This was the first Daniel had heard of it. 'Whoa, stop the car,' he said. 'I'm going to finish the race.'

The driver thought he was delirious, that he must have hit his head. 'No, no, no, you're injured. You need to go to hospital.'

'I'm serious,' Daniel replied. 'For God's sake, I need to get back in the race!'

Daniel won the argument and eventually finished the stage, bloody and battered, in seventeenth place. He went to hospital that night in Nyagatare and they patched him up, but the next day he was brutally stiff and had miserable luck with a puncture; he could only place twentieth. The next day was the final stage, back to Kigali, and he battled through it to finish. He had come fourth overall and his reward was 300,000 francs – £300 – more money than he had ever earned or even seen in his life. Sat in the Umucyo Saloon, his smile was as wide as the Nyabarongo River as he remembered the moment.

As I listened to Daniel tell the story, re-enacting his crash using Coke bottles for the participants, showing me the still-vivid scars, it was hard to believe that he lacked passion for cycling, as Rafiki had suggested. What about aeroplanes? Was he afraid of flying? 'No,' he replied, looking confused that I had asked. 'I remember the first time, I travelled on a plane to Gabon, I was really excited. I felt like a star. But I was a little confused about how to use the toilets. The first time I didn't even go to the toilet, because I thought, *I don't want trouble here*.'

Daniel's cycling career offered a less satisfying perspective on the Team Rwanda experiment. After winning the single-speed race at the 2006 Wooden Bike Classic, he took home a Schwinn mountain bike, but then it went quiet. The first he heard about Team Rwanda was a news item on the radio in 2007 that the five riders had been sent to the United States. He said that he had not even been called in for testing. When

Jock decided to widen the team, he invited Daniel and another rider who tended to place well in local races, Obed Rugovera. They joined up with the team in late 2007, trained with them, but while the original riders were now on a salary, those two would receive only food and lodgings, plus a share of any prize money that the team won at races in which they competed.

The Tour de la Tropicale Amissa Bongo in Gabon in January 2009 was Daniel's first international race – he was selected, along with Nathan's younger brother, Nicodem Habiyambere, because Adrien and Nathan were now riding professionally in South Africa. The racing was hotter and faster than they had experienced before, with well-known teams from Europe – including Tour de France stalwarts Française des Jeux and Bouygues Telecom – setting the pace, but the new riders acquitted themselves well. As important to Jock was how they coped with the cultural experiences. 'Daniel and Nicodem would never be the same,' he noted at the time. He painted a particularly vivid picture of the swimming pool at their hotel in Libreville. 'The last time Daniel was ever surrounded by water was in his mother's womb! He had NEVER before been in a body of water.'

At the Umucyo Saloon, Daniel took a short while to recall the experience in the swimming pool. Eventually he said, 'It was not so memorable to me.' A greater concern to Daniel back then was that he was still not being paid to ride with Team Rwanda. He had a wife and young baby, and he was broke. He had been training with the team for more than a year by that point and the money he had saved was disappearing. He had begun to think that maybe he was better off with Emmanuel Mayaka's Ciné Elmay team, when at least he could rely on a regular 5,000 francs each week. 'Whatever we do is to raise our families,' Daniel said. 'What's the point of a lavish hotel if

I came home empty handed, facing my family with nothing? It doesn't attract me. It was just some momentary pleasures.'

He tried to explain his position to Jock, but with only Rafiki to translate, Daniel was never sure that Coach understood. In February 2009, Daniel was selected for the Tour d'Egypte; he told Rafiki who told Jock that he did not want to race. The reply came back that he didn't have a choice, the plane tickets and hotel rooms were already booked. He could be slung in jail if he pulled out now; Team Rwanda denies any such threat was made. Either way, Daniel boarded the plane, but decided to race in a way that brought the minimum risk of personal injury. He refused to ride in the main pack, but hung back a few metres behind it, so that he'd avoid any crashes. He did this some days for the entire stage, with Jock screaming at him to race properly. Team Rwanda did not perform well at the Tour d'Egypte, not helped by Daniel's show of defiance. At the end, each rider's share of the prize money was just 3,000 francs – £3 – for a week's racing of up to 120 miles every day.

'I could earn that in one day if I went back to work my land or did something else at home,' said Daniel. That was where the story of his fear of flying came from, he thought. 'I just couldn't face the humiliation of going on an aeroplane all the time any more. People in my village thought I was famous and when I came back I couldn't even buy them a drink!'

When Daniel returned home, he retired from cycling; he was twenty-seven, he should have been at his peak. Ciné Elmay still existed, but Mayaka had stopped supporting individual riders after Team Rwanda selected the most talented ones. Daniel gave his racing bike back to Jock and he sold the mountain bikes he had won at the Wooden Bike Classics in 2006 and 2007. With that money, he trained to become a barber. He charged 150 francs (fifteen pence) for boys, 200 francs (twenty pence) for men and 300 francs (thirty pence) for girls and women – about a third of the prices in Kigali. Still, he had never made less than 3,000 francs in a day. He had not ridden a bike seriously since he came back from Egypt in 2009, but he still watched the races. Whenever the Tour of Rwanda passed his shop, he flagged down a motorbike and followed the race up the road for a few miles. In the old days, people in his village would listen for reports about his races on the radio; now I was the first person to have spoken to him about cycling in years.

I asked Daniel if he enjoyed being a barber. He shrugged. 'It's fine,' he said, 'but don't be surprised if next time you pass through here I'm doing something else.' He would rather be riding his bike, but what choice did he have? He had another child now, two young boys to support. 'There has to be a cut-off point,' he said. 'If I'd have continued like that, digging into my savings, I'd be dead now.'

Rwandans never spend much time thinking about the future. This is, after all, a country without winter; nestled under the Equator, the year-round temperature is mostly in the mid-twenties, just some months it rains more than others. The academic John Mbiti, who was born in Kenya, lived in Uganda and studied at Cambridge University, discovered that none of the East African languages really concerned itself with any time beyond the present day. 'What would be "future" is extremely brief,' he wrote in his influential 1969 book, *African Religions and Philosophy*. 'If the event is remote, say beyond two years from now, then it cannot be conceived, it cannot be spoken of and the languages themselves have no verb tenses to cover that distant "future" dimension of time.' In the West, they plan; in Africa, they react.

Such a generalisation could sound absurdly broad-brush,

but Mbiti's argument made sense when I talked to Daniel and Abraham, both of whom grew up in old-fashioned, rural parts of the country. In the villages, a person's worth is judged by the prosperity of their family. These indicators have been unchanged for decades, if not centuries: how many cows they owned, the number of coffee trees on their plot, and so forth. Being a member of Team Rwanda made Daniel a local celebrity, but it did not put cement on his floors or water in his taps. More than that, it left his family on their knees, severely undermining his reputation and social standing. He was humiliated that he had nothing to give family and friends when they asked for financial assistance. Jock could have told him that he would be a millionaire in five years' time, riding in the great cycling races of Europe, and it would not have made any difference. That future didn't exist for him.

Obed Rugovera – Daniel's old team-mate, who stayed on unpaid and eventually started to receive a salary – spent the summer of 2012 in the United States learning to teach yoga and massage. What were his impressions of the country, he was asked when he came home. 'Everything is different than Rwanda,' he said. 'In the US many people have jobs, everyone works. Everyone has a plan for each week and they have goals. Americans think of the future.'

Jock set the rules, but the Rwandans had to play by them. Daniel must have come across as ungrateful to him, maybe even greedy; Abraham, too. Jock often repeated the mantra that Team Rwanda was not about the bike: how else would the average Rwandan fly on an aeroplane or stay in a plush hotel or use a flush toilet or learn to speak English? It was these precious moments that the fundraising was paying for. Speaking with Daniel, however, it occurred to me for the first time that maybe not all Rwandans wanted these life-altering experiences. They were Western aspirations, not Daniel's own.

It should be no surprise that Adrien and Rafiki, the most worldly and educated of Team Rwanda's riders, both prospered under the system. Daniel, the runt of fourteen kids, for whom everything in life had been scraping by, day to day, had not fared so well. Abraham, whose life had often been reduced to the most gruesome soap opera, had taken years to adapt to the regime and was now past his racing prime. 'When you have a family, you become distracted,' said Rafiki. 'If Abraham had the same head as Adrien, he would be the best. No one would get close to him.'

It was also revealing that Adrien and Rafiki were the only members of Team Rwanda in those early days who had not worked as bicycle-taxi riders. For the others cycling was a job: they rode bikes not always because they loved doing it but because that was how they made their living. Team Rwanda came along and offered to pay them more money to do basically what they had been doing for years and they jumped at it. The situation was more emotive for Adrien and Rafiki: they chose a career in cycling because it was their passion. As a child, Rafiki had doodled bicyles in his school books, while Adrien had grown up hearing about the legendary feats of his uncle, Emmanuel Turatsinze. The sport had an all-important romance that perhaps for some of their team-mates it lacked.

When new riders – from Eritrea, Ethiopia, Rwanda or wherever – arrived at the African Continental Cycling Centre in South Africa, the first lesson JP Van Zyl taught them had nothing to do with the bicycle. He sat them down and they had to learn how to use a knife and fork. 'They're used to eating with their hands,' he explained. 'I've seen so many people say: "Ah, look at how they're eating like pigs." So you have to teach them and tell them why. Sometimes I can't even explain why they need to change! But if they go to an important dinner with sponsors, they're going to immediately judge them. So it's for their own good. Even when they ask you why: "Well, this is what the Western people want, so do it when you get there."'

Adrien was an exceptional rider, on roads and on a mountain bike, but he was also comfortable with a set of cutlery. His greatest quality, though, was to gaze into the future and embrace a vision that he could never have imagined on his own. That was why, when the riders' house was broken into in Potchefstroom that Sunday night, he knew he had to stay in South Africa.

8

BOYS ON TOUR

The night before the 2011 Tour of Rwanda passed through Adrien Niyonshuti's hometown, Rwamagana, I went to the local bicycle-taxi rank. A young man came over, hustling for a fare; his name was Jean-Claude Hategekemana. He was twenty-four, the same age as Adrien, and he said they had been at primary school together, but in different classes. Would he watch tomorrow? 'Of course, everyone will come to see the cyclists, this whole place will be full,' he predicted. Would people be screaming for Adrien? 'Well,' he paused, 'some of us are upset that he is competing for South Africa. We would prefer him to race for Rwanda. But we will shout for him anyway.'

Jean-Claude was not the first Rwandan to make this point to me: Adrien would be fronting the squad now called MTN-Qhubeka, selected by Douglas Ryder. But the Tour of Rwanda would also feature two Rwandan national teams, overseen by Jock Boyer. Many locals believed that Adrien had somehow flipped allegiances. The subtleties of racing – that it is perfectly commonplace to race for a team based in another country, but also compete under one's own country's flag – were irrelevant for many Rwandans. They wanted to see their cyclists taking on the world, wearing their national colours and holding their own. It made them proud, even hopeful. Of Team Rwanda, Jean-Claude was only familiar by name with Adrien and Abraham. 'There was a big rivalry between them, but now Adrien is stronger,' he said, as a crowd milled around us. 'But the *muzungu* has done a good job training them. I think they will do well.'

Jean-Claude's own story was familiar enough, a version of something I had heard often from the riders in the team: he came from an outsize family and his father died when he was a child; he lived with his mother and had left school in his early teens to find work. Bicycle-taxis suited him well enough for now, but the job was punishing and he planned to save money and take his motorcycle licence. That was, he felt, a more prestigious profession. He had started work that morning at six o'clock, and thirteen hours later, he was hoping for one last commission as Rwandans filed out of Mass – it was a Sunday – before clocking off. He had earned around 2,000 francs – £2 – that day, pretty typical, but he had to hand over 400 francs of that to his friend, from whom he rented the bicycle. Had he ever considered racing? 'I don't have time for that!' he said, as if I'd suggested that he devote his weekends to making a matchstick model of Rwamagana Cathedral. 'I'm too busy making my livelihood.'

The middle class in Africa might be growing – it is predicted to exceed a billion people by 2060 – but I found it hard to spot in Rwanda. This is partly explained by the genocide – Tutsis traditionally filled that intermediate position – but there are deeper, systemic inequalities. In the cities, there are plenty of people for whom life is good. They dress smartly, drive 4x4s, take holidays to Europe and the waistband of their chinos is gently distended. Not all well-to-do Rwandans are carrying a few pounds – President Kagame was memorably described by the writer Philip Gourevitch as being so thin that in official state photographs he looked like a cardboard cut-out – but it is frequently a giveaway. Lunches, and often dinners, in the more affluent parts of Rwanda are typically buffets; this custom dated to the seventies, when it was felt that civil servants took too long for their lunch breaks. The hotplates are piled high with carbohydrate-heavy staples – potatoes both sweet and 'Irish', rice and beans – and diners can fill their plates as often as they like.

Outside of the main conurbations, Rwandans tend to be lithe and toned, their muscles naturally conditioned from walking miles each day, often carrying half their bodyweight in produce. It is no surprise that when Tom and Jock arrived, they saw potential athletes everywhere they looked. Rwandans are still, overwhelmingly, subsistence farmers, and many survive on less than sixty pence a day. The government may have been spending five per cent of its gross domestic product on science and technology, but the trickle-down has been glacially slow. For visitors to Rwanda, there is an unsettling absence of the middle ground: they can spend an hour zipping around Kigali on a moto-taxi and pay £1, but if they want to rent a car for one day it costs at least £100, the annual earnings of some rural Rwandans. The chasm between the lowest earners and the most prosperous must sometimes feel impossible to breach for the poorer strata, no matter how hard they work.

Cycling was one of the few professions that offered any degree of upward mobility. The riders were not rich by any means: Adrien was the only one of the team to have running water and electricity in his far-from-grand house; less than eight per cent of Rwandans had access to electricity, and the supply that was available was centralised, three-quarters of it in the capital Kigali. Still, through their sweat and efforts, most of the Team Rwanda members could now consider moving out of the family homes into their own houses. They could think about finding a wife, too. If they wanted to propose, they would need money to buy a cow – the traditional gift for the bride's family – which normally cost upwards of £400. The riders might not be the middle class yet, but from where they started, they were climbing the ladder.

The progress of the cyclists neatly dovetailed with President Kagame's plans for the country. The government's Vision 2020 development programme, unveiled around the turn of the millennium, imagined Rwanda as a 'middle-income country' in World Bank terminology; moving up to the ranks of emerging nations that included Brazil and Thailand. The per-capita income would rise to £600 – four times what it was in 2000 – and the country's gross domestic product would be boosted sevenfold. Half of the subsistence farmers would be found paying jobs. These are ambitious goals, and a dozen cyclists were barely a drop in Lake Victoria. But Kagame knew the value of role models and these young men on their bicycles, no different from millions of their compatriots, had a personal connection to the population that government policy would probably never match. For the duration of the Tour of Rwanda, they were practically a rolling billboard for the future of the country.

In the post-genocide landscape, sport has been identified as an area of potential reconciliation and healing for Rwanda. 'That's the great thing about sport and the creative industry,' said Albert Rudatsimburwa, the head of Contact FM radio station. 'When a footballer is playing or when a singer is performing, you don't wonder, "Is this guy a Hutu or is he a Tutsi?" I have never, never, never heard anything in that direction at a concert or a sports event. And I tell you: in the army, it's the same thing. No one in a war says, "Who's Hutu? Who's Tutsi?"'

Cycling has some democratic advantages over other sports. Usually spectators have to travel to a stadium and pay an entrance fee; a degree of effort is required. With so few televisions in the country, most Rwandans interacted with their sports heroes only through reports on the radio. But cycling came directly to the people. All they had to do was stand by the roadside at an assigned time, updated by the radios clamped to their ears, and the riders passed so close that they could stare into their eyes. They would fly past like a storm, a kaleidoscope of flashing colours. Every seat was the best in the house. It was what the French called a *jour de fête* and, in a country starved of entertainment, these were rare pleasures. Even better, it was free. 'It's a moment of joy,' Joseph Habineza, the sports minister, told me in 2010 not long before he resigned after incriminating images turned up on the Internet. (The eleven photographs showed 'Minister Joe' posing with five women, none of whom was his wife.)

For many of the cyclists on Team Rwanda, the adulation of the crowds made the suffering they endured worthwhile. Rafiki talked with warmth and nostalgia of the early Tours du Rwanda that he attended as a child. Sometimes, he reflected, spectators would become so excited that they would give their favourite rider a live chicken, or in extreme cases a cow, to show appreciation of their efforts. The racers would return home in a Toyota Hilux pick-up loaded with their bicycle and their clucking, mooing spoils. These days, riders were more likely to be given cash and perhaps a motorbike. 'It was very ceremonial back then,' Rafiki said ruefully. 'It's become too sophisticated. The interaction is not the same.'

Cycling might not be especially high-tech, but it has turned out to be the perfect expression of the new Rwanda: a country that has not forgotten the genocide, but is also trying not to be defined by it. In the early days of Team Rwanda, the Americans imagined that its greatest impact would be seen outside its borders. The achievements of the riders on their bicycles would confer legitimacy on a country that many in the West dismissed as brutal and medieval. Wherever the riders travelled, they would be ambassadors for a nation. But it turned out there was more to the story than public relations. The Tour of Rwanda sent a direct and powerful message to its own citizens – millions of whom came out to watch – that self-improvement was possible for anyone prepared to work hard enough.

All bicycle races are, at some level, advertisements for the places in which they are staged. The Tour de France is a three-week tourist brochure: a selective showcase of the country's natural and cultural wonders seen at their best from a helicopter. The Tour of Rwanda is similar: relentlessly scenic, it presents a young, vibrant nation that is clearly on the way up. But a universal truth of bicycle races is that there is only so much that can be stage-managed. Rwanda, like any country, has its murky corners and embarrassing secrets that it might prefer outsiders not to see. Following the Tour, it became clear that it wasn't only Minister Joe who was up to no good – scratch the surface and there were feuds, petty jealousies and even a pimp on a BMW motorbike.

The Tour of Rwanda, on one level, has a family resemblance to cycling events the world over. Thin men in colourful kit huff and puff over a terrain and distances that have long stopped being pleasurable for them. The leader of the event wears a yellow jersey, and the most efficient hill climber sports a spotted red-and-white one. There is no prize for sprinting, because there are not enough flat roads on which a sprint could be organised. There are podium girls, but they would never do anything so forward as kiss the winners. Motorcycle outriders cruise around making sure the roads are closed, while irascible policemen whack children on the legs with sticks to keep them in line. Behind the riders is a snake of vehicles, including a race referee, a handful of VIPs, the team cars, journalists and a medic.

At the end of each stage, the highest-performing riders receive a doping test. Like any race, riders will cut corners if they can get away with it, though in Rwanda cheating is likely to entail a rider holding on to the side of their team car on a severe slope, not receiving a blood transfusion in their hotel room at the day's end. The idea of willingly submitting to a blood transfusion in central Africa is, I would hazard, still a few years distant.

The race has been overseen since 2009 by GSO, a French-based organisation that has a hand in running cycling's annual World Championships. Before 2009, the Tour of Rwanda had mostly been of national interest, featuring local riders and an exotic but usually under-prepared selection of competitors from neighbouring countries. But in late 2008, the race became sanctioned by the International Cycling Union and accorded a rating of 2.2, one level below events such as the Tour of Britain. The UCI had been looking to expand the sport in Africa, and Rwanda's ambitious progress had caught its eye. With UCI points on offer, the guest list for the 2009 Tour of Rwanda took an abrupt upgrade. Among those invited was Lance Armstrong himself: 'He could have talked about the war on cancer,' said Aimable Bayingana, president of the Rwandan cycling federation. The American declined but an experienced

Moroccan national team came and, spurred on by recent criticism from their king, Mohammed VI, won six stages out of eight. The Rwandan riders did not take a stage, but Adrien Niyonshuti finished third overall and Abraham Ruhumuriza was fifth.

The 2010 edition of the race went to another level again. With extra UCI points available for Olympic qualification, nine teams became sixteen and the line-up now included professional and semi-professional squads from France, Belgium and the United States. The race lasted almost two weeks and the average speed increased from twenty-two miles per hour, as it had been in 2009, to an impressive twenty-four miles per hour. Morocco, so dominant before, barely made a dent. This time the Eritrean national team, led by their modest but exhilarating superstar climber Daniel Teklehaimanot, swept all before them. The boss of the Americans, Phil Southerland from Team Type 1, an outfit committed to representing athletes with type-one diabetes, admitted that he was completely unprepared for the raw talent of the competition. 'We got our asses handed to us,' he said after the final stage. Teklehaimanot won, as everyone suspected he might when we saw that he had come prepared with a matching all-yellow uniform. Again, Adrien was the best-placed Rwandan in eighth; Abraham, because of disciplinary issues with Team Rwanda, was not permitted to race.

It would be invidious, however, to present the Tour of Rwanda as just another bicycle race. One French journalist said that following it made him feel that he was covering an anarchic early edition of the Tour de France. There is certainly none of the commercialisation of modern-day cycling: in European races, a publicity caravan precedes the riders, ramping up excitement for their arrival; sponsors toss out keyrings, hats and jelly sweets. At the 2011 Tour of Rwanda, 'the caravan' consisted of a solitary battered pick-up truck, with teenagers piled precariously in the open back, blasting hip-hop from an enormous speaker. One of the motorcycle outriders, a well-built man with dreadlocks, was said to be operating a prosperous sideline organising introductions between local women and the assembled dignitaries for a fee. The competition, too, did not necessarily conform to the rigid strictures of European stage racing. At the Tour of Rwanda in 2010, I asked Dan Craven, a professional cyclist who was born in Namibia but had done most of his racing for UK-based teams such as Rapha Condor, how he rated the Rwandans. 'Tactically, they're naïve,' he replied. 'But it's not just the Rwandans, it's all riders at this level. They just don't really know what they're doing.'

At the back of the peloton, it was even more lawless. There were vast discrepancies between the abilities of the riders and, as soon as the race went uphill, the field would be obliterated, strung out along the road. In most cycling events, the rejects from the main group bunch together: it means they can share the effort as they ride and there is the added advantage that they are not disqualified if they finish outside the time restrictions. Not in Rwanda. 'They just attack, attack, attack,' marvelled Simeon Green, a British rider who rode the 2010 Tour. 'Generally, Africans don't have that much experience, but they are extremely strong, so they can hurt you. There's also a bigger pride element: in Europe, cycling has been around for more than a hundred years, so you understand that if you're not going to win, you roll in nice and easy.'

The disparity between the privileged and the disadvantaged teams actually appeared to expand each year, not narrow. The 2011 Tour of Rwanda was launched with an individual time trial: each of the fifty-five riders in the race set off on his own, at two-minute intervals, on a two-and-a-half-mile route around

Kigali. Team Rwanda had set up camp in the shadow of the national stadium, the Amahoro, which in the local language means 'Hope'. It is a symbolic destination for many Rwandans, having safely harboured many thousands of Tutsi refugees under UN protection in 1994. The intensity and professionalism of Team Rwanda's preparations was something to behold. The riders were cordoned off to avoid distraction from the thousands of friends, family and rubberneckers. Before they went out on the course, they worked up a sweat for half an hour on a static bicycle. Then they slipped on their special teardrop-shaped helmets and climbed on to their machines. Fresh from the plane, these were a fleet of Eddy Merckx EMX-7 carbon-fibre bicycles, with one previous owner: the Belgian professional team Quick-Step. A month before, they had been used by riders such as former world champion Tom Boonen and Sylvain Chavanel, who had worn the yellow jersey for two days at the 2010 Tour de France.

It was impossible, at this moment, not to marvel at how far the Team Rwanda riders had come. Less than five years before, they were using decrepit bikes with either no gears or shifters that they had to lean down to change on the top tube. Now they were on 'Tornado Tom' Boonen's space-age machinery, wearing aerodynamic helmets. A pair of *soigneurs* would caress and pummel them after each stage. I half-expected to find out that Jock, inspired by Team Sky's marginal-gains philosophy, in which the British outfit hunted down every minuscule competitive advantage, had arranged for his riders to sleep on ergonomic mattresses with hypoallergenic bedding, while an air purifier hummed away in the corner of the room. I actually asked, but no: while the race was in Kigali, the team was staying at the £10-a-night Centre d'Accueil Saint Francois d'Assise. They were low on funds again this year, and a church hostel was all they could afford. The morning of the time trial, the lucky ones had cold showers, but some of the team had no water at all.

The 2011 Tour of Rwanda seemed destined to be a week-long, cross-country victory parade for Adrien. As well as the duration being reduced, the competition was weaker than previous years, only ten teams and neither of the past two winners: Eritrea couldn't afford the airfares, while Morocco pulled out the week of the race. The Algerian national squad was also a no-show, while Libya and Egypt were otherwise engaged as the Arab Spring rumbled on. Adrien, meanwhile, as Jean-Claude on the Rwamagana bicycle-taxi rank had noticed, would be the lead rider for his professional team MTN-Qhubeka, the strongest road outfit in Africa. Friends are crucial in cycling and, in the past, Jock had recognised that the Rwandans lacked the strength in depth to support Adrien during the most testing stages. Now Adrien would be able to rely on his five team-mates from MTN-Qhubeka, plus unofficial-but-everyone-knew-it assistance from the two teams of six riders from Team Rwanda. That made seventeen allies from a field of fifty-five; his success was not a formality but it certainly represented the best opportunity for a Rwandan to win the Tour since it had become an UCI-endorsed international event.

MTN-Qhubeka were clearly fully committed, too. For the prologue in Kigali, they had lugged Adrien's bespoke time trial bicycle with disc wheels, worth more than £5,000, from South Africa. It seemed a lot of effort for a course not even three miles long – in a competition where most of the athletes were warming up with a few turns round the car park of the Amahoro stadium – but it sent an unmistakable message of intent. Team boss Douglas Ryder had flown up from Johannesburg to watch, even though it was his fortieth birthday that week. Long-standing Team Rwanda benefactors Tom Ritchey and Peb Jackson missed the start because they had a meeting with President Kagame and they could not stop him talking.

Adrien was the last rider to set out and he zipped round the course at an average speed of more than thirty-two miles an hour. He took every corner at full pelt and, on the straight sections, he made full use of the aerodynamic reach of his handlebars. He had clearly brought his best form, which was why it was surprising that when he crossed the line he had recorded only the fourth-best time, behind three members of Team Type 1. The next day, a split stage from Kigali to Rwamagana in the morning and then back in the afternoon, it was a similar story: despite frenzied fan support, both races were won by Kiel Reijnen, a twenty-five-year-old American. Reijnen, who had just returned to racing after a year-long mystery illness, either didn't know or didn't care that he was spoiling the party for the homecoming hero. He eschewed local food: instead he had brought fifteen kilograms of supplies in his suitcase – an impressive larder of dehydrated camping meals, quinoa, olive oil and fresh garlic, plus a rice steamer – and he cooked each evening in his room. When I heard that, it imparted the same ominous feeling I remembered from the 2010 Tour when Daniel Teklehaimanot unveiled his head-to-toe yellow kit. Reijnen was clearly not here to make up the numbers.

Still, there was no need to panic. The race had not gone uphill yet: 'We will see tomorrow if the yellow jersey is a climber,' said Adrien, with uncharacteristic steeliness. He was talking about the hundred-mile run from Kigali to Gisenyi, the most brutal stage of the whole race.

It turned out that Reijnen, who hails from Boulder, Colorado, in the foothills of the Rockies, had seen a mountain or two in his time. But something more noteworthy took place on that stage: the Rwandans, who were supposed to be bolstering Adrien's attempts to take the yellow jersey, appeared not to have received the memo. At one point, two riders – Abraham and Gasore Hategeka – broke away in a bid for personal glory. Even Reijnen was taken aback. 'I don't know what their tactic was,' he told me afterwards.

Douglas Ryder was furious. 'It's tough for Adrien because he has opportunities none of the Rwandan riders have,' he said. 'He's had fame and fortune and so I think there's a lot of jealousy. Last year he came to this race and rode on the Rwandan national team – they were good enough for him then – and this year he brings his MTN team. So now those guys are racing against him. They want to show that they're actually better than we are. It's tough for him, he's a bit angry about it. But he wants to win this race badly. He'll never let go.'

At this stage, the damage was minimal: Adrien was only eighteen seconds behind Reijnen, a gap that could easily be overhauled in the remaining days of the Tour. But then Adrien walked past Douglas and me as we sat on the balcony of the team's hotel in Gisenyi. He had strapping on his right shoulder; the bandage was intense white, but blood was already seeping through. He had another dressing on his elbow and one more on his knee. 'The knee's good, Adrien?' Douglas asked. Adrien gave him a tired smile. 'Look!' Douglas exclaimed. 'He laughs. He's got a flipping gaping wound in his leg. He's just amazing.'

Adrien had tumbled off his bike not during the long, difficult stage, but on the gentle one-mile roll downhill to the hotel after the finish. He had been freewheeling, holding on to the car that Jock was driving, when they went over a speed bump. Adrien had lost control and been upended head-first.

When Adrien was out of earshot, Douglas's frustrations boiled over. 'Jock, interesting guy, eh?' he said, his Afrikaans brogue becoming more pronounced. 'Look at all the articles that have been written about Adrien in the last two years, especially with his build-up to the Olympics, there's never been a mention of MTN-Qhubeka's commitment and our involvement with Adrien. And we've built Adrien. We've coached him, we've supported him, he lives in South Africa. He's got a bank account, a work permit.

'He wants to create his own little empire, old Jock,' Douglas continued. 'We're not doing it for personal glory, to put our name in lights, and he is a bit. I think he needs to justify his existence here and the impact that he makes, so I think he's getting a bit clouded. So we do bang heads a little bit every now and again.'

Adrien's innocuous crash, witnessed by only a handful of team staff, turned out to be the defining moment of the 2011 Tour of Rwanda. At the start line the next day, he could barely grip the handlebars of his bicycle, an insurmountable disadvantage when he was spending all day climbing hills. His knee was so sore that he had to keep it moving constantly to prevent it seizing up. He found it hard to sleep at night. It would be more than three months before he was fully recovered physically from the spill. He probably should have pulled out of the race, but his pride would not allow it. In the end, he finished sixth overall, but he managed to string together enough solo efforts to take the King of the Mountains competition. Reijnen won the race, and Nathan Byukusenge was the highest-placed Rwandan in fourth. The wait for a Rwandan winner of their home tour in the UCI era would continue.

*

If this was the first sign of divisions within Team Rwanda, it would not be the last. Innocent Uwamungu was one of the most irrepressible characters in the set-up; he had a wide smile with a gap between his front teeth (a sign of fertility in these parts) and a raucous heh-heh laugh. He rode the 2011 Tour on the 'B' squad, Akagera, named after the national park in the east of the country, but he had a mouth full of abscesses and tooth fractures so he had not been at his best. But the main reason that Innocent was hard to miss was that he had sight in only one eye, his left; behind his Oakley shades, his right eye was almost closed over. His story contained all the heart-warming and most disconcerting parts of the Team Rwanda project.

Jock had spotted Innocent riding on 25 December 2009. Training on Christmas Day is often taken as a sign of great dedication from an athlete, but that wasn't why Innocent was doing it. 'Everyone enjoys themselves on Christmas Day because they have money,' he explained. 'But I didn't have any money at the time, so it was a way of staying busy so the day would finish faster.'

The bike had been his father's: he was a deliveryman for a local bakery and he would often cover seventy miles in a day on bread runs. The family – father, mother, Innocent and his sister – was displaced during the genocide and they spent two years in refugee camps in Zaire. They returned in 1996, but the area where they lived – north-west Rwanda, the former heartland for Hutu Power – was still fiercely contested and a year later Innocent's father was killed by Hutu insurgents. Life was hard after that: his mother sold tomatoes at the market to support the family and, although he was not even ten years old, Innocent left school. When he could reach the pedals, he became a bicycle-taxi rider, using his father's battered single-speed. He got married, to Monique, and they had a baby daughter, Honorine.

The road between Ruhengeri and Gisenyi was mostly empty that Christmas afternoon, but Jock and the team mechanic Maxime were out on their motorbikes. When they saw a muscular rider powering up a hill, they turned their BMWs round and flagged him down. An impenetrable conversation took place – Innocent spoke only Kinyarwanda, no English or French – and a policeman came over to rebuke the Rwandan for bothering the *muzungus*. Still, somehow Jock communicated that Innocent should present himself at the team headquarters the next morning at ten o'clock. He was wearing a T-shirt emblazoned with the logo RockShox – a brand of bicycle suspension – so they called him Rocky. When he turned up on time the following day, Jock was impressed. A day later, he tested him on the Velotron, an upgraded version of the CompuTrainer: Rocky wasn't the next Armstrong, or even the next Adrien, but there was no doubting his determination. His new nickname turned out to be a good fit and soon even his friends and family took to using it. When he was selected to train at the African Continental Cycling Centre in South Africa, Jock arranged a passport: for Rocky's birth date he selected 6 July, Sylvester Stallone's birthday.

Life changed quickly for Rocky after he joined Team Rwanda. Before, he estimated, he would sometimes earn only 10,000 francs – £10 – in a month; his family rarely went without food, but new clothes or shoes were impossible dreams. Now he had enough money to buy a plot of land and build a house. It is hard to explain the life-changing significance of owning property for Rwandans. 'It is the most important thing for us,' said Rocky, as we sat in his living room. He was wearing a Cameroon football jersey with the name of their star striker,

Samuel Eto'o, on the back; when I pointed this out, he rushed to his bedroom, embarrassed, and swapped it for a Team Rwanda shirt. He continued, 'Nobody can come and say, "Give me my house, go and find another one, the rent you're giving me is not enough." I'm very happy now.'

One day in June 2011, he had just finished training. His house was set back from the main road in the town of Mukamira, perhaps 150 metres across a patch of bumpy volcanic rock. He slotted his sunglasses into his helmet, lifted his bike on to his shoulder and walked past a group of labourers who were extracting pumice to use in the construction of an outside wall. At that moment, one of the men struck the rock with a hammer and a shard flew into Rocky's right eye. It was a tiny nick but it penetrated down to the optic nerve. At first, Rocky could still see, but his vision was blurred. He knew he should go to hospital, so he caught a bus to Ruhengeri, fifteen miles away. When he arrived there, he waited for a couple of hours, but the doctor eventually told him that they did not have the skills to treat him. He needed to go to Kigali. It was dark now, so Rocky had little option but to return home to Mukamira on the bus.

He did not sleep that night, and early the next morning, his sight deteriorating rapidly, he caught the bus to Kigali. At the hospital there, they determined they couldn't treat him either, but they recommended an eye specialist from the United States, who worked in Kabgayi, one hour to the south. Rocky was back on the bus again, but in Kabgayi, he was told that the American had gone home and would not be back for a month. At this point, Rocky spoke to Jock and an appointment was made with a doctor back in Kigali. Finally, after three days, the wound was dressed properly and he was given antibiotics. But now he had no vision at all and it was too late to save the eye.

At the 2011 Tour of Rwanda, Rocky had not yet been fitted with a glass eye – that would be another long and frustrating drama – but, apart from the week after the accident, he had never stopped cycling. At first, he borrowed rollers from Jock, which allowed him to ride his bicycle in his living room. But before long, he was back on the road. It was strange initially: if it rained or when he had sweat in his left eye he was practically blind; he found that his peripheral vision and his awareness of depth of field were erratic, too. Rocky's solution summed him up: he decided he would just ride at the front of the group, so there were fewer riders to bump into. His spirit – or perhaps just his desire not to return to his previous life – was indomitable. Two weeks after the Tour, on a Sunday morning in December, I saw him finish second in a one-day race around Kigali against the best riders in the country. His prize money was 200,000 francs (£200), which he planned to use to put a wall around his property. At Jock's instigation, he was even thinking about the Paralympics.

Rocky's was a freak injury, but it was a reminder of the unconventional struggles that were everyday hurdles for the riders in Team Rwanda. The lack of qualified doctors is simply one issue: there's just one medical school in the country, turning out around forty students a year to serve a population of nearly eleven million. (This doesn't even take into account the brain drain that affects sub-Saharan Africa: it has been said there are more Ethiopian doctors in Washington, DC, than in Ethiopia.) Rocky described what happened to him not with outrage or injustice, but with calm acceptance. Indeed, as we spoke, men worked on his land, extracting the pumice with hammers to create the wall that his recent windfall was funding. There was a constant dink-dink-dink of metal on rock, a noise that should have given him nightmares. 'I'm not angry, I'm doing good,' he insisted. 'The only problem is that I realised that some of my neighbours were happy when they heard about the injury. Also some of my team-mates, they were pleased, thinking, *He won't go further*. But in the race last Sunday I showed that it is possible.'

So, other members of Team Rwanda felt they would profit from his loss of sight? Rocky nodded his head. 'It's with the young riders that I saw that. The older ones are happy to teach us what we don't know. Coach tells us to help each other, but there is a lot of competition within the team and not everyone wants you to improve. That's why we're not doing so good at the moment.' His team-mate Gasore made a similar point. 'One of the great weaknesses of Team Rwanda – and Rwandans in general – is that we compete between ourselves,' he said. 'Teamwork is not really sinking in: people want to get that credit on their own or for their clubs.'

With inequality there will always be envy, and Rwanda is no exception. Rocky didn't have much, but every time he got ahead, an invisible hand seemed to pull him back. Not long before we met, he had come home to find that his family – he now had a son, Fabrice, too – had been robbed of all their clothing by a jealous neighbour.

Equally, that infighting and petty jealousies existed within Team Rwanda should also not come as a surprise; it is a sports team, after all, and egos are inevitable. But, because of the country's history, there was a peculiar frisson hearing these issues expressed. Unity is a national obsession in Rwanda: 'There is no Hutu or Tutsi,' I was often told. 'We are all Rwandan now.' This was a place, after all, that had developed a criminal offence called 'divisionism'. Although legally vague, it had been defined as, 'The use of any speech, written statement or action that divides people, that is likely to spark conflicts among people, or that causes an uprising which might degenerate into strife.' Newspapers and political parties had been punished, and individuals imprisoned; such an environment meant that disagreements often simmered, unspoken, just beneath the surface. Critics, meanwhile, complained that divisionism allowed President Kagame to skim over the fact that Tutsis – just fifteen per cent of the population – were disproportionately represented in business and in the government.

If there was any resentment towards Adrien in Team Rwanda, no one was explicitly calling it that. But Adrien did admit that he would never live in the country while he was still racing, even if it did mean that some of his compatriots believed he had switched nationalities. It was simply too hard to concentrate, on and off the bike. 'In South Africa, I just have to focus on one thing: cycling,' he said. 'If I have to focus on lots of things, I get headaches. It's very difficult for me to stay in Rwanda and do proper training because there's a lot of problems with my family and sometimes neighbours will come and say, "Adrien, I have problem, you have to help me." They think you are getting millions and billions, so you have to give them money for free.

'That's life in Africa, for all Africans,' he continued. 'Take the example of soccer, like Didier Drogba or Eto'o: Eto'o works hard to get that money, Drogba works hard to that get that money. So for me, when I come here, people think I'm rich, that I have a lot of money and that it's easy. They ask me for money – 5,000 francs, 10,000 francs – or they say, "Adrien, you have a lot of bikes. You must give me a bike. I want a tyre, I want an inner tube."' He sighed a deep, world-weary sigh. 'I have to give them, but actually it's not easy to get money.'

9

THE MOST FAMOUS RWANDAN

'Are you planning to write about President Kagame in your book?' a Rwandan friend, who wanted to remain unidentified, asked me one day. I opened my mouth to reply, but the question was a rhetorical one. 'Please do not. Really, what is his connection with the story of cycling in this country? It is one of the only things that he does not control in Rwanda.'

He had a point. Team Rwanda existed not because of presidential decree, but because of the vision of Tom Ritchey and the persistence of Jock Boyer, allied to the hard work of young men driven to improve their lives. When Rocky needed a new glass eyeball, it was paid for not with government funds, but by an appeal on Facebook that was answered by the Jorgensen family from Tacoma, Washington. If airfares were required for the riders, the money came from a similar source. The only claim one could make for Kagame's direct relevance was that if he didn't want Team Rwanda to exist, then it would not.

But Kagame remains ever-present in the Rwandan psyche.

According to legend, at night, while the rest of Kigali sleeps, the Boss – as he is known in his party, the Rwandan Patriotic Front – tours the city in an unmarked car. As he is driven around, whenever he spots something he doesn't like or doesn't recognise – a new building development, say – he makes a note. The next morning, when his ministers arrive at their desks at seven o'clock prompt, there is a directive to investigate and report back. Every public official was set *imihigo*: targets that they would be ruthlessly assessed on attaining. Nothing escaped Kagame's attention. His sombre portrait glared down, reproachfully to some eyes, from behind almost every hotel check-in desk, bar and shop counter in Rwanda. The message echoed the one that Jock had hissed at his riders: 'I listen to *everything*. I see *everything*.'

Sometimes I would ask a Rwandan who the second most famous person in their country was. Their reaction was always beautiful: they would fall silent, then they might laugh, shake their head, maybe giggle some more. Perhaps it was Paul Rusesabagina, the manager of the Hôtel des Mille Collines during the genocide, but his celebrity was much greater outside the country than within it, and he now lived in South Africa. One person suggested the silverback Titus, the star of a BBC documentary *Titus the Gorilla King*, but animals were stretching the rules and he had died in 2009 anyway. There were no serious contenders from the arts. All of its neighbours – the Democratic Republic of Congo, Tanzania, Uganda and Burundi – have an enduring cultural heritage of literature, dance, music and theatre, but Rwanda has an oral tradition and had yet to produce individuals of note in these fields. There were no entrepreneurs, fashion models or captains of industry.

Even sport did not throw up potential candidates. While dynamic, powerful West Africans have made their mark in every football league in Europe, no Rwandan had ever – with respect to Elias 'Baby' Uzamukunda who played in France's fourth division with Cannes – made it to a high level. The country has never come close to qualifying for a World Cup. East Africa, meanwhile, churns out the world's most formidable distance runners. Kenya sits just the other side of Lake Victoria, but Rwanda, its people incubated in the same thin air of the highlands, has no great tradition of athletics. Uganda, to the north, produced the champion 400-metre hurdler John Akii-bua – one of forty-three children from his father's eight wives – who became a star of the 1972 Munich Olympics. Even Burundi, which has similar dimensions to Rwanda and is much, much poorer, had Vénuste Niyongabo, the winner of the men's 5,000m at the 1996 Games in Atlanta. Rwanda has never won a medal of any colour at the Olympics.

The Olympics, with its opening procession of more than 200 nations, can make the world feel very small and connected. In 2012 there were rowers from Nigeria, swimmers from Equatorial Guinea and a lone female sprinter in a hijab from Saudi Arabia. It isn't, really. Rwanda had sent a team to each Games since 1984, but the reality is that most people in the country have never even heard of the Olympics. The first time this came up, I was taken aback. I was speaking to a safari guide called Thomas: he was in his twenties and well-educated; he came from the capital city Kigali, not the sticks; he spent a lot of time around Westerners, his English was good. No question, he was Rwanda's one per cent. He knew everything about Arsenal FC and would go to a bar every weekend to watch their matches. Yet the Olympics were a blank slate to him. I fumblingly explained that they are a four-yearly collision of sports, nations and abilities. 'Sounds interesting,' he said, not sounding too interested. 'Maybe I watch next time.'

One might imagine that Rwanda's institutionalised under-achievement has dented the morale of its sports fans, inclined them towards pessimism, even defeatism. It is worth restating: no Rwandan has ever won a sporting event of international significance; only a handful have qualified by right – as opposed to by wild card – even to compete in those competitions. Not a bit of it. They demand success and really do regard second place as failure. 'We don't like to lose – at all!' said the sports minister Joseph Habineza. 'It's a problem and a big challenge for me because I have to educate people, to say, "Listen: to be a sportsman, you have to know how to win *and* to lose."'

What kind of country does not produce exceptional individuals? And how must it feel to live in a place with so few successful role models? The Tour of Rwanda provided an annual airing for these questions. In 2009, when foreign competitors joined the race, no Rwandan was able to win a stage. It was the same story in 2010. There were times watching the Tour when it seemed almost inconceivable that one of the home riders would not snatch a victory. On that rainy day in 2011, when Abraham and Gasore broke clear against team instructions, they were minutes ahead of the field and it appeared they only had to roll down the hill to Gisenyi and contest the sprint between the two of them. Somehow – and no one who was there that day could explain exactly how – they were overhauled by an American a few hundred metres before the finish. The problem had to be a psychological, rather than a physiological one. Were Rwandan sportsmen so conditioned to finishing second that they found it impossible to claim victory?

The 2011 Tour of Rwanda appeared to be following a well-worn script: seven stages down, seven foreign victories. Then on the last day, as the field rolled back into Kigali, a twenty-three-year-old new boy from Team Rwanda called Joseph Biziyaremye launched a solo attack eight miles from the finish. It had been a long week and the main contenders had agreed an informal armistice, but Joseph became restless with the stalemate. His aggression looked impetuous and, as he disappeared into the distance, no one took it that seriously. Even Jock did not regard him as an exceptional prospect. A former bicycle-taxi rider, he had been with the team for only six months. He spoke only Kinyarwanda and didn't appear to register a single word of what Coach was telling him. Jock organised a place for Joseph at the UCI's Continental Cycling Centre in South Africa, but he was still on African time and missed his flight.

On that day, however, Joseph's timing was rather good. He built up a lead and, even though he weaved up the hill towards Nyamirambo stadium in Kigali like he had spent an evening drinking banana beer, he had established enough of an advantage to win by nine seconds. Fifty metres beyond the finish line, he tumbled off his bicycle. He sat bolt upright, with his legs splayed, seemingly unable to speak or move. For minutes, as a posse of photographers and journalists swarmed around him, he remained mute, scarcely blinking. A buzz went round the crowd: a Rwandan had won! Joseph gave the impression that he was in shock.

Rwanda did once qualify for the African Cup of Nations football tournament: the year was 2004 and the finals were held in Tunisia. It was a landmark moment for Rwandan sport, maybe its greatest. Never mind that the starting eleven of the *Amuvubi* – the Wasps, as the national team are known – comprised mostly Congolese, Ugandan and Burundian nationals playing on hastily arranged passports and the team were knocked out in the group stage. There was one highlight, though: they played Congo and, against expectations, the *Amuvubi* triumphed one-nil, with a late goal scored by Said Makasi. The result did not go down well in Congo. Makasi was born and raised in Bukavu, on the Congolese side of Lake Kivu and after the match there was a riot in his hometown. Fans called Makasi a 'prostitute' and they burned down his parents' house.

Not long after the tournament, the football federation decided to redirect the money spent on naturalising mercenaries into creating an academy for young Rwandan players. The first intake of teenagers started living and training together in 2009. Within two years, the Junior Wasps had finished as runners-up in the African Championships and qualified for the under-seventeen 2011 World Cup in Mexico.

The under-seventeen team attracted considerable attention outside of the country, in part because most of the players had been born in 1994. A BBC documentary, *Rwanda-17: Healing a Nation*, followed the team and filmed an emotional scene in which the reserve goalkeeper, Kabes Hategikmana, was reunited with his father, who was in prison for crimes committed during the genocide. But again, like the cycling team, their enduring legacy was destined to be in the hearts and heads of their compatriots. After years of filling its ranks with outsiders, it turned out that Rwandans could play football after all. They had just never had the opportunity and backing before.

In the course of the under-seventeen African Championships, which were held in Rwanda, the Junior Wasps beat Burkina Faso and Egypt, and even the mighty Ivory Coast in the semi-finals. Crowds for the matches started small, but as the tournament went on they became raucous sell-outs and all-day parties; President Kagame attended the semi-final and final. It was further proof of the unifying potential of sport in modern Rwanda.

Rwanda's young players were every bit as talented as any

others that came out of Africa, believed Richard Tardy, their coach. Tardy was French; confidence in home-grown talent had not yet extended to management positions. Recent coaches of the *Amuvubi* senior team have included three Germans, a pair of Serbs, a couple of Croats, a Swede and a Ghanaian, but never a Rwandan. (Jock, of course, was another example of a foreign boss.) But Tardy knew what he was talking about. He had worked in France alongside the one-time Liverpool and Aston Villa manager, Gérard Houllier, and then spent a decade coaching in Ivory Coast, Algeria and Morocco. Three of his young Rwandan players were quickly taken on for trials with first division French clubs; perhaps this was the start of European scouts looking beyond West Africa for the stars of the future. Tardy even felt that if the team stayed together, Rwanda could make an impact at the 2018 World Cup in Russia, when most of them would be twenty-four, or four years later in Qatar.

This was an exciting dream: Rwanda could qualify for its first World Cup, with a team of local players that its fans had watched grow up in front of their eyes. Tardy, however, recognised some challenges remained. 'The players are good enough,' he sighed. 'But we must not only look in the next two years, it must be the next five, six years. This is difficult in Africa: in Africa you need to immediately have results. If you lose one game it is the end. It's finished for football.'

President Paul Kagame, Richard Tardy and Jock Boyer were all faced with the same problem. They had to convince Rwandans that they were winners – despite what the evidence suggested. The president decided that his secret weapon was the diaspora. He made assiduous efforts to court Rwandans who had been successful outside the country's borders, and encourage them to bring their expertise home. They became central to Vision 2020 as role models, and the smarter bars in Kigali always contained a smattering of people who had returned to the country from Belgium, the United States or Canada. Some were encouraged by Kagame directly; if their skills were particularly valuable to Rwanda – as happened with a drug researcher who worked for GlaxoSmithKline in America – he would even offer them a ride home on the presidential jet.

If they were not prepared to leave their lives in the developed world, Kagame would still put a financial squeeze on. In August 2012, he launched the Agaciro Development Fund; *agaciro* means 'dignity' in Kinyarwanda. The aim was to raise money from expatriates so that Rwanda no longer had to rely so heavily on foreign aid, which still made up half of the country's budget each year. 'Why should a citizen of another country have an obligation to feed me for ever,' the president said at a fundraising lunch in October 2012. 'That is almost blasphemy.' The appeal for 'solidarity' reaped immediate benefits: in the first two months, twenty billion francs, more than £20 million, poured in. A Twitter feed kept a rolling update of donations, with Rwandans encouraged to pledge 500 francs – fifty pence – by sending a text from their mobile phones.

The timing of the Agaciro fund was, however, no accident. During the summer of 2012, Kagame faced accusations that Rwanda was arming the rebel group M23 in the Democratic Republic of Congo; Human Rights Watch denounced M23 for committing 'a horrific trail of new atrocities', including summary executions, abductions, torture and mass rape. M23 was formed from the remains of the National Congress for the Defence of the People (CNDP), a group dominated by Congolese Tutsis and led by the flamboyant and vicious Christian warlord Laurent Nkunda. A former Pentecostal preacher who wore white robes and had a matching white pet goat called Betty,

Nkunda was born in Congo to Rwandan parents. He had joined the Rwandan Patriotic Front during the genocide and then fought alongside Rwandan forces when they first invaded Congo in 1996. In 2007, Nkunda's CNDP launched offensives against another local militia, the Democratic Forces for the Liberation of Rwanda (FDLR), which was mostly made up of Congolese Hutus, including fugitive *génocidaires*.

Kagame strenuously denied covert involvement outside Rwanda's borders, but he was adamant that the security of the country was compromised so long as the FDLR still existed. Rwanda first moved into eastern Congo in 1996: so soon after the genocide, chasing down the Hutu perpetrators in flight, it appeared to have right on its side. But the First Congo War became the Second Congo War and then the 2008 Nord-Kivu fighting; the bodies were piling up and there were multiple accusations of war crimes and ethnic massacres levelled at Kagame's soldiers. By 2013, more than five million people were estimated to have died in the ongoing campaign for control of the Congo. It was the deadliest conflict since the Second World War.

Where Congo is enormous (ninety-times larger than Rwanda, practically the size of Western Europe), sprawling and chaotic, Rwanda is focused, disciplined and efficient. There are almost 2,000 miles between Congo's capital Kinshasa, in the west of the country, and the provincial capital of Goma, on the Rwandan border, and Rwanda has taken advantage of the absent authority of the Congo president, Joseph Kabila, in these areas. The idea, though, that Kagame was acting in pre-emptive self-preservation was becoming unsustainable. The FDLR may have still had the stated aim to overthrow the government in Kigali, but its threat was practically non-existent by 2012. In January 2009, Congolese and Rwandan troops launched Operation

Umoja Wetu (Our Unity) against the FDLR and over the next three years around 4,500 FDLR combatants were repatriated to Rwanda through the United Nations, a number thought to be more than seventy per cent of their entire force. As part of the same covert deal between Kagame and Kabila, Nkunda, who had evidently outlived his usefulness for Rwanda, was detained under house arrest in Kigali, though criminal charges were never brought.

So, if Rwanda was not defending itself, why was it still linked with the M23 rebels in 2012? The situation was complicated to unpick, though it was clearly connected to a breakdown in relations between Kagame and Kabila. One recurring accusation was that Rwanda had a continuing strategy to plunder eastern Congo's lucrative deposits of gold, diamond and coltan. A metallic ore that contains tantalum, coltan is essential for mobile phones, computers and many other gadgets. Congo contains as much as two-thirds of the world's coltan reserves, and it had become so valuable that it was known as 'grey gold' or the 'blood diamonds' of the tech world. In Congo, the fighting was called '*Les Pillages*'; with coveted exports at the centre of the dispute, there were chilling echoes of the Belgian-driven 'rubber terror' of the late nineteenth century. Once again, it was the impoverished Congolese citizens who were paying the price.

In 2012, a growing number of nations began to suspend donations to Rwanda: Sweden, Germany, the Netherlands, the United States and finally the European Union froze part or all of their aid programmes. The British government, the second-largest bilateral donor to the country after America, delayed a £16 million payment due for July, but later reinstated it; half of the sum was allocated to the general budget, while the rest was 're-programmed' into support for specific areas, such as education. That decision was personally taken by Andrew

Mitchell, a Conservative minister, on his last day as International Development Secretary. Mitchell – who was forced to resign from his next posting as Chief Whip for allegedly calling a Downing Street policeman 'a pleb' – had been a regular visitor to Rwanda, with eight trips between 2007 and 2012.

But any special relationship between Britain and Rwanda was about to be tested. When M23 scuttled the much larger but ill-disciplined and underpaid Congolese Army and occupied Goma in November 2012 – receiving 'direct support' from Rwandan troops, according to the UN, and taking orders from General James Kabarebe, Rwanda's minister of defence – Britain announced it was withholding a £21 million aid package for Rwanda due to be handed over in December. Eventually Mitchell's successor, Justine Greening, reinstated £16 million of the payment, but the funds were now targeted to specific forms of aid, not simply added to the government's coffers. Overall, the aid freeze left Rwanda with a shortfall of an estimated $200 million and the World Bank delayed convening a meeting of its board to discuss the payment of a further $125 million.

These were figures that would have a serious impact on Rwanda's long-term development, however much coltan it could fill its pockets with. Kagame, a fiercely proud and independent man, needed the Agaciro Development Fund to work so that he no longer had to put up with his knuckles being rapped in public by the Western donors. There followed an intriguing development in March 2013, when Bosco Ntaganda, the leader of M23 and former chief of staff of the CNDP under Nkunda, left Congo and travelled to Rwanda in disguise to turn himself in to the American embassy in Kigali. The warlord, known as 'The Terminator', asked to be sent to the International Criminal Court, where he was wanted on charges of war crimes.

Ntaganda's move confirmed the disintegration of M23, as scores of its members had already fled to Rwanda. Whether Kagame was involved in this surprising turn of events was unknown – and there is a chance we will never find out.

Kagame had long polarised opinion, but still his fall from grace was emphatic. For years, foreign leaders had gone soft in his calm, confident presence. From the entrepreneurial ambition of Vision 2020 to its far-reaching social reforms, Rwanda was the success story of the continent. Aid and loans were assigned on favourable terms, while private investments poured in, particularly from the United States. Rwanda's story – the country's astonishing recovery from rock bottom; Kagame's counterintuitive faith in reconciliation over punishment – was what drove the project forwards. The president may not have wanted his nation to be defined by the events of 1994 – it was respect, not pity, he wanted to invoke – but it would be disingenuous not to acknowledge the narrative power of the genocide in the period of growth and dramatic transition that followed it.

'The most fascinating element to me in Rwanda was the forgiveness factor,' said Peb Jackson, a vice-president of Saddleback Church and a long-standing supporter of Team Rwanda. 'What I heard about and witnessed was the almost incomprehensible nature of forgiveness and reconciliation that has been occurring in this country since the genocide. A society where maybe even the perpetrator moves in next door to the family after he had murdered several members. So that's been something that attracted me and every time I have brought people to the country that has interested people.'

The best advertisement for the new Rwanda was always its inspirational president. 'The thing that really continued bringing me back here and galvanised my desire to be helpful to the country was Kagame,' Jackson told me. 'I looked at other countries in Africa – a failed continent, essentially – and there very few examples of successful leadership, very few examples of successful entrepreneurship and the attraction of capital, except for maybe natural resources. Then I got to know Kagame, I saw his commitment to rule of law, safety, his pride in the country, the humility of his leadership. I saw all this and I thought, *The problem in Africa isn't so much poverty and disease and drought. It's leadership*. I felt like Kagame represented a new era of leadership that was not just something for Africa or Rwanda, it was something for the world.'

Growing evidence of Kagame's alarmingly autocratic streak therefore represented a serious problem for Rwanda's wholesome image. Before the 2010 elections – which he won with ninety-three per cent of the vote, a slip on the ninety-five per cent he returned seven years earlier – three of the main opposition parties were struck off the ballot and two of their leaders dumped in jail. A pair of newspapers in Kigali were shuttered and an editor working for one of them, *Umuvugizi*, was shot in the face outside his home; he had been investigating the botched assassination of a former Kagame ally in South Africa. Amnesty International uncovered evidence of illegal detention and torture in the run-up to the same election and there was particular concern over the 'Rehabilitation and Vocational Skills Development Center' at Iwawa Island in Lake Kivu, which was commonly compared to a tropical Alcatraz. In March 2011, Rene Claudel Mugenzi, a Rwandan émigré living in London, called into a BBC radio phone-in and asked Kagame whether a revolution, similar to the Arab Spring, was possible in Rwanda. Two months later, police from Scotland Yard hand-delivered a letter to Mugenzi that read: 'Reliable intelligence states that the Rwandan government poses an imminent threat to your life.' The President, of course, denied the existence of any such global hit squad.

Kagame began to seem thin-skinned, even despotic, a man who didn't know where his remit might stop: in early 2012 he took to Twitter to call for the resignation of the Arsenal FC manager, Arsène Wenger. (His Twitter rants were famous, replete with spelling mistakes, teenage abbreviations and Yoda-style syntax – 'Wrong u r'.) There was growing evidence, in fact, that the President had a violent temper that he struggled to contain. In an interview with Jeffrey Gettleman of the *New York Times* in 2013, he admitted to physically abusing his staff and there were more serious allegations that he physically whipped government employees he believed guilty of quite trivial errors; for example, a driver who used the wrong truck.

The truth of Kagame was that he never substantively changed. From the beginning he was ruthless, expedient and completely single-minded in his determination to improve the fate of his nation. He was schooled on the pragmatism of military strategy not diplomacy. He graduated from the trenches, not a smart Western university. What had changed was that Rwanda was no longer a soft target, a country that the big beasts of the international community felt they needed to stand up for. The stories coming out of the Democratic Republic of Congo in 2012 proved how outdated this perception had become. What remained less clear was ultimately how damaging the revelations would be. If aid was not fully reinstated and foreign investment declined with it, Rwanda's ambitious recovery could very quickly look fragile and compromised.

In December 2012, the National Intelligence Council, America's centre for long-term strategic thinking, produced its four-yearly Global Trends Report for the incoming president, a recently re-elected Barack Obama. Rwanda was highlighted as being at an elevated risk of becoming a failed state by 2030. One recurring concern was its population explosion. Rwanda was already the most densely populated country in Africa and – despite measures such as a new programme offering free vasectomies – women were still having five or six children on average. The question of where everyone would live and what they would eat was an issue that was threatening to overwhelm the remarkable strides Rwanda had made since 1994.

Tiny Rwanda, with its close-knit and obedient population, was a place that could turn as fast as the weather. That was witnessed during the one hundred days of the genocide and it has been seen again in its recovery. No one wanted to see such a dramatic turn again.

President Kagame's standing abroad inevitably had implications for Team Rwanda. If he damaged the nation's brand, then Jock would feel it, too. The long-term financial strategies of the country and the cycling team were, in fact, somewhat similar. Both needed to rely on donations to help them find their feet, but both ultimately wanted to be independent and self-sustaining. Team Rwanda was always intended to run as a business: 'It's not aid,' Jock often insisted. The plan was that the budget would be covered by corporate sponsorship when the team became successful, but until then they had to find around $200,000 every year from donations. Here, Rwanda's painful history and the emotive stories of the riders was the crucial selling point; it would be much harder to raise funds for Burundi, say, a country of similar if not greater need but with a much lower international profile. Without adversity, the project could not exist. It was clearly easier to solicit pledges for a cycling team that was a beacon of hope and reconciliation than for one that represented a rapacious aggressor with blood on its hands from the seemingly endless conflict in Congo.

Jock did not really keep up with politics, although the topic was hard to avoid living in a city, Ruhengeri, not far from the Congo border and where there was a grenade attack – killing one and injuring five at a bus station – in March 2012. But the first time I sat down to speak with him in 2010 he accepted that a message of unity was at the heart of Team Rwanda. 'The country's got a horrific past, and this team transcends a lot of things,' he said. 'The team members come from all different regions, the groups that were fighting against other, we have both sides and they're getting along and they work for each other. So that really is a big plus.'

He had met the president a couple of times. 'President Kagame has been a supporter of Team Rwanda from the very beginning,' Jack said. 'He had the riders for dinner at his house and told each of them that every place we go these guys are ambassadors for Rwanda.'

With apologies to my Rwandan friend, it is impossible to discuss *anything* in modern Rwanda without reference to Kagame. He had been the architect of the rebuilding of the country since 1994 and many of its very young population would have no memory of a time before he was in power. One of the ever-present questions in Rwandan life is what happens when Kagame stands down, which the constitution requires that he does in 2017. Many people were convinced that he would just stay on, that it was impossible to imagine the country without him at its head. But if that happened, Kagame had admitted, 'It's a failure.' And if the country failed, Team Rwanda went down with it.

10

A GOOD MACHINE

If Team Rwanda was offering a second chance to the riders, it was doing as much – if not more – for the colourful cast of helpers, most from the United States, who were passing through. Some stayed for months, others for years; everyone had their particular reason for landing there. But after a while, a pattern emerged: no one came to Rwanda if everything was going right in their life.

Kimberly Coats was Jock Boyer's right-hand woman. With her bottle-blonde hair and toothy smile, she had the look of a professional golfer's wife. She had grown up in Kansas, got married, and opened a few restaurants with her husband in Kansas City. Back then, she was convinced she would be a millionaire by the age of forty and retired by forty-five. After that, she'd travel the world with her husband. She almost pulled it off, too: in 2003, when Kimberly was in her mid-thirties, the couple moved to Las Vegas to expand their restaurant empire. But the project unravelled.

'I lost it all,' Kimberly recalled in her online journal (which has the subtitle: 'A Life of Living Fearlessly'). 'I lost my business, which ironically I hated anyway but never had the balls to confront my feelings due to the haze of Benjamins which poured into my bank account. I lost my second business simply for bad business decisions. I filed for bankruptcy and a year later I gave my house back to the bank: a victim of the housing freefall in Las Vegas. And then I lost my marriage – still the saddest part of the whole master plan.'

In late 2008, Kimberly, now forty-two, read about Team Rwanda in an American magazine, *Outside*; by April 2009, she was on a three-month volunteer placement with Jock. After five weeks, she phoned her boss in the States and quit her job as a business development manager for Sysco, the behemoth of restaurant suppliers in the United States and Canada. Then she went home, filed for divorce and returned to Rwanda. She shared an abrupt, no-nonsense manner with Jock, and was also a devout Christian; she was made logistics and marketing manager for the team, a fancy job title that covered just about anything that needed doing, and they became a couple and then, in 2013, married. She channelled Jock so effectively that I started to feel I could treat them as one person.

Maxime Darcel, the mechanic, projected a more laid-back vibe. His father, Serge, ran a bike shop called Vélo 9 outside Paris and had been a mechanic for one of Jock's teams in the eighties. As the project in Rwanda became more serious, Jock asked Serge if he knew anyone who might want to help the team and he volunteered his son: Maxime was in his early twenties, unsure what to do with his life. His joined Jock at the Tour of Gabon in 2009 as a trial and, like Kimberly, he never left. He was friendly but sometimes fiery; he got so fed up with Rwandans shouting *muzungu* at him that he took to yelling *kazungu* – 'black person' – back at them. Young, not obviously religious, he sometimes seemed an odd fit for a quiet backwater like Rwanda, but he reasoned that it was not for ever. 'If I didn't come here, I don't know what I'm supposed to do in France, perhaps continue to work with my father or to stay on bicycles, or maybe to travel around,' he said. 'Sure, I miss Paris a lot. But it's okay, I know I'll be back one time and have a good party then.'

These were the permanent residents of the Coach's House in Ruhengeri, but there would often be a ragtag crew of visitors. One of the most intriguing of these was an American in his early twenties called Scott Nydam, who came for three months at the end of 2010 to coach the riders. I met Scott at the Tour of Rwanda, when I was offered a spot on the back of his motorbike for one of the stages. 'Hey, I'm Scott,' he said, pulling his hand out of a bulky leather bike glove, and offering it. He was handsome, with pointed, elvish features, and he had a slightly squeaky voice. He looked like a cyclist, so I enquired if he was one. 'I used to ride, but I was diagnosed with a TBI. That's a traumatic brain injury.' He handed me the helmet that had been looped through his arm. 'The doctors told me that if I had one more blow to the head it could kill me.' I looked down at the motorbike: it was a grey BMW F650 Dakar and the carbon-fibre chassis had scuffs all over it. Scott put his helmet on and tucked in a pair of earbuds.

'Is that race radio?' I asked. In most serious cycling races, an official in the lead car behind the cyclists updates the rolling caravan of vehicles behind them – team managers, organisers, media – on the status of the race.

'No,' replied Scott. 'Just a little ambient music to keep me awake.' Suitably reassured, I clambered on and we were off.

Scott had taken a circuitous path to professional cycling. He came from Colorado and studied sociology at college. He planned to become a social worker, but somehow in his early twenties he found himself in construction, working for an

Australian builder in California and Tasmania. He did some rock climbing on the side and, in his mid-twenties, he entered a winter quadrathlon in New Mexico, an attritional event that combined road cycling, running, skiing and snowshoeing. He finished second, but he really enjoyed the biking, something he had never done seriously before. He moved through the amateur cycling ranks and in January 2006, at the age of twenty-eight, he quit his job and decided to see if he could make it as a pro.

The team he joined, BMC Racing, was one of the most ambitious in North America. Scott moved to Sebastopol in northern California and began training with Lance Armstrong's one-time wingman Levi Leipheimer. Scott's improvement was dramatic. He won the King of the Mountains jersey at the 2008 Tour of California, the biggest race in the United States. Then in April 2009, he lined up in the Tour of the Battenkill in upstate New York. Battenkill was the closest America had to a Classics race, the legendary one-day tests of endurance in Europe: 'Pretty @!*$=%&# Hard' was how *Bicycling* magazine described it. It was 124 miles, on- and off-road, and Scott won it the tough way: he broke away on an eighteen per cent dirt climb early on and then rode solo for sixty miles to record his first professional victory. The talk was that BMC Racing would make their debut in the Giro d'Italia and the Tour de France the following year. 'A whole world was opening up to me and it kind of had an exclamation mark on it with Battenkill,' said Scott. 'Then the very next week it all shut down.'

Scott was always a fearless racer, prone to spills. Soon after Battenkill, he crashed at the Tour of the Gila in New Mexico, coincidentally one of the early foreign races that Team Rwanda entered. The first he knew about his accident was when he woke up in a helicopter, concussed, on the way to a neurological trauma centre in Texas. The doctors were anxious: it was the fifth time he had knocked his head, the fourth time he had been out cold. A few months later, he underwent tests at Stanford University in California and his results placed him in the lowest twenty per cent for brain function. That figure could bounce back, but the membrane protecting his brain, the meninges, was almost non-existent. 'You can't afford to hit your head again; you could have another bleed,' Dr Jaime Lopez told him. 'We think you're done racing.'

Scott took a sabbatical from competing for BMC Racing, but continued riding. One day he went out with Tom Ritchey, on the road and tracks near Tom's ranch in Jenner, northern California. It was a cloudless afternoon and, after a sapping climb, they crested King's Ridge and looked out over Highway One to an infinite Pacific Ocean. Scott couldn't quite believe he was expected to give this up. When he got home, an email popped up from Tom, one he had sent to others before. It read: *Have you ever thought about going to Rwanda?*

A visit to Rwanda was probably not something that Scott's neurologists would have recommended. The country's roads are some of the most hazardous in the world and car wrecks – preceded by the telltale tree branches on the tarmac, which serve as makeshift warning triangles – are a common sight. Laws on speed limits and alcohol intake are rather casually observed. If Scott were injured, there would be only a fractional chance he would receive the specialist attention required. On the motorbike that day at the Tour of Rwanda, we stopped by the side of the road to let the race streak past. 'My wife Jennifer and I went out on a motorbike and two little girls walked out right in front of us and we hit them. We hit one of the girls,' Scott told me, still obviously shaken. 'She went flying and landed on Jennifer in a ditch. We trashed the motorbike but everyone was just about okay. As a Westerner, you go, "They're so stupid, they're not thinking!" But that's too simple an answer. There's just a much different mindset and the mental map we have laid out in front of us, what to expect, doesn't necessarily equate.'

Jock made a similar point. 'It is highly stressful living here,' he said. 'The amount of casualties we see on the road is just incredible, deaths all the time and that is not easy to watch or deal with. The other day I hit a guy on a taxi-bike who at the last minute made a U-turn in front of me on the motorbike. It's a miracle I haven't killed someone in four years. That was the first time I actually hit somebody. They have no concept of inertia here, that a two-tonne object will take more than a millisecond to stop and will kill you if you come in its path and it can't stop. They just don't understand that.'

Scott worked with the Team Rwanda riders for three months in the build-up to the 2010 Continental Championship and the Tour of Rwanda shortly afterwards. He had an offbeat, questioning mind, and he wrestled to make sense of the country. For one thing, the oranges there are green: 'What are you supposed to do with that?' he asked. 'Do you still call them oranges?' After the accident, he had been kept on by BMC Racing doing coaching and odd jobs for the team. But the transition was proving harder than he had imagined. At one point in Rwanda, he went on a motorbike with his wife to a swampy bog in a rainforest looking for the source of the Nile, imagining himself the protagonist of a Wes Anderson movie. He drank a cup of water from the spring and thought the pilgrimage might somehow bring him closure on his racing career – it didn't work. 'It's like hanging out with your ex-girlfriend or something,' he said. 'The whole bicycle thing, as positive as it was, is equally as devastating to me in a way. That's the skinny, that's the truth of it.'

What really perplexed Scott, though, was what drove the Rwandan cyclists. Soon after arriving, he went for his first ride, with Gasore Hategeka. Everyone who met Gasore developed a soft spot for him: he was gentle and humble, and his story – which emerged slowly, over months – seemed to encapsulate everything that Team Rwanda was about. When Gasore first turned up at the Team Rwanda base in June 2009, aged twenty, they thought his name was Alex; he spoke no English or French, so the mistake went uncorrected for a few weeks. He had a decrepit Eddy Merckx bike that had been re-welded so many times that the solder resembled blobs of chewing gum on the frame. There was no electricity the afternoon he was meant to be tested on the Velotron, and none again the next morning so Jock and Kimberly gave him a road bike, a Scott CR1, on trust. It did not take long for him to prove that it was a smart investment. When the power returned, Gasore tested better on the Velotron than any Rwandan ever had. At his first race, two weeks later, he rode with the Team Rwanda veterans the whole way before crashing near the finish. 'I knew from the second I saw him ride he was special,' noted Kimberly. 'Physically he is small, extremely strong, very lean and most importantly he has the intensity. He has the "it".'

Gasore couldn't read or write a single word; even his Rwandan team-mates found him introverted. On the bike he was either lacklustre or inspired, but Jock felt that if anyone had the potential to match Adrien Niyonshuti it was Gasore. In February 2010, Team Rwanda went to the Tour of Cameroon, racing against squads from Africa and Europe. On the third stage, Gasore was riding with the main pack when he got a puncture, repaired by Maxime in the back-up car, then another. He fought back each time and rejoined the field; despite the mechanical problems, riding his bike that day felt like the easiest thing in the world. At the bottom of a steep hill, he accelerated away from the field and established a lead. Jock screamed at him to keep going. Gasore didn't look back again until he crossed the line, becoming the first Rwandan to win a stage of an international race.

Bicycles were integral to the lives of many Rwandans, but for Gasore they were a lifelong obsession. His mother had died when he was young, and his father was a heavy drinker who rarely came home. North-west Rwanda, where he lived, was a Hutu Power stronghold and after the genocide – when Gasore was perhaps six or seven – his family had fled for the Zaire border. Not long after they returned, Gasore's father was beaten badly by government soldiers and died from his injuries. Gasore never found out exactly why and didn't ask. He became a *mayibobo*, one of Rwanda's legions of street children, and had to fend for himself. Initially he would scavenge any food he could find and after a while he picked up work shunting huge sacks of potatoes. The pay was just a few coins, but he had a formidable work ethic and he was a good saver. When he started to cycle seriously, his shoulders and arms were too big from hauling the hundred-kilogram bags; even years later, Jock fretted that Gasore was carrying an extra four kilos of unnecessary muscle.

If anyone was proof that a bicycle could change lives in Rwanda, it was Gasore. It had taken him years of scrabbling around to save up the 35,000 francs, around £35, to buy that first Eddy Merckx bike. His only extravagance when he was living on the streets was occasionally paying a bicycle-taxi rider to borrow his ride for an hour. 'When I was learning to cycle, I'd get three hundred francs and pay to hire a bike to try to improve,' Gasore told me one afternoon, as we chewed on barbecued corn in his modest rented house in his hometown of Sashwara. 'I never saved any money: everything I made would go into improving my cycling skills. Do you know the wooden bikes? I'd help someone who was pushing the loads, just so I could get a ride when they finished offloading. The same with the single-speed bikes. I'd push them for someone for free and in return, when they had dropped off the luggage, I would get a chance to cycle and learn.'

Gasore continued, 'When I was young, very small, I would look at kids of my age who could cycle and feel, *They are better than me*. So I needed to learn and be like them. Then when I was at their level I would see someone above me at the next level and I'd want to be like them. Even now, I think that.'

On Scott's first ride, as he and Gasore passed through Sashwara, they had a conversation in pidgin English about his victory in Cameroon. Then Gasore pointed to Scott's bike, 'It's a good machine, a good machine.' Scott was riding the carbon-fibre BMC that he had won the Tour of the Battenkill on, and originally he thought he must be referring to that. Only later did he realise that Gasore hadn't even looked at the frame. He was making a grander statement: a bicycle, in Gasore's eyes, represented both work and freedom; it put food on his table and money in his pockets. A good machine, indeed. The exchange had a profound impact on Scott: when he flew back to the United States after three months, he decided to leave his bike in Rwanda; he was done with serious riding. 'It's certainly one of the better decisions I've ever made,' he said. 'I feel very good about it: that bike's still living, it's still racing. If it was here with me it would be sitting in a garage or on a wall. But now it's on the Africa Tour, it's in Eritrea.'

When Scott became a professional cyclist, he could see there were plenty of gifted athletes who never made it. 'In the US a lot of guys come and go who just simply had it too good,' he said. 'If you are sitting on a trust fund and you have all your basic needs taken care of, you're not going to push yourself to the verge of death on these climbs to hold on to certain wheels. What I do know is that, if you want to make it, it's going to take every bit of you as a rider, as a person, to apply yourself and then, *even then*, you may not have it to make it to the finish line.'

In many ways, Gasore was an extreme version of what Scott was talking about. For years, he had dedicated every waking hour, directly or indirectly, to success on the bike. He had applied himself to it with such foresight and dedication that it was almost as if he had a premonition of Tom and Jock's arrival in the country. When the Americans did finally come, he doubled his efforts. He joined his local bicycle-taxi association and ferried passengers and cargo all over the relentless hills of north-west Rwanda. He trained every morning on his own before work, then he came home, splashed some water on his face and put the padded seat on the back of his bike for customers. Team Rwanda would often pass in formation close to where he lived and he would attempt to keep up with them, even on his balloon-tyred single-speed. He pestered them to find out when they were coming past next, so he could ride with them for a little longer.

When he finally won a place on the team, he worked even harder. Gasore never missed a training camp, and was typically the first to arrive on Mondays and the last to leave on Fridays. He helped wash the dishes and clean up around the house; many Rwandans were scared of dogs, but he played easily with Zulu, Jock's giant South African Boerboel. Gasore was learning to read and write, and the team's English teacher described him as the most improved student. He was the only rider to apologise to Jock for not following his instructions.

'I had no one to look after me, so I had to look after myself,'

Gasore told me. 'I didn't have the chance to go to school, but I realised that what I had was physical strength. I just had to use that strength to make a breakthrough. Some Rwandans want to relax, that's their problem, but for me I have to use the energy I have now to the full, so that when I'm old I don't have any regrets.'

Yet, here was the strange thing: Gasore's career began to splutter and then stall. In March 2011, at the Tour of Cameroon, he looked set to build on his success of the previous year. He won an early stage, and as the race came to the final day, he was in fourth position. With a strong performance, he could finish on the podium. But, on the last stage, he was completely listless, almost disinterested. Jock shouted at him from the team car to push himself, but it didn't make a difference. Soon after they came back from Cameroon, Gasore was sent to the UCI's World Cycling Centre in Aigle, Switzerland, for two months with Nicodem Habiyambere. There, they would have the best facilities, expert coaching and the opportunity to completely focus on riding. But Gasore actually deteriorated. 'When they arrived at the centre, Gasore is much better than Nicodem,' explained Michel Thèze, their coach in Switzerland. 'But when they leave . . .' He crossed his arms, like lines on a graph, one rising, one plummeting. 'I don't know why – *c'est bizarre*!'

Scott, who knew exactly what it took to become a professional racer, could not make sense of it either. 'These guys are coming from Rwanda, they are coming from poverty, they should jump right on it,' he said. Scott shook his head: this was where the project lived or died. 'The big question I have is: do these guys want it? Rwandans are very communal. I don't think their desire to succeed is as individually based as it is for cyclists in Europe or the United States. They want to look out for their families and they want to make themselves stable financially.

It's not necessarily primarily winning bike races that these guys are getting keyed into.'

In the early days of Team Rwanda, it might have been enough to turn up to races and for the riders not to embarrass themselves. But now, Jock in particular expected more. Adrien, as usual, set an example that the rest found impossible to emulate. At the 2009 Tour of Ireland, Adrien's first race in Europe with MTN Cycling, Lance Armstrong heard about the Rwandan genocide survivor and asked to start next to him on the first day. Photographers and television crews from ninety accredited press agencies recorded the moment for posterity. Armstrong even suggested they go for a beer, presumably not realising that Adrien was a devout Muslim. In the men's road race at the 2010 Commonwealth Games in Delhi, India, Adrien spent the first half of a gruelling race in a lead group of six riders before his front derailleur disintegrated and he was forced to abandon. Nathan and Abraham Ruhumuriza went on to complete the 104-mile course, while Gasore and Nicodem dropped off the pace and withdrew.

Adrien was recording his best endurance mountain bike results at the same time. He claimed his first international victory, the one-day Nissan Hazeldean race, against some of South Africa's hardiest professionals in June 2010; at the 2011 Cape Epic, paired with the Namibian Mannie Heymans, they took the jersey for best African team, finishing ninth overall. Then, with Max Knox, he won the Subaru Sani2c three-day event in May 2011 ahead of more than 600 pairs. Few riders anywhere in the world could shift so seamlessly between road and rough terrain. Studying the data from the SRM powermeter on Adrien's bicycle, Dr Carol Austin, the director of health and performance at MTN-Qhubeka, found he was developing an uncommon ability to ride just under his anaerobic threshold for hours on end. Put simply, Adrien would keep going when everyone else gave up.

Back at home in Rwanda, the race invitations kept on arriving as the international fame of the team grew. As well as traditional haunts, such as Morocco and Gabon, the Tour of Rio in Brazil was added to the schedule in 2011 and the Tour of Eritrea for 2012. Riders continued to be dispatched for training at the UCI centres in Switzerland and South Africa, and also to the United States. Victories, however, remained elusive. 'We're not here to make up the numbers,' said Jock, when he arrived with six riders in Rio de Janeiro in August 2011. But that was exactly what they were doing. The veteran Obed Rugovera was eliminated during the first stage for failing to make the time cut, while the other riders rode with heart, but were invariably off the pace on the harder stages.

Many of the Rwandans retained incorrigible technical weaknesses. One example: Emmanuel Rudahunga, whom everyone called 'Boy', looked like a cyclist created by God, or at least by a team of aerodynamically fixated sportscar designers. He was young and rangy with impossibly long, swooping legs. I remember pulling up alongside him during the Tour of Rwanda one day: he was alone powering up a steep hill, and we followed behind in a press car, wheezing in first gear. 'Oh my God,' exclaimed the ex-professional sitting next to me, 'he's in the big dog,' using Australian slang for the larger, more punishing chainring. Yet Emmanuel's mouth was clamped shut, he barely seemed to be breathing. But here also was his big problem: he was on his own because he was afraid of cycling in a pack, so day after day in races, he would launch near-suicidal solo breakaways from the main field that were spectacular but invariably had the longevity of a firework.

Cycling had brought the riders, Gasore among them, relative

comfort and prosperity. In early 2012, Jock and Kimberly found out that Gasore was engaged. He had not told them, perhaps mindful of their preference that riders should not get married until the end of their careers. Adrien's girlfriend, as the Americans often reminded his team-mates, was his bicycle. Gasore's bride was called Marceline; she was also an orphan, but had somehow managed to put herself through secondary school and now worked for the government. Gasore had met her at the Adventist church that they both attended. Gasore tried to keep their relationship a secret, but word got out because he had spent all his money on moving to a bigger house and a cow, costing £400, which he gave to Marceline's uncle as a wedding present. He had run out of money for food that month: 'Forward thinking is not their strong suit,' wrote Kimberly.

This was a problem of running a competitive bicycle team that was also an economic development project. By the latter model, Gasore's story should have been regarded an unqualified success. The former *mayibobo* was now a homeowner, with a wife and a well-paid job. By the end of the year, Marceline and Gasore had a baby, Anthony. But as a cyclist, his career was in danger of sinking fast. In the space of a year, he had gone from being the most promising rider in Team Rwanda to no longer making the first squad of six in 2012. It confused and saddened everyone involved with the programme. 'Do we want it more for him than he wants it for himself?' asked Kimberly. 'Is this it – as good as it gets for his life?' There was discussion about whether they should suspend his salary until he performed better in the races.

When he returned to the United States, Scott asked himself the same unsettling questions. 'I've never had one Rwandan say to me: "I want to go to Europe and race my bike,"' he said. 'It's always been somebody else's dream for them. It's once-removed. It's Jock's dream for them. Not one of those riders has ever been able to say that to me. They may parrot it back to you, if you asked them, "Hey, what's your dream?" They'd pull the string on the back of their neck and they'll tell you what they've heard maybe Jock say: "I want to race in the Tour de France." And that might be the difference with Adrien; he has his own personal ambition.'

Scott was right: the Tour de France did not exert a significant tug for the Rwandan riders. It was Jock's obsession as an unhappy, bicycle-mad teenager growing up in California, not theirs. He could show them videos of iconic races from the past, but they must have felt remote, even unreal. Their ambitions were smaller, closer to home. Gasore's second-ever race was the 2009 Kwita Izina, an event that celebrated the naming of newborn baby gorillas in the Volcanoes National Park. Again, Gasore had a puncture at an inconvenient time, and once more he raced back to rejoin the leading contenders, which included Abraham Ruhumuriza, Nyandwi Uwase and the most experienced riders in Rwanda. When the race finally snaked through the streets of Kigali, he sprinted over the line in fourth place.

At the presentation, the emcee called the top three riders to the stage; Gasore stood to join them and the organisers had to tell him to return to his seat. But he had done enough to win an envelope stuffed with prize money. He twirled it in his fingers for a few seconds and eventually snuck a look inside. There was around £150, more money than he had ever held in his hands. He closed the envelope again, looked down, opened it once more and checked the money was still there. He rubbed the purple and brown banknotes with his fingers and finally took them out of the envelope and stashed them in his pocket. He could not have been any happier or more proud if he had just won the Tour de France.

11
SPARE PARTS

At the end of men's races in Rwanda, I would often see a group of young women, some with bicycles, perhaps a couple wearing Team Rwanda shirts. They were described to me one time as 'groupies', but this did them a disservice. They were interested in their own racing, more than the men's; it was just that their opportunities were more sporadic. In a good year, they might have three races to show what they could do. These events would feature the most talented female racers, plus a man called Raiza, who had lost one of his legs in a car accident. 'There was a problem about where to put him,' explained Jeannette Uwimana, Rwanda's best female cyclist. 'He couldn't compete with the men, so they stuck him with the ladies.'

Rwanda has a global reputation for women's rights. In the immediate aftermath of the genocide, the population was seventy per cent female; it had since settled at closer to fifty-five per cent. In 2003, the new constitution stipulated that women should make up at least thirty per cent of the parliament, but in reality they fared rather better: by 2008, women held fifty-six per cent of the seats, making it the first country in the world where women were the majority of parliamentarians. There were also high-profile postings in the cabinet: Louise Mushikiwabo was Rwanda's forthright foreign minister, and women headed the health and agriculture portfolios. The Supreme Court chief and police commissioner general were also women. 'Equality' became as much of a buzzword in the President Kagame era as 'reconciliation'.

Even if female political representation was a little misleading – no one, man or woman, exerted really meaningful influence apart from Kagame – there had also been important changes made to women's legal rights in the aftermath of the genocide. Archaic patriarchal laws were thrown out: women could own land or property in Rwanda, and no longer had to pool their assets with their husband when they married. Inheritance laws were changed so that a man's property would be split when he died equally between his wife and both female and male children. A free police hotline was created for women who experienced domestic violence, while men convicted of rape faced proper prison sentences, in contrast to some of Rwanda's neighbours.

Equality would take longer to reach cycling. Kimberly Coats talked at length and with passion about the creation of a women's team to run alongside the men's, but even if the intentions were noble, there were never the funds to commit to the ambition. In the end, support amounted to an invitation for some riders to attend a couple of training camps in Ruhengeri. The first of these came in late 2010 before Rwanda hosted the African Continental Championships. The race itself attracted only twelve entrants and was dominated by the South African women, with Jeannette the best-placed Rwandan in seventh. The following year, another promising rider called Angelique Mukandekezi came out of an open day called 'race what you bring', organised by the Rwandan cycling federation in

Nyamata, a small town not far from Kigali on the road to Burundi. Angelique was given 30,000 francs – around £30 – by Team Rwanda to take a month's break from working in the fields, and there was hope that she and Jeannette would form the nucleus of the women's squad.

When I met Jeannette, in May 2012, she was still riding but had not competed for almost a year. She came to meet me in Kigali from a self-imposed training camp in Byumba, in the chilly, damp north of the country. She was trying to shed a few pounds to get down to race weight; Kimberly had been explicit on this point. 'She's a decent rider, however she weighs the same as I do and she's six inches shorter,' she commented. 'That's a lot of junk in the trunk to move up these hills.' Jeannette was solid certainly, but looked more powerful than flabby. She started off our meeting shy, talking so faintly that the recorder barely picked up her words, but gained in confidence gradually. She had a disarming smile and her exuberant braids, which gave a hint of her day job as a hairdresser, swished when she became impassioned.

Jeannette had been to secondary school, a rare thing in Rwanda, where only one in nine girls do so. It was a discrepancy that President Kagame was keen to address in order to hit his prosperity targets for the country. Rwanda's population had nearly doubled in the two decades since the genocide and one year of extra schooling had been shown to reduce fertility rates by ten per cent. The government was now offering incentives for girls to attend school, which might be a pint of cooking oil at the end of each week, extra milk or prizes for girls who performed particularly well in science. Campaigns encouraged girls to settle down later. In 2009, the Ministry of Youth launched *Sinigurisha*, which means 'I am not for sale'. It developed into a specific attack on *shuga dadis* or 'sugar daddies':

men who would typically offer rides home from school, mobile phones or food in exchange for sex. A 2006 Rwanda Behaviour Surveillance study reported that one in ten girls had their first sexual experience with a man at least a decade older than them.

Both Jeannette and Angelique had what Kimberly called 'the conversation'. It essentially set out that they could not get married or have children if they wanted to ride with the team. Jeannette, who was in her early twenties, did not need any convincing. 'Most of my friends have two or three children now,' she said. 'It's only because I love cycling that I don't. I want to be at least in the top three women in Africa, and I will get there. Until I do that, no husband and no kids. Can you put the baby on your back and cycle? It doesn't work!'

Feminism did not have much of a foothold in Rwanda, but, in her quiet, determined way, there was something of the pioneer in Jeannette. In mixed races, she would often beat men. 'They think cycling is a joyride,' she said. 'But those who come and feel the pain, they run away!' Rwanda could be a conservative place; did Jeannette scare some men? I wondered. She laughed. 'People have different tastes. There are some men that say, "That's the one for me!" And there are others who are afraid and say, "Ah! I don't even dare to get close to her!" So it depends. But my country needs me and even my bike needs me. I love my bike and I won't disappoint my bike.'

The reception that Jeannette and Angelique received on the road was unpredictable. In the countryside, they would often be cheered by pedestrians as they flashed past them, particularly by the women, who tended to carry the heaviest loads on their heads while the men used bicycles. But sometimes there were minor issues. On one of her early outings on a road bike, Angelique had a puncture; Jeannette and Kimberly stopped to help her and, soon enough, they had a crowd of fifty, mostly young men, around them. When Angelique clipped back into her pedals, one of the men grabbed hold of her back wheel, fooling around. She didn't know what to say, but Kimberly didn't hold back, bawling at the man to let go. 'Thank you, Kim,' said Angelique when they were back on the road.

Kimberly had problems of her own. One day when she was out riding with Angelique and Jeannette, they went through Sashwara, Gasore Hategeka's hometown. Team Rwanda was a familiar sight there, which made what happened particularly surprising. As Kimberly rode past, a man raised a discarded inner tube above his head and whip-cracked it across her back. She slammed her brakes on and turned round. The man bolted and a pair of bystanders went in pursuit. They caught the man in a shop and dragged him back to the road, smashing their fists on his head. Fortunately for the man, Kimberly was feeling more New Testament than Old that day and instead of slapping him, as had crossed her mind, she demanded only an apology. The experience, however, did increase her unease with the country. 'Every day it is a struggle here,' she reflected. 'Rwanda is not the "Kumbaya" place people make it out to be. I used to ride alone. I do not any more. I bury myself in the training camps and stay close to my compound and wait for the day I get to travel to South Africa or Kenya for a reprieve.'

Jeannette took note how Kimberly reacted. 'She is just like a man,' she said, with reverence. 'I really want to be like her!' It was inspiring talking to Jeannette, but again the lingering emotion was unease. She was training, as hard as she had ever done in her life, in an effort to shed weight. Yet there were no races on the calendar and she received no money from the federation or Team Rwanda to cover her costs. Hers felt like a futile quest. 'There's no support,' she admitted. 'We just have to train on our own. The federation will schedule a race and at the last moment they'll say, "Sorry, you're not in." It gets really dispiriting. When they let us down like that, it is actually painful. Not a light pain, but a really deep pain, because we've spent our time and energy and we're just ignored.'

For Team Rwanda, the development of a female squad in a country where women's rights were a nascent concern made the right noises – and potentially a prosperous revenue stream for fundraising. 'Maybe it sounds pie in the sky,' Kimberly told *Run Like A Girl*, an American website dedicated to women's sport in 2011, 'but I think we can change the society for women, one bike at a time.' The reality was not quite as promising, but Jeannette refused to become downcast. 'Women now have many more rights than they did in the past,' she said. 'When I was a young girl, women would be beaten very often by their husbands, but now that doesn't happen. It's unlawful. I can't wait for a time when women have the same opportunities as men in cycling. Even if I don't see that in my lifetime, I want to see my children getting those chances.'

There was certainly no lack of enterprise or ambitious ideas in Team Rwanda. In 2008, not long after arriving, Jock oversaw the purchase of a plot of fifteen acres and planted jatropha, a scrubby tree that thrives in the tropics and has been hailed as a life-changing biofuel. *Scientific American* magazine called it 'green gold in a shrub' in 2007. The team's aim was that their micro-plantation would supply a community of sixty households with sufficient fuel to power an eleven-kilowatt generator at sixty per cent output for sixteen hours a day. 'Ideally all of our riders will be able to "grow" their own fuel,' said Jock. 'Our ideal is to be a totally green team, the first zero-carbon-imprint team in the world.' The team was also in discussions with a company called Renewable Fuel Products in Silicon Valley to buy a reactor that turned oil-seed crops into diesel fuel, but the £100,000 price tag proved prohibitive.

Meanwhile, as new riders such as Gasore had come through, others fell by the wayside. The first of the original five to leave the team was Nyandwi Uwase. Like Abraham Ruhumuriza, he had rarely had a straightforward relationship with the management: he would fall out with Jock, storm off, run out of money and then return repentant. The pattern would then repeat. At the 2010 Tour of Rwanda, Scott called him 'the prodigal son'; at the end of one stage, Maxime offered Nyandwi a bottle of water, he brushed him off dismissively and Maxime took offence. The pair had to be separated as they bashed each other with empty water bottles. Jock began to lose patience.

'Of the five, all the others saved their race money and bought houses,' Jock told me. 'But Nyandwi spent all his race money on frivolous things and had nothing left. He thought he was indispensable, but he was infecting the other riders and at international races he never performed. Never once. They get exposed to good food and lots of food; I tried to temper their diets because they would get to buffets and eat three times what they should be eating. But he wouldn't listen to me. Whether he will learn or not, I don't know.' Nyandwi eventually moved to Pretoria in South Africa and rode occasionally with the local Velo Cycling Club.

Of all the schemes implemented by Project Rwanda, the biggest disappointment was the coffee bike programme. In the beginning, Tom Ritchey dreamed about supplying half a million bicycles to coffee farmers in Rwanda; the eventual total, however, was closer to 3,000. The problem, in Tom's mind, was pure economics. The price of the bicycles had settled at around $200, which in Europe or America might sound reasonable, but was far beyond the aspirations of rural Rwandans, some of whom would take most of a year to earn that. 'It's crazy, it's way too expensive,' reflected Tom. 'I remember on my second trip here, Bishop John Rucyahana told me, "Tom, the first thing you have to realise is that poverty is expensive." The difference between value in the United States and in Rwanda is just shocking. A box of chocolate-chip cookies costs $2 in America, and it costs $10 in Rwanda. Even if the bike cost $50, people would not be buying it. The barrier of ownership was beyond what I ever thought it would be.'

One of the main hurdles was transporting the bikes. 'We didn't know this, but it turns out that Rwanda is the second most expensive country in the world to ship to,' Tom said, with a wry smile. 'Yeah, and the first is Antarctica. It's landlocked by 1,500 miles: there's no railway in the country, it's got tariff issues, it's got all kinds of things.' Tom was not exaggerating: for all Kagame's reforms, there was still practically no domestic infrastructure in Rwanda; a government study revealed that on average it took a lorry four days and $864 in bribes to make it from the nearest major port, Mombasa in Kenya, to Kigali. During that journey it would typically stop at thirty-six roadblocks and ten weighbridges, many of them overseen by thugs in uniform. There were long-term plans for a rail link between Kigali and the Indian Ocean port of Dar es Salaam in Tanzania – Dan Cooper, who went with Tom on that first trip to Rwanda, was among those working on it – but that was at least five years and $5 billion away.

Project Rwanda stopped importing bicycles around 2008, and then they spent a few years trying to sell off existing stock. Tom's conclusions on the collapse of the coffee bike programme were confirmed by a 2010 study compiled by four visiting students from the Harvard Business School. The numbers just did not stack up.

Tom was distraught as he talked about the experience; he had thrown time, money and expertise at the problem, everything he knew from almost fifty years of riding and creating bicycles. He summed it up with a comment that almost everyone involved with Project Rwanda made at one point. 'If you can do something in Rwanda, you can do it anywhere,' he said, 'because you chose the hardest place practically on the face of the earth to do it.'

There was only one problem with this analysis of the coffee bikes: none of the Rwandan coffee farmers agreed with it. This became clear when I spoke to Celestin Nemeyimana, who was one of the first pair of Rwandans to try out Tom's prototype 'Hope Bicycle' in 2007. After his first ride, he had loudly proclaimed: 'This bicycle will make me a rich man!' There was an obvious question as we sat in a bar in the market town of Gikongoro, deep in the Southern Province: Had it?

Celestin nodded his head and smiled. He was still a member of the Karaba coffee cooperative, and was now aged thirty-nine. When the bicycle arrived, he tended around 300 coffee trees, but, thanks largely to his newfound productivity, he had expanded the operation to 730 trees. For his family – he now had a wife and two children – he grew beans and cassava, and he had a small orchard of fruit trees: pawpaw, passion fruit, banana and pineapple. But his main income came from the coffee, and the price had been increasing every year.

'It was a fantastic bike, totally different from anything I had seen,' said Celestin. 'It would take more than 150 kilos, so you could carry anything: luggage, produce, cement, soda bottles. From my house to this town, it would usually take an hour and a half on a normal bike; on the coffee bike it took fifty minutes and I would not have to get off and push at any point.

I could pedal all the way. There is no way you can compare it to a normal bike.'

Celestin spoke with intense passion; the bicycle really had changed his life, just as Tom might have hoped. He could carry more coffee beans, faster, to the Karaba washing station, and so received a higher price for them. The quality of his coffee was improving because the cherries had less time to deteriorate. He had competed every year since the bicycle arrived in Rwanda's Cup of Excellence, where the best coffees in the country were auctioned to foreign buyers. But work was only one part of it. Every Sunday, Celestin would wash the bicycle and oil the moving parts before going to church with his family piled up on the metal rack at the back. 'It improved my status in the village, because I was the one who had to explain to people how the bikes worked and how to use the gears,' he said. 'I was not married when I first had the bike, but I used it to prepare for the marriage and to get money for the wedding. My wife loved having rides on it. Sometimes I'd have to refuse her and say, "No, no, no, we can't spend all our time on the bicycle, we need to do other work."' Celestin stopped, and with genuine emotion said, 'So it's sad they don't have the spare parts.'

Celestin used the bike for eighteen months without any problems, but eventually it started to groan with wear and tear. Tom Ritchey's son Jay had set up a spares shack at the Karaba cooperative, so Celestin went there and bought the parts he needed. But a year later, he was riding so much that he started having bigger problems that were more complicated to repair. He needed a new rear derailleur and the chain had stopped rotating properly; the tyres were bald. The spares shed drew a blank with these, so he tried to fix them with locally available parts. The patch-up did not really work and eventually he had no choice but to park up the bike. He had ridden to meet me that day on his old Chinese-made bicycle. He did not like it as much, but it was easier to keep it on the road.

Wasn't the coffee bike just too expensive? Celestin shrugged. 'When they stopped selling them the bicycle cost 135,000 Rwandan francs' – which is $200 or £135 – 'but people still bought it. If I could buy a brand-new one now I would buy it at any price – even without spare parts – because I know that by the time it breaks down, after two or three years, I would have recouped my initial investment. And it's not only me: all the other farmers at the Karaba cooperative would buy one, as well.'

It was a confusing conversation; it didn't match up with anything I had heard from Tom or the people behind Team Rwanda. (I had even met an American intern who had a placement to sell off the final bicycles, so they could close up the project: he had a couple of hundred bikes sitting in a factory in Kigali with no takers; he would offload the occasional one to a *muzungu* looking for a souvenir of their stay in Rwanda.) We finished our Fantas and paid the bill, but Celestin asked my interpreter, Ayuub, if he could make one last comment. 'I want to thank you very much: the fact that you've come to talk about this bike after all this time shows there is goodwill somewhere,' he said. 'If you ever talk to the people who made the bicycle, please tell them that it inspired us to make good-quality coffee and despite the fact that the bicycles are broken down we have continued making good coffee and they will keep getting good coffee.'

In late 2011, as we drove around rural southern Rwanda, where most of the country's premium coffee is grown, Project Rwanda's coffee bikes were a common sight on the roads. They were not hard to spot with their loud colour scheme. Many of them were still riding well, but most had been patched up with substitute parts. When we flagged them down, every single owner wanted to talk about spare parts. They mentioned the same words – derailleurs, gear shifters, chains and wheels – so often that I started to recognise those words in Kinyarwanda. They were so insistent that at one point Ayuub turned to me and said with complete seriousness, 'The bicycles are a good business, I think. If I had the money, I'd invest in it.'

At Maraba, the other coffee cooperative that participated in the scheme from the outset, we met the head accountant, a studious man called Jean de Dieu Shema. He sat behind a tidy desk underneath an inscription that read, *One finger alone cannot pick up a stone*. He explained that 253 farmers from Maraba had taken the option to buy the bikes, and all but twenty of them had fully repaid their loans. They had not heard anything from the Americans since 2007. 'We could not get enough of the bikes,' said Jean de Dieu. 'The farmers did not care about the price. It was fair. They never complained. Some of them even sold their bikes to petty traders, men who did not work in coffee, at a higher price. The problem is only the spare parts.'

Back at the Karaba cooperative, we walked past the washing station and the terraces where the coffee cherries were sorted to the kiosk that Project Rwanda had built for maintenance of the bicycles. It was a brick hut, with a concrete floor, about three metres square. As we entered, my jaw dropped and so did Ayuub's: we had spoken for hours about the lack of spare parts and this room was filled from floor to ceiling with all manner of bicycle accessories. There were more than a dozen frames, front forks going rusty, a foot pump covered in cobwebs. 'Ahh, but all the things they brought were the parts that didn't break,' explained Bonaventure Safari, the manager of Karaba. 'That is why the project failed.'

*

The situation was a mass of knots that only became tighter as I tried to unravel it: the Americans insisted that no one wanted to buy the bikes, while the Rwandans were adamant they could not get enough of them; everyone complained about the lack of spare parts, and yet there was a kiosk throbbing with them. Even if they were not the right ones, at some point there had been a willingness to confront the issue. What everyone had to agree on, though, was Bonaventure Safari's reluctant conclusion that the initiative had 'failed'.

The whimpering demise was a familiar one among NGOs: the developing world was full of expensive projects that had broken down because there was a minor glitch and no one was around to repair it. Kimberly Coats directed me to a presentation given at a TEDx ideas conference by David Damberger, a Canadian who was a founding contributor of Engineers Without Borders, and who had been a director of their southern Africa programmes. For Damberger, the enduring problem with aid projects was that the providers are in love with supplying 'hardware' solutions (in Project Rwanda's case: bicycles) but lose concentration when it comes to 'software' (that is: fixing them). That is why so many ingenious-sounding ideas died. 'At first you're like, "Whoa, software, of course you have to do maintenance,"' he told his audience in Calgary in 2011. 'But when you think about people donating to charities it makes you feel a lot better to know that your money went to something tangible: like a well or a school or giving a family a goat. It's not sexy to tell your friends that you helped fund a water committee or pay for teachers' salaries.' Engineers Without Borders had even adopted a new slogan: *It's not sexy. It works.*

In Portland, Oregon, I found the embers of the Bikes to Rwanda non-profit organisation established in 2006 by Duane Sorenson, the intrepid coffee hunter behind Stumptown Coffee

Roasters. In the early days, Stumptown had bought a few hundred coffee bikes to give to farmers and paid the salary of a CEO to oversee the investment, but the company had long stopped bankrolling the charity and Bikes to Rwanda was now little more than the post-office box. It had a new committee, but despite their good intentions, none of them had ever been to Rwanda and any contacts they once had with the coffee cooperatives had dried up. They owed Tom Ritchey $70,000 (a debt that he had graciously written off) and there was vague awareness of a container of bicycles that had been lost somewhere between China and Dar es Salaam. 'If we were making some money, it would be a great scam,' admitted Dan Powell, one of the new committee members. 'But we can't even do that!'

Powell designed bicycle accessories for a living, and had taken an interest in Bikes to Rwanda because the charity combined two of his passions: cycling and coffee. (One of Powell's signature innovations is the 'Bar-ista', a holder that attaches to bicycle handlebars and allows a rider to store their coffee cup as they ride.) Still, he was not optimistic about being able to resuscitate the project. 'If you said Rwanda to someone eight years ago, they might have a little more of an idea a) where it is on a map and b) what happened and c) why this is a great thing to do to effect change there,' said Powell. 'Now, there's been several other countries in Africa where atrocities have happened, Ivory Coast or Somalia or any number of places that are maybe more in the forefront of people's minds.'

An additional problem for Rwandan coffee, particularly from around 2007 onwards, was an imperfection called the 'potato defect' that had started to blight some of their speciality coffee. It was most likely caused by a stink bug – a technical term, surprisingly – called antestia, which infects the beans. Of all the thousands of tastes within a brew, potato was just about the worst: 'It's almost like raw asparagus,' winced Aleco Chigounis, who was the chief coffee buyer for Sorenson at Stumptown, 'very off-putting and undesirable.' It mainly affected Rwanda and its neighbour Burundi and was near impossible to eliminate: the bacteria were practically invisible. 'The trouble with the potato taste defect is you can't see it,' explained Thomas Miller, a professor of entomology at the University of California, in *Scientific American* in 2012. 'It's not really clear what steps you need to take to prevent it from happening. It's a great big mystery. You've got yourself a nice twenty years of work before you figure out what's causing it.'

On the bicycle side, one hope was that Tom's initiative might be subsumed by the charity World Bicycle Relief, which was set up by Frederick K. W. Day in 2005 to match bikes with underprivileged riders. Day's story was not so different from Tom's own: FK, as everyone knows him, was a college dropout who loved riding. In 1987 he created SRAM, which made bicycle components, with his brother, an MBA student called Stan. Helped by some high-profile endorsements – Lance Armstrong was an early adopter – SRAM became the largest bicycle-parts company in the United States, the second-biggest in the world, with around $500 million in annual sales. Stan did the numbers and FK pushed innovations.

World Bicycle Relief was born after the 2004 Indian Ocean tsunami, which killed more than 200,000 people and wiped out communities across Asia. FK flew to Sri Lanka to see how he could help. One idea was to ship containers packed with second-hand bikes given by Americans to the devastated areas, but FK thought it too risky. The bikes could be damaged in transit and when they arrived there was a risk that no one in these countries would have the parts or expertise to keep the myriad machines on the road. Instead, FK – again, much as Tom would do – decided to design his own: World Bicycle Relief shipped out almost 25,000 bikes to Sri Lanka, which cost a little under $100 each, paid for mostly by donations.

FK shifted the programme to Africa after requests from NGOs there, and set up bases in Kenya, Zimbabwe, Zambia and South Africa, where it partnered with Qhubeka, the charity with which Douglas Ryder's MTN team later formed an alliance. By the end of 2012, World Bicycle Relief had supplied more than 120,000 bicycles, almost seventy per cent of them to women and girls: an initiative intended to keep them at school longer and steer them away from early marriages. For every fifty bikes it distributed, it trained one mechanic and supplied them with basic parts and tools. The bicycle had been adapted a little since the first batch sent out to Sri Lanka and was now called the Buffalo Bicycle (or '*Nyati*' in Swahili-speaking countries). It was not as striking a machine as Tom's coffee bike – certainly heavier and less innovative – but at $134 per unit it was cheaper. There were plans to expand the operation into Rwanda in 2013.

It was too early to speculate whether World Bicycle Relief would ultimately be much more successful or enduring than Project Rwanda. Even FK Day was cautious. 'You can have all the goodwill in the world,' he told *Forbes* magazine in 2010, 'but if what you're doing isn't driven by the invisible hand of Adam Smith, you're doomed to fail.' Like many other Westerners before him – Tom, Jock and Duane Sorenson among them – FK was inspired by an altruistic desire to help provide solutions for Africa, but the repeated aid failures and the cast-aside projects of well-meaning outsiders showed there was no blueprint for how best to achieve these goals.

The issue was at the heart of what Jock was trying to

achieve with the cycling team, too. Jock's model took the existing cycling training plans and sensibilities from Europe and America and asked the Rwandans to adapt to it. Adrien had done so effectively, but there had been others – Nyandwi, Gasore, Abraham, Daniel Ngendahayo – whose potential it had failed to unlock. But Team Rwanda was not the only project that believed that the future stars of world cycling would come from Africa. Across the continent, programmes were being set up in Kenya, Eritrea and Ethiopia. Each of these experiments asked similar questions, though it was becoming clear that their solutions were often radically different: Was a Western approach best? Might a specifically African methodology work better? There was not even a consensus on what counted as 'success'. Was it a race to produce the first black African to ride the Tour de France? Or was it enough just to improve the lives of a few individuals on the globe's most challenging continent?

12 AFRICANISATION

Not so long ago, Africans were not known for distance running. Until the nineteen-fifties, Finland was considered to be the great athletics powerhouse; New Zealand had a period of dominance, too. Then, at the 1960 Olympic Games in Rome, an Ethiopian called Abebe Bikila – who was trained by a Finn, Onni Niskanen – claimed an unexpected victory in the men's marathon, becoming the first sub-Saharan African athlete to win a gold medal. At the start line, a commentator had asked: 'And what's this Ethiopian called?' He was meant to be wearing Adidas shoes, but he turned up late and grabbed a pair that didn't fit, so he ended up running over the city's cobbled streets barefoot. Bikila, a member of Emperor Haile Selassie's Imperial Guard, would go on to repeat the success four years later, despite having his appendix removed just forty days before the race. That time he did wear shoes.

But it was in 1968 that African athletics definitively arrived with the duel between Jim Ryun and Kipchoge 'Kip' Keino in the 1500m at the Mexico City Olympics. Ryun was the corn-fed, all-American superstar from Wichita, Kansas, who had started running as a child on his 4.30 a.m. newspaper round. Tall and lean, with a distinctive flat-top haircut, he broke the four-minute mile shortly after his seventeenth birthday. He entered the final in Mexico as the world-record holder, unbeaten at the distance for more than three years. More than the numbers, he just *looked* like an athletics champion. Sprinters could get by on raw explosive power, but longer distances called on cerebral qualities such as focus and discipline. The determination and stamina required, it was said, made it the domain of the Anglo-Saxon.

Keino was a police officer from Kenya who escaped a cheetah at the age of twelve by shinning up a tree and lashing himself to a branch overnight. He had never beaten Ryun and the omens couldn't have been much worse in Mexico: a German doctor diagnosed him with gallstones and he had to run two miles to the Estadio Olímpico Universitario before the final when his bus was caught in traffic. In the race, his tactics appeared either naïve or desperate. He sprinted from the gun, soon establishing a lead of twelve metres. Keino was running suicidally fast, but instead of Ryun reeling his rival back with his famed finishing kick, the lead edged out to fifteen and finally twenty metres. It was the widest margin of victory in that event in Olympic history. Afterwards, Ryun was attacked in the American press: his defeat inexplicable and somehow inexcusable. He briefly retired, though he was only twenty-one. 'Some even said I had let down the whole world,' he recalled. 'I didn't get any credit for running my best and no one seemed to realise that Keino had performed brilliantly.'

Many Kenyans and other black Africans have followed in Keino's footsteps since 1968. He had exploded many long-held beliefs about athletic dominance and he reinforced the point four years later, at the 1972 Olympics, when he won the 3,000m steeplechase, an event for which he had not even trained. Any distance from 800 metres to the marathon and beyond would never be the same again. Just one example is the London Marathon: between 2003 and 2012, the men's race was won eight times by Kenyans and twice by Ethiopians. But Keino's name also came up frequently when I spoke to cycling coaches from different countries in Africa. Their logic was hard to fault: as much as they were unbeatable runners, these Africans had exactly the right physiological traits (huge lungs, spindly but powerful legs) to do well in cycling. All that was needed was one pioneering individual – a cycling Kipchoge Keino – who could take on, and beat, the best competitors from the Old World. Then the floodgates would open. It sounded simple when they put it like that.

At the Tour of Rwanda each November, it became clear that Jock Boyer was not the only person who believed he could inspire an African cycling revolution. Jock – along with Douglas Ryder, and his South African-based MTN-Qhubeka team – chose to pursue, broadly speaking, a Western agenda. They set their sights on the Tour de France and the storied races of the European cycling calendar. They hooked their riders up to high-tech power meters to measure their efforts and instructed them in the current thinking on tactics, strategy and physical conditioning. The riders had the best equipment and they were typically found winding down at the end of the stage with a recovery drink and a post-race massage. Such an approach would not raise an eyebrow at most races in the world, but in Rwanda it felt like an unfair advantage, almost cheating.

Then there were the *more African* African teams. These varied hugely in quality, from the explosive Eritreans to the impoverished Tanzanians and the really pretty appalling Burundians. By the 2011 edition of the Tour of Rwanda, the home nation had stopped inviting their southern neighbour,

Burundi, as well as other perennial backmarkers Uganda and Ivory Coast, believing that they lowered the tone of a serious bicycle race. These teams stayed in fleapit hotels, and often the only food they ate was the complimentary breakfast served at their lodging and an evening meal at the destination town. There may have been some great natural talents among this group but they were in desperate need of a fairy godmother – or failing that, just some sustenance during the stage.

Finally, in a classification of their own, there were the Kenyan Riders, who were like no other cycling team in the world. On the road at the 2011 Tour of Rwanda, the Kenyans were hard to miss: in part, this was due to their garish purple uniforms, but mostly it was because they cycled together all day, every day, rarely breaking out of formation. No cycling textbook in the world would have advised them to ride like that; a core premise of professional cycling is that a team picks its strongest rider and his team-mates surround him like worker bees defending their queen. But in a race dominated by unfathomable tactics, there was something serene about their progress. 'I'm really ignorant of everything,' admitted their coach Rob Higley, an Australian running expert finding his way in a new job. 'So for a non-cyclist, I had to decide what was the best thing to do. I thought, *Let's just groom these guys so they're a really well-oiled machine that works together and does not just break up and leave every man for himself*. We train like that every day, gradually raising the percentage of the effort, week by week, month by month, until previously very tough paces become very comfortable.'

While other coaches rushed around before a stage barking orders, Rob could usually be found sitting in a team car with his head buried in a book. Everything about his approach was unconventional. 'My biggest value is that I know how to work with Kenyans,' he said. 'I'm a bit of an oddball, I don't really fit into the Western world. It's all a bit stressful for me, a bit competitive, a bit forced. But in Africa you can let it flow, you can let it evolve.'

At the heart of the Kenyan Riders team was a philosophy they called 'Africanisation': in essence that it is a huge blunder to treat African cyclists as if they are Europeans or Americans. Africans, Rob believed, had become the greatest distance runners on the planet not by copying established methods, but by adapting their own. If he was right, then Jock and Douglas Ryder were frittering away millions on a mostly futile quest. 'It's not about making money or even winning gold medals, it's about making the most out of individuals,' explained Rob. 'But I'm cocky enough to believe that if I get this right, the gold medal will come as well and maybe the Tour de France.'

The story of the Kenyan Riders began with a splinter. Nicholas Leong, a commercial photographer then in his late thirties, was holed up at home in Singapore waiting for his body to discharge a shard of wood lodged in his foot. An obsessive fan of the Tour de France since he was fourteen, one day he started wondering: how would the best marathon runners fare if they were stuck on a bicycle? They had the bodies of the Italian climbing star Marco Pantani, at least to Nicholas's eyes. Could they ride like him?

Singaporeans have a reputation for order and practicality, but that has never been Nicholas's way. A roly-poly man with irrepressible enthusiasm, he did national service for two and a half years (as all men in the country are required to do), then he left and somehow ended up spending three years on the Thai–Burma border with Burmese rebel soldiers and refugees. While he was there, Aung San Suu Kyi's National League for

Democracy party won the 1990 general election, only to have its victory nullified by the ruling military junta and Suu Kyi placed under house arrest in Rangoon. Nicholas remembers feeling the outrage and, more than that, thinking: If he had an idea that was larger than himself, and that took all the lessons he had learned from Burma, he would not walk away from it. He went back home and became a photographer. He did well, but he had a growing, gnawing realisation that every advertisement, billboard and annual report he shot could easily have been done by another photographer. 'At the end of my life,' he said, 'there really would be nothing I could point to and say, "I did that, and if I hadn't, it would not have been done at all."'

All of which goes a small way to explaining the rather extraordinary behaviour that followed. Nicholas booked a plane ticket to Nairobi for the evening after the 2006 Singapore Marathon. He had a hunch that the marathon runners would be returning home on it. At the airport, he walked up to a group of skinny black Africans; out of the first fifteen runners to cross the line that morning, thirteen were from Kenya. He asked, 'Who's the guy who won the marathon?' Amos Tirop Matui, the smallest of the bunch, came forward. Nicholas said, 'Okay, I'm following you home!' He had never been to Kenya before. Everything he knew about cycling he had gleaned from videotapes of the Tour de France. 'I'm like the guy who sits there on Saturday and watches Manchester United and has watched Manchester United for thirty years, so he thinks he knows everything about the game,' he told me.

At Nairobi airport, the runners had organised a *matatu*, a shared minibus, and Nicholas sat in the front next to Matthew Birir, the gold medallist in the 3,000m steeplechase at the 1992 Barcelona Olympics. He had been in the country five minutes, and had already met an athletics legend. *Only in Kenya*, he thought. The bus was headed for Eldoret in the highlands of the Great Rift Valley, the birthplace of mankind, some say. Nicholas hung around aimlessly for two weeks, went home for a couple of months, and then returned to Kenya for half a year. 'I got cheated by a lot of people, I lost a lot of money, the kinds of things that happen when you're new in Africa,' he remembered. 'At that time, I probably had far more money than I had sense. Now I feel that I have a lot more sense, at least in Africa.' He paused. 'But I have far less money.'

Nicholas decided to base himself in Iten, fifteen miles from Eldoret. There were only 4,000 residents of Iten, but many of them had gold medals and world records to their name. The 800m runner David Rudisha, a star of the 2012 London Olympics, went to school in the little town and Mary Keitany, winner of the 2011 and 2012 London Marathons, lived there. The land is flat with a temperate, year-round climate; athletes benefit from living at nearly 2,200 metres above sea level, their lungs ballooning as they become accustomed to the barely-there air. A 1990 study by the Copenhagen Muscle Research Centre took professional runners from Sweden – a nation that traditionally performed well at middle and long distances – to Kenya to compete against the St Patrick's High School athletics team in Iten. It was a salutary experience for the Swedes. Dr Bengt Saltin, who conducted the study, estimated there were at least 500 schoolboys in the region who could beat the best Swedish man over 2,000 metres.

The problem that Nicholas found in Iten was that none of the runners wanted to swap their spikes for bikes. Perhaps it shouldn't have been much of a surprise: prize money for a major city marathon is typically around $100,000, while even $10,000 for a lower placing would be a life-changing amount. Nicholas had in mind a monthly wage of something closer to $100. The skyline of Eldoret had been completely reshaped by the success of its athletes: there was a five-storey shopping centre, large office blocks, flats and private schools, all built by returning heroes. The runners themselves lived in mansions behind imposing concrete walls. With such conspicuous success, young Kenyans were dubious about making the switch.

Eventually Nicholas met Zakayo Nderi Mwai, an Eldoret shoeshine, who woke up each morning at five o'clock to ride his bike, a single-speed Black Mamba roadster that weighed nearly twenty kilograms. Nicholas offered to train Zakayo and three other riders in Singapore on proper racing bikes for a couple of months. Then he picked a pair of them – Zakayo and bicycle-taxi rider Samwel Myangi – and in 2008 headed for L'Alpe d'Huez, the most famous climb in the Tour de France. It was a stunt, mostly designed to raise awareness and boost fundraising, but it turned out to be a revealing experiment, as well. The night before, Zakayo dreamed of slaying a lion; the next day, a Thursday-morning mass-start event, he scampered up the twenty-one famous hairpins in forty-two minutes ten seconds. That was only three minutes outside Lance Armstrong's time in the 2004 Tour de France. If Zakayo had been racing that day, he would have placed in the top twenty. Not bad for someone who had never ridden a bike with gears before Nicholas showed up.

There were obvious parallels between what Nicholas was doing in Kenya and Jock's Team Rwanda, but their methodologies were very different. For one thing, Nicholas's approach was not remotely scientific. He did not have a CompuTrainer or a SpinScan program to assess riders, so he found a seven-mile hill between the town of Biretwo and the Catholic church in Tambach, which rose 700 metres at a gradient of about six per cent. He then invited anyone who wanted to join the team to ride up it on a Black Mamba. Nicholas figured that the world's best on their race bikes would probably do it in twenty-six minutes, so he set the cut-off at thirty-four minutes. There was a cash reward for anyone who succeeded and a place on the Kenyan Riders squad. As a selection process, it was far from foolproof. 'Some guys can do it and they don't become very good cyclists,' he said. 'Because of other things: discipline problems, drinking and chasing women.'

After Zakayo's initial breakthrough on L'Alpe d'Huez, the Kenyan Riders began to stall. They were training harder than ever, but they were actually performing worse not better. It was in 2010 that Nicholas decided to call in Rob Higley, someone who knew even less about cycling than he did. Rob had travelled the world for three decades in a humble quest to find 'the perfect human running model'. The search had led him inevitably to Kenya and then Iten, where he became a coach at St Patrick's College. One of his protégés was David Rudisha. Rob was initially dubious about switching sports, but he began to think he could help. 'A lot of my coaching career has been to return power to an athlete, to an ageing athlete, to an athlete that has burnt out a lot of natural talent,' he said. 'So I felt like I could do it if they were prepared to get *off* the bike.'

The set-up that Nicholas and Rob created in Iten was an eccentric one. The riders trained on mountain bikes bought from the supermarket for less than £100 and modified with locally available accessories. They lifted homemade barbells that were actually buckets filled with cement, and Rob, who had once been a physical education teacher, introduced all manner of odd games into their daily routine. In one exercise, the riders would stand in a circle and toss a two-kilo medicine ball at each other at random; they had to clap before they caught it, or else drop down on to one knee, then both knees, and so on. Another game involved a pair of riders wrestling each other; they were allowed to do anything apart from move their left feet. (I half-expected to hear that if a rider forgot his kit, he would be made to do the session in his underwear.) Yoga, pilates and intense stretching balanced the dynamic efforts. The idea was to increase an individual's explosive core power when they returned to the bike – that the exercises built team spirit and broke the monotony of long hours in the saddle was a bonus.

Partly the thriftiness was inspired by necessity – Nicholas by now had emptied his six-figure life savings and he had no support from the Kenyan cycling federation – but there was also a deeper faith in 'Africanisation'. Kenyan runners proved themselves running barefoot on dirt tracks before they were ever given kit and a set of spikes. Nicholas felt that no one should come to their training camp and think that they needed money to be a cyclist or that technology provided all the solutions. There were no heart-rate monitors, smartphones or Garmin GPS devices; the project needed to be sustainable. Even when the Kenyan Riders went to foreign races, they rode fairly basic aluminium racers. 'Our bikes would not be considered good at all, no,' admitted Nicholas.

There was an abundance of reasons why a Kenyan cycling project should not be successful. Nicholas had long accepted that his original idea of putting a great marathon runner on a bicycle was simplistic and impractical. Millions of children in Kenya dreamed of becoming great runners. The vaunted Kenyan system was, in fact, notoriously wasteful. Promising athletes would cover extreme distances – up to 150 miles a week at unrelenting race-level intensity – and the rate of attrition was appalling: many would fall ill, pick up injuries, become demoralised; even successful competitors would be brilliant one year and disappear the next. But there would always be another exceptional individual coming through.

Such profligacy was not an option for the Kenyan Riders. There were no cycling heroes for the riders to emulate and the coaches could not afford to waste any talent. In short, substandard equipment was being ridden by athletes whom other sports had rejected. 'We just have a very small pool,' said Nicholas. 'There are literally fifty guys in Kenya who are taking cycling seriously enough for me to be serious about them. Five. Zero. That's the pool. If you go to France the pool is tens of thousands. If you go to anywhere in the world, the pool is tens of thousands, perhaps even hundreds of thousands.'

But, despite these drawbacks, Nicholas and Rob's work was producing results. At the 2010 Tour of Rwanda, the best-placed Kenyan finished in eighteenth place, thirty-three minutes behind the winner. The next year, he finished twelfth, thirteen minutes in arrears. Then in 2012, a former milk delivery man called John Njoroge Muya made the podium, coming third, less than two minutes behind the yellow jersey. He had beaten all the riders from Eritrea, Rwanda and Ethiopia; ahead of him were just two experienced professionals from South Africa. 'The thing Kenya does have – that I haven't seen in Rwanda, for example – is a kind of hunger for sporting success,' said Rob. 'It's an absolute belief in their ability in a way that comes from the Kipchoge Keino days: "We're the best, it's as simple as that. Maybe we won't win today but we will win next time."'

It was easy to underestimate Nicholas Leong, as he zipped around the Tour of Rwanda on the back of a moto-taxi with a camera dangling round his neck. Or Rob Higley, who at times sounded more like a benign cult leader than a cycling coach. But after the 2012 race a heretical thought was becoming hard to suppress: *what if they were right, and everyone else was wrong?*

*

The best cyclist in Africa, however, was from neither Kenya nor Rwanda. He was an Eritrean called Daniel Teklehaimanot. Eritrea, a small triangle of land on the Red Sea that is occupied by five million people, had one advantage that those two countries did not: an established cycling culture. A long-time colony of Italy, the Italians had left behind their love of bicycles, along with streets of incongruous modernist architecture and an enthusiasm for cappuccinos. There are around 200 full-time professional cyclists in Eritrea and, unlike the rest of the continent, there are hard, technical races every week of the year. Spectators pay to watch, and the larger teams have boisterous fan clubs. The Tour de France is shown each year on state television.

Until recently, no one knew that Eritreans were mad about cycling, but then there was much that outsiders did not know about the country. On the World Press Freedom list, compiled in 2012, Eritrea ranked 179 out of 179 countries. That was behind North Korea, Iran and Turkmenistan. There was no independent media in the country at all, and no foreign correspondents were based in its capital Asmara. Eritrea had more journalists in prison than any other African country and they were often detained in overcrowded shipping containers in the desert that were sweltering in the day and freezing at night. Reporters Without Borders called it a 'black hole' of information.

The snippets of news that did come out of Eritrea were rarely positive. The economy, never particularly robust, was in collapse: in 2008, exports totalled less than £10 million. Unicef estimated that forty per cent of Eritrean children were malnourished. There were frequent power outages in Asmara, and water was sometimes only available between 2 a.m. and 4 a.m. The regime operated a shoot-to-kill policy of anyone who tried to flee to the refugee camps over the border in Sudan or Ethiopia. They let it be known that if a citizen did escape, their family would be punished. The country had always had conscription, but since 1998, when it restarted a long-running dispute with Ethiopia, military service had been open-ended. It was common to find men in their thirties still conscripted; some soldiers were said to be in their seventies.

Being a member of the national cycling team – or other sports teams – was one of the few legal ways to avoid conscription. Or at least to defer it; they might still have to do a stint at the end of their career. It also provided a rare opportunity for foreign travel – and potential escape. Despite the government's dire threats, Eritrea had one of the highest defection rates in the world, perhaps second only to Zimbabwe. Among the diplomatic cables unearthed by Wikileaks in 2010 was one titled 'Eritrea's squabbling colonels, fleeing footballers, frightened librarians'. It told the tale of how the entire Eritrean national football team absconded in 2009 during a regional tournament in Kenya and sought asylum. 'Only the coach and an escorting colonel reportedly returned to Eritrea,' wrote the United States ambassador Ronald K. McMullen, before adding in parentheses, 'One wonders why, given their likely fate.'

Daniel Teklehaimanot was one of the few Eritreans to make it out of the country with permission. Already a national champion by the age of nineteen, he was spotted at the African Continental Championships in Morocco in November 2008 by Michel Thèze, a coach at the International Cycling Union. Daniel had finished only eighth, but Thèze liked his aggressive instincts: 'I'm not obsessed with results,' he said. 'It's how you behave in a race. Either you are a follower or you take initiative.' In January 2009, Daniel was sent to the UCI's World Cycling Centre in Switzerland for a prolonged period of training. Soon after he arrived, tests showed that one of his legs was shorter than the other; it could be corrected, but it is not ideal for a professional cyclist. He had never been near a dentist in his twenty years so his teeth were a graveyard. But the major issue was his heart: when he fully exerted himself on a bike his heart rate spiked to 260 beats per minute. He was diagnosed with tachycardia, an irregular heartbeat that is dangerous and, for a sportsman, life-threatening. There was a chance he would never ride a bicycle again.

But there was one more thing they discovered about Daniel in the physiological tests. Even with tachycardia, his power output and his ability to sustain intense effort exceeded almost anything the coaches had ever seen. In fact, only one UCI graduate came close: Chris Froome. Froome, who was born in Kenya and educated in South Africa, arrived at the centre in 2007; six years later he won the 2013 Tour de France. 'Looking at Daniel's results I was not sure if I should cry or laugh,' said Thèze.

The heart operation went without complication and Daniel was soon winning every race on the African circuit. I met him at the 2010 Tour of Rwanda. He was tall, almost six-foot two, and had three per cent body fat, which was about the same amount as a competition bodybuilder. He had intensely dark, tightly ringed black hair and was unfailingly polite and deferential off the bicycle. On it, though, he was an assassin. He had just swept the board at the African Continental Championships, winning the road race and the individual time trial for himself, and the team time trial with the Eritrean squad. The Tour of Rwanda was billed as being a shootout between him and Adrien Niyonshuti. In the event, it turned out to be not much of a contest: Adrien fought desperately, but Daniel won with panache. He was on the podium so often that the bombastic

Rwandan emcee even created a signature tag for him: 'Tek-Tek-Tek-le-haimanot!'

The only debate was how much his formidable Eritrean team-mates had contributed to the victory. 'Daniel's impressive, but he didn't put out much this race, he had a really strong team,' said Jock, a little ungraciously. 'The only way to see which of Daniel and Adrien has the most potential is to get them in a race that is above both their heads and see who does best. But Adrien was stronger in this race than Daniel without a question in my mind. Had Adrien been on even ground with Daniel he would have been ahead of him.'

Daniel's talent was too obvious to be ignored by the major cycling teams and in 2011 he was signed by GreenEdge for the following season, their first in the professional peloton. Bankrolled by Gerry Ryan, whose Jayco caravan and camping business had built him a £120 million fortune, GreenEdge was billed as Australia's answer to Britain's Team Sky. Out of thirty riders, seventeen were Australian. It looked like a good fit for Daniel: he spoke a little English, and the team was strong enough to qualify for all the major races, including a precious invitation to the Tour de France. He was, the management said, 'a project': a rider – then twenty-three – whom they were looking to develop for the future. He signed a two-year contract for 33,000 euros a year, GreenEdge's minimum wage, although it was a step up from the $20 a month he would have been paid in the Eritrean military.

Daniel was not selected for the 2012 Tour de France, that was never the plan, but he was picked for the nine-man GreenEdge team for the season-ending Vuelta a España, Spain's most important race and one of the big three on the cycling calendar. When he rolled down the start ramp in Pamplona for the opening team time trial, he became the first black African to compete in a Grand Tour. In another glimpse of the future, Ji Cheng, a twenty-five-year-old rider with the Netherlands-based Argos-Shimano team, recorded the same distinction for China. There are 500 million cyclists in the country, and a formidable track-racing programme, but Ji was the closest they had come to producing a top-level professional on the road.

More significant than the historical footnote was Daniel's performance at the Vuelta a España. He raced hard and worked unstintingly for the team. At the beginning of the third week, he made it into a group of riders who had broken away from the main pack but crashed on a descent. He was going fifty miles an hour and landed on his shoulder in a ditch, bashed up and bruised. He finished the stage last, in 182nd place, half an hour back. He was still suffering the next day and lost another thirty-five minutes. But he reached Madrid to complete the race. (Ji also made it through, in last place overall, completing the event four and a half hours behind the winner, Spain's Alberto Contador.)

Shayne Bannan, general manager at GreenEdge, was impressed with Daniel's resilience; much as Jock had been with Adrien. 'You don't get where he's got, leave your home country, come and live in Europe, if you're not mentally tough,' said Bannan. 'He's that, no question.'

The debate was now not if Daniel Teklehaimanot would race in the Tour de France, but when, and whether he would be the first black African. (The first black rider of any nationality competed in the Tour de France only in 2011 when Yohann Gène from Guadeloupe was selected for the Team Europcar squad. The British commentator Phil Liggett, who had been covering the Tour for forty years, became momentarily ruffled, referring to the 'coloured cyclist' and inspired a virtual mailbag of complaints from viewers.) Riders typically hit their peak in their late twenties and Daniel was becoming physically tougher and more tactically shrewd with each race. Bannan, not a man given to overblown pronouncements, believed he could become a top-twenty finisher, perhaps higher. He would have to achieve those ambitions away from GreenEdge, however, as in late 2013 he signed a two-year contract with Douglas Ryder at MTN-Qhubeka. Douglas was able to offer him 'a leadership position' with the team – and an end to visa complications he had been experiencing – but a big part of the attraction was representing an outfit from his home continent. 'I've chosen this team because it's an African team,' he said.

Meanwhile, in August 2012, Daniel's Eritrean team-mate Natnael Berhane joined Team Europcar for the 2013 season. Natnael was just twenty-one but he was already the road race champion of Africa in both 2011 and 2012. Shorter and more powerful than Daniel, he was a *puncheur*, strong on short climbs and with a spirited finishing kick. He might not have the endurance and climbing power for a multi-day event, but Europcar fancied that he could take out a stage here and there or win a one-day Classics race. He immediately proved his potetial when he won the hardest, 'Queen' stage of the 2013 Tour of Turkey (the summit of Elmali, 'Turkey's L'Alpe d'Huez', no less); he went on to finish second overall. Adrien was not out of contention as a future Tour rider, either.

Across the continent, some very different programmes, all working independently, were converging on a moment in history. Eritrea had unparalleled strength in depth and was finally allowing its riders to gain international experience. Jock had expertise and a bulging book of contacts to help Rwanda. Kenya had neither of those advantages, but perhaps it had the most naturally gifted athletes. Phil Liggett had better start brushing up on his pronunciation and terminology. 'I'm sincerely convinced that the future winners of the Tour de France are here in Africa,' said Jock. 'It's just going to take time. It could be five years, it could be ten years, but it will happen.'

For Jock, everything came back to race experience. The tactics of a bicycle race can often seem impenetrable, particularly compared to the pared-down simplicity of athletes lapping a track. To win any event, on any given day, a rider needs physical strength and determination, but also mental fortitude and cunning, and often a huge slice of luck. The Tour de France has been decided by as little as eight seconds; scarcely a blink during a three-week race. It was often described by previous winners as more of a draining psychological assessment than an athletic achievement. 'Cycling is not a simple sport, it's very complex,' said Jock. 'It's got gears, it's got tactics, it's got wind, uphill, downhill, rainy weather, cold weather, muddy weather, cobblestones – there are so many variables. It's not like jumping in a pool and swimming fifty laps. By the time I was a junior I had raced more than all of these Rwandan guys put together. That's significant when you look at cycling.'

Jock believed that the quickest way to get his African riders up to speed was immersion in the latest training philosophies coming out of Europe and the United States. One of the supporters of Team Rwanda was Chris Carmichael, whom Jock had raced alongside in the pioneering American team 7-Eleven in the nineteen-eighties. Carmichael's own cycling career was cut short in 1986 when he shattered his right patella in a backcountry skiing accident that left him in intensive care for a week, but he quickly moved into coaching the United States national team. One of the first cyclists he worked with was a brash eighteen-year-old Lance Armstrong, and their relationship continued throughout his Tour de France campaigns.

Carmichael's celebrity grew with that of his most famous client: at its peak, his company, Carmichael Training Systems, had 115 employees and dispensed fitness advice to more than 2,000 private individuals. In July 2005, *Men's Health* wrote: 'Without Chris Carmichael, there'd be no Lance Armstrong.'

Jock implemented Carmichael's approach with Team Rwanda and, in 2012, Carmichael Training Systems coaches began arriving in the country to coach the riders directly. Carmichael leaned heavily on technology and regular testing to track changes in performance. But the core of his philosophy was intense, unstinting hard work. At the highest levels, his programme encouraged what might seem obsessive behaviour: during the racing season, Armstrong took to travelling with a digital scale to weigh every mouthful of food he ate; reflecting on a life spent in performance labs and wind tunnels, contorting his body into the most efficient aerodynamic positions, he referred to himself and other top riders as 'computer slaves'. Not everyone could sustain the regimen, but Carmichael would argue that there was only one winner of the Tour de France each year. 'Who hits more practice balls every day than any other golfer?' he said in 2002. 'Guess what? It's Tiger Woods. Well, Lance trains more than his competitors.'

The Kenyan Riders coach Rob Higley had only passing familiarity with Carmichael's methods, but had little interest in using them on his Kenyan cyclists. Not that he didn't think they would work: 'It's actually the most economical way to go if you want success,' he conceded. 'Bring in as many fairly talented people as you possibly can, push them through a grinding programme, a really barbaric programme, and you know the cream will rise to the top. You see that with the runners in Kenya. But I really care about my athletes, they are my family, and I don't want to let them down.'

At the end of the 2012 Tour of Rwanda, following John Njoroge Muya's podium finish, Rob spent a couple of days with Jock in Ruhengeri. It was not entirely a meeting of minds. 'They told us a lot about their programme, but asked us no questions about ours, which was kind of interesting,' he said. 'I think they really believe in what they are doing – and they should; that system has been in place a long time. But instead of asking what we were doing, they readily suggested that we disperse our group: send some to the UCI camp in South Africa, send some to an amateur squad in Europe. You know, it was almost like they were very keen for us to water ourselves down just in case we were on to something new and revolutionary that was likely to blossom into something quite extraordinary. That's just human nature. That's not critical of any individual. Everybody will defend what they have and hope like hell that somebody hasn't discovered something unique that is going to be better.'

For now, Rob and Nicholas Leong were content enough with their supermarket mountain bikes and primitive barbells. 'We won't succeed if we think, *Oh well, Alberto Contador has this, Lance Armstrong has this, how do we get this?*' said Nicholas. 'This is the only way we can get this done. We're far more interested in how David Rudisha does it.'

There may have been no consensus on the best way to put African cycling on the map, but maybe that was for the best. What everyone did agree on was that the breakthrough was going to happen, and once African riders were given a chance it would be impossible to hold them back. 'It feels like an idea whose time has come,' said Nicholas. 'You hear about Thomas Edison inventing electricity or the Wright Brothers inventing flight. But actually, if you're a student of this stuff, you realise that at the same time there were two, three or four people working on the same idea and one of them succeeded.'

Did Nicholas feel confident that he could be the one everyone remembered? 'History hasn't been written yet, so I don't know if our model is going to be the most successful,' he replied. 'But for now we'd argue that what we're doing is a viable model, there's really no doubt about it.'

13

THE RACE

The first time Adrien Niyonshuti saw the 2012 Olympic mountain bike course he was too scared to actually ride it. He took one look at the wall of rocks and told a friend from his MTN-Qhubeka racing team, 'I'll break my neck if I go down that.'

It was June 2011, a year before the London Games, at Hadleigh Farm, near Leigh-on-Sea on the Essex coast, where the 2012 race would take place. Technically, Adrien was still a novice. His first experience of mountain biking was the Wooden Bike Classic organised by Tom Ritchey in 2006 and since then he had concentrated on road racing and marathon mountain bike events in South Africa. These races, which lasted for up to eight days and covered 450 miles, tested endurance more than skill. The Olympic race was a sprint in comparison: seven laps of around three miles; just twenty-two miles in total, with the winner taking about an hour and a half to cover them. High-level mountain bike races operated an 'eighty per cent rule': the tracks were so narrow that if a competitor dropped too far behind the leaders – eighty per cent of the course give or take – they were eliminated from the race by the organisers. That's what Adrien meant when he told Clive Owen at the Criterion Theatre that he would be happy just to finish.

Despite his initial misgivings, Adrien had flown in from South Africa, so he knew he had to return to Hadleigh Farm. The site has been owned by the Salvation Army for more than a century and it was a late-notice stand-in for the Olympics when the original venue, Weald Country Park, was deemed insufficiently challenging. The new designers took this as an invitation to imagine a monstrous rollercoaster ride. They imported 2,500 tons of crushed stone to surface the route and another 1,500 tons of boulders, which they scattered around like tasteful mini-avalanches. A once-featureless expanse of parkland became a steep and technical playground of rock drops, gap jumps, step-ups and switchbacks.

When Adrien did finally dare to ride the course, he might as well have had stabilisers fitted on his bike as he gingerly picked his way through the obstacles. At the end of a week's practice, the organisers held the Olympic 'test event', the Hadleigh Farm International. Adrien was yanked from the field after just five circuits as France's two-time Olympic champion Julien Absalon loomed ominously. After that race, the course was made 'higher, wider and harder' in response to rider feedback. Adrien thought it was plenty tough enough already.

Almost as soon as Adrien qualified for the Olympics there was concern that, rather than being the greatest day in Rwandan cycling history, it could be an embarrassment. 'It's wonderful Adrien making it to the Olympics but we want to see him finish,' said Tom Ritchey. 'He's good on strength, but he doesn't have the snap, the discipline, the hardcore technical skills. With the lap timing of twelve minutes, a lot of riders are going to get pulled, they're going to get lapped. They won't even be allowed to finish.'

So it was that in May 2012, three months before the biggest race of his life, Tom shipped Adrien off to mountain-bike bootcamp in Switzerland with his friend Thomas Frischknecht. The Americans might have invented the sport, but the Swiss are perfecting it: at the 2012 Mountain Bike World Championships, they took four of the top five spots, including all three podium places; seven out of the first twenty finishers were Swiss. 'Frischi', as everyone calls him, is a pioneer of the sport in the country; a multiple world champion in cyclo-cross and mountain biking, no one in history has won more World Cup races. He took silver in the cross-country mountain bike race at the 1996 Olympics and the next day he competed in the road race – ostensibly for fun – finishing in the main pack. Now in his early forties, he remained an irrepressible competitor, but mostly he coached; his Scott-Swisspower team included one of the favourites for Olympic mountain bike gold, the Swiss rider Nino Schurter.

Before Adrien arrived with Frischknecht, he warmed up with a couple of World Cup races. In mid-May in Nove Mesto na Morave, Czech Republic, he was forced to abandon with two laps still to finish as Schurter threatened to overtake him. A week later, in La Bresse in France, it was even worse: he was eliminated from the race with three laps remaining. At times, he was reduced to walking with his bike across sections that the best riders – in fact, everyone else – were riding over. He lacked explosive power on the uphill sections and on the descents, to borrow the withering self-beration of Gianni Bugno, an Italian racer from the nineteen-nineties, 'a priest in a *soutane* could have made it down faster'.

I asked Frischi how he rated Adrien as a mountain biker when he arrived in Switzerland. 'I'd say, for an Olympic level, he was a bad rider,' he replied. 'I was actually kind of shocked.' He didn't mean to be brutal; he just had the same directness and lack of euphemism in English that sometimes made his compatriot the tennis player Roger Federer sound so boastful. He was also just stating facts: Schurter had competed in his first mountain bike race aged six, two decades ago; that was quite a head start. Geography was simply not on Adrien's side. 'There's a reason why there are no skiers from Africa and why there are no surfers from Switzerland,' said Frischi.

To prepare for the Olympics, Adrien summered like a Euro banker: shuttling between St Moritz in Switzerland and the Colline Metallifere, high in the hills of Tuscany, surrounded by vineyards and olive groves, with a flying visit to London to carry his nation's flag at the opening ceremony of the Olympics. Under Frischi's instruction, Adrien pounded the trails every day for hours; sometimes with Schurter and Florian Vogel, two members of the Swiss Olympic team, but more often with Frischi himself or his eighteen-year-old son Andri, the second-ranked junior in the world, who were more his speed. At Gasthaus Spinas, an Alpine lodge overlooking the Engadin valley, he built his confidence, riding on swooping trails through wildflower meadows. He had fondue for the first time, a barbecue almost every night. From some angles, Rwanda looks like Switzerland, but they must have felt a million miles apart. 'Usually I eat meat or fish only once a week,' Adrien told Frischi, embarrassed almost, after one meal. 'If I just eat beans or rice, that's totally fine with me.'

Adrien had a lot to learn but he was picking it up fast. He entered local training races on Wednesday evenings, alongside sixty-odd Swiss riders, and began to hold his own; at the last one before the Olympics, he finished fourth, beaten only by national-level competitors. Mostly, he enjoyed being in the pack at the head of the race, being part of the competition rather than a backmarker waiting to be eliminated. Throughout his life, he was accustomed to riding at the front: he was the best in his country, one of the top competitors in Africa; his pride had been stung. Jock Boyer arrived in St Moritz in late July and challenged him to a race. Jock was in his mid-fifties, but his competitive instincts had not dimmed from his Tour de France days. When Adrien tried to laugh him off, he insisted. Adrien gave Jock a ten-minute start to make it interesting, and ninety minutes later he finished a full five minutes ahead of him.

His next race would be the Olympic Games. How good was Adrien after his two-month crash course? 'Decent,' said Frischi. High praise indeed.

The sun was high in the sky as Adrien – number forty-four – waited on the start line at Hadleigh Farm on 12 August 2012. It was a Sunday, the final day of the Olympics, and there was an end-of-term feel among the spectators and even the organisers. After years of escalating local pessimism, the London Games had been a success beyond any rational expectation: more home medals won, less travel chaos; the nation had discovered a unity that it had previously reserved for defending its shores from foreign invasion. Now the pressure was off, and everyone could relax. Mountain biking was a rare cycling discipline that Britain did not greedily dominate. Liam Killeen, a thirty-year-old from Malvern, was the sole British competitor and only an outside shot for a medal.

Adrien had spent the previous evening speaking on the telephone to his family in Rwanda and also to Jock, who had not made the trip to London. They laughed about the old days: dodgy equipment, missed aeroplanes and chaotic foreign trips. Adrien admitted he was nervous; Jock told him that, whatever happened the next day, he had already made his country proud, he had changed Rwanda for ever.

The odds were stacked up against Adrien just a little higher by the starting protocol, which dictates that the riders lined up in rows that correlated to their world ranking. Adrien was currently rated 209th, meaning he would be on the sixth and last row of the forty-seven competitors at Hadleigh Farm. A couple of riders along from him was Derek Horton, a thirty-nine-year-old from the Pacific island of Guam who worked in a bike shop and had scraped together £4,000 of his own money just to make it to London.

There may have been forty-odd riders ahead of Adrien, but millions of people were behind him. 'Each time Adrien is riding, Africa rides with him,' said Aimable Bayingana, the president of the Rwandan cycling federation, before the race. 'The whole continent will be on his side.'

'I don't feel any more special than other athletes selected for the Games,' Adrien insisted. Still, his story had a knack of drawing people to it. Team Rwanda had the offbeat charm of the Jamaican bobsleigh team, the underdogs who made it to the 1988 Winter Olympics and were immortalised in the 1993 film *Cool Runnings*; each time he rode his bike he went some way to expunging the negative associations that persisted with his country. Adrien was, for the most part, comfortable with his role as an ambassador for a reborn Rwanda. He might even have been the second most famous person in the country now. 'The crowd should go wild now because this man has been the story of the Games: Adrien Niyonshuti,' said the announcer, introducing him to the 20,000 spectators being seared pink in the midday sun. 'The man of Rwanda bringing hope to a country that twenty years ago didn't have any.'

As the starting gun popped, the leading contenders – Absalon,

Schurter, Jaroslav Kulhavy, the 2011 world champion from the Czech Republic, and Burry Stander from South Africa – shot off. For Adrien and the riders at the back of the pack, it was a less explosive beginning: they had to wait for those in front of them to clear, like fun-runners inching across the start line in a big-city marathon. Adrien was riding a Trek 29er hardtail – a bike with no rear suspension and large, twenty-nine-inch wheels; he had borrowed a light carbon-fibre pair from Frischi because, in the Swiss's opinion, 'the equipment he had was not really Olympic standard'. Even still, his bike weighed a kilo and half more than Schurter's. That might not sound like much, but this is a sport where the best frames weigh less than a bag of sugar; some competitors even eschew a paint job because it adds an unnecessary sixty grams.

The course swept down an incline and then straight up a hill to separate the field a little. It wasn't long before Adrien realised that this was the fastest mountain bike race he had ever been part of. Road riders have the Tour de France, but for cross-country mountain bikers, the Olympic Games are everything. For four years, all the riders save themselves for this day, all of them had brought their best form. Part way through the first lap, Absalon punctured. Riders carry a canister of liquid latex to flash-repair flat tyres, but by the end of the first lap he was in twenty-seventh place, already a minute behind the leaders. He pulled to the side and ripped off his race number to audible gasps from spectators when images were shown on the big screen. Adrien passed him and noted that at least he had outlasted the Olympic champion from 2004 and 2008.

Competitors were taking extreme risks to find any advantage. On the second lap, Liam Killeen, who had been zipping niftily through the field, careered down a treacherous staircase of boulders called Deane's Drop and was catapulted off his bike at the bottom. He fractured his left ankle and also had to withdraw. Adrien was stuck behind that crash for a while, and could only watch as the riders in front powered off into the distance. He opted to keep a steady pace, picking his way carefully through the technical downhill sections like the Rock Garden and making up time climbing the six sinuous hairpins known as Snake Hill. The demands of a cross-country race are like no other in cycling: competitors have to combine the raw torque of a sprinter, the technical skills of cyclo-cross, the endurance of a time trial rider and the power-to-weight endurance of a climber. Unlike road cycling, they can find no respite in a pack or be sheltered by a rival's back wheel; they are constantly at their limit or beyond it.

With one lap to go, race officials decided that they needed to clear out some of the backmarkers because the leaders, Kuhlavy and Adrien's training partner Schurter, were closing in fast. Two riders would be eliminated: China's Weisong Tong and Horton from Guam. 'I just wanted to conquer my biggest fears,' said Horton, as he unclipped his shoes from the pedals. 'That stupid Rock Garden. I did that today.'

Adrien had made it. Not by much, but he'd done it. As Schurter and Kuhlavy fought out a thrilling sprint finish, narrowly edged by the Czech, Adrien completed his final lap. His eyes were shielded by mirrored Oakley sunglasses and his face betrayed no hint of the pride he must have been feeling. Still, a crowd roar chased him round the course; as he sprinted up the final hill, the ovation was scarcely less intense than the one the leaders had received thirteen minutes earlier. He had finished thirty-ninth. He could barely stand up when I spotted him just past the line. He was so tired that he would not even attend the closing ceremony of the Olympics that evening. 'I'm just so thankful to finish,' he said. 'I feel, like, broken. That was so hard.'

It was left to others to assess his achievement. 'What Adrien's been through, it's such a unique case,' said Burry Stander, twice a Cape Epic champion, who finished fifth in London; he was killed in January 2013 when he was hit by a taxi during training in Shelly Beach, South Africa. 'We all talk about preparation, but I think Adrien's had probably the toughest life preparation for this event. For him just to be on the start line is a victory in itself. But seeing Adrien race in South Africa over the last few years I've noticed quick enough that for him just lining up isn't a victory. A year ago, he wouldn't have even finished this course, to be quite honest, but he's gone to Europe, he's done the hard races, he's really worked hard at it. So hats off to him: he might not know it but he's a big inspiration even to us front guys.'

'I'm really proud with what he did,' said Thomas Frischknecht, who was at Hadleigh Farm commentating for Swiss television. 'For me, personally, his thirty-ninth-place finish is as big an achievement as Nino Schurter's silver medal. Nino had his best race ever, even though he didn't win, and Adrien as well did the best performance of his whole life on a mountain bike. That's what counts.'

Even immediately afterwards, Adrien's thoughts turned to the Rio Games in 2016 – whether it would be him participating, aged twenty-nine, or someone else. 'We will learn a lot from the Olympics, so next time there will be other riders from Rwanda,' he said. 'It's really important for me, the federation and the government that we have opportunities for cycling.'

As Adrien spoke, I imagined hundreds, thousands, perhaps millions of Rwandans, young and old, crowded round transistor radios in Rwamagana, or piling in to bars in Ruhengeri to track his progress halfway round the world in London, shrieking with delight every time his name was mentioned on the commentary. The message would have been unmistakable to all of them, however scratchy the sound or pictures: Rwandans are capable of greatness.

Epilogue:
A NEW HOUSE

If you are a building a house and a nail breaks, do you stop building, or do you change the nail?

Rwandan proverb

Adrien Niyonshuti was not the only person pondering Team Rwanda's future. Since the team had been established, the Olympics had been a driving inspiration; now that ambition had been ticked off, what next? Thomas Frischknecht, who had followed the team since riding with them at the 2007 Cape Epic, was concerned. 'The story is told now,' he said sadly. 'Realistically, I don't think Adrien will ever make it to the podium in a World Cup mountain bike race or a world championships or Olympic Games – that's out of reach for him. I'm a little bit afraid that the interest slows down after the Olympics. That created a great story, but will all the people that brought him to the Olympics also support him in the near and longer future? That's the big question mark.'

There was good news then when, in November 2012, the UCI confirmed that MTN-Qhubeka had become the first African squad to gain Pro Continental status. That was a rung below

Team Sky and GreenEdge on the World Tour, but meant that the team would now be doing the bulk of its racing in Europe. Team principal Douglas Ryder bolstered the roster for the 2013 season with a smattering of experienced European riders, including the German sprinter Gerald Ciolek and Giro d'Italia stage winner Ignatas Konovalovas from Lithuania. But the line-up was still seventy per cent African and included Adrien, three Eritreans – Ferekalsi Debesay, Meron Russom and Jani Tewelde – and Tsgabu Gebremaryam Grmay, a twenty-one-year-old from Ethiopia, who might have the greatest long-term potential of all. At the same time, Douglas formalised his relationship with JP Van Zyl to run an all-African 'feeder' team comprised of younger riders who would race on the continent. That squad included more Eritreans and Ethiopians, and one Rwandan: Janvier Hadi, who grew up in Sashwara and had once shared a house with Team Rwanda's Gasore Hategeka. Douglas's goal was that MTN-Qhubeka would ride the Tour de France by 2015 and ultimately it would do so with an entirely African squad.

'This team will be revolutionary,' predicted Douglas. 'For years I've had the dream of African riders and everyone's looked at me like I've smoked some cheap herb. But I promise you that every single race organiser is going to want our team to ride because there has never ever been a team like ours in the history of the sport. In ten years' time world cycling will be very different. The Americans had their time and the British are now having their time, because Sky invested a lot at the Olympic Games, signing stars. But wait, Africa is coming.'

The timing of MTN-Qhubeka's elevation was auspicious. In October 2012, the United States Anti-Doping Agency (USADA) released hundreds of pages of eyewitness testimony that detailed 'the most sophisticated, professionalized and successful doping programme that sport has ever seen'. At its centre was the seven-time Tour de France champion Lance Armstrong. For weeks, cycling made headlines for regrettable reasons: Armstrong's sponsors supported him and then, one by one, reconsidered; his Tour victories were expunged from the record books; he was counter-sued by newspapers and insurance agencies whom he'd won judgments against in the past. The UCI emerged from the scandal deeply compromised: its board had accepted a donation of more than $100,000 from Armstrong in 2002; this conflict of interest was described by Travis Tygart, the head of USADA, as 'totally inappropriate'. There were near-universal calls for the governing body's president, Pat McQuaid, and his predecessor, Hein Verbruggen, who remained an honorary president, to be censured.

An injection of fresh blood, to use a metaphor Armstrong would recognise, was therefore rather welcome for the sport. If the UCI was looking for a clean start, who better than riders from a continent entirely untainted by cycling's dark past? Professionals talked of riding *paniagua* – on 'bread and water' – but Africans were lucky if they had even that. 'It's a new frontier for cycling,' said JP Van Zyl, who was employed by the UCI beyond his work with MTN-Qhubeka. 'With everything going on in professional cycling, Africans have no idea of systematic doping and all that nonsense in Europe. This will be the saviour of cycling.'

As the clamour for McQuaid's resignation grew, there were rare voices of support from Africa. The UCI had spent millions developing the sport on the continent: it supplied equipment, including all of Team Rwanda's race bikes; it sent out coaches and race commissaires to events in Africa; it also paid for all costs when African riders were sent to train at their centres in Switzerland and South Africa. McQuaid himself was a regular visitor to the African Continental Championships. 'The UCI is instrumental to cycling in Africa,' commented Kimberly Coats. 'Without the UCI, African cycling would struggle to continue growing at the current pace. If the UCI goes down, African cycling will be the collateral damage.'

There are two visions for the future of professional cycling. In one of them, the financial and technological arms race escalates and rival teams pump in more and more money to overhaul the richest set-ups, notably Team Sky, which is backed by the Murdoch media dynasty. This would not favour African riders. But another view imagines a reformed, more wholesome sport, one that is perhaps cleaner than ever. Teams would be forced to scour the globe for riders who naturally have the athletic qualities that previously could only be created with doping programmes. Then it would become a numbers game, and Africa always wins: by 2100, there will be more eighteen-to-twenty-five-year-olds on the continent than even in China. It will be the biggest sporting mass population in the world.

Adrien featured prominently in the publicity photographs for MTN-Qhubeka in a special, all-white kit as the national champion of Rwanda. He was set to move to Lucca in Tuscany for the 2013 season and Douglas Ryder was convinced he could play a major role in the team's European plans. 'He's the most driven, passionate, committed individual that I've ever met,' he said. 'With a lot of other riders, you get all the bullshit. With Adrien, you know that when he's finished at a race, he's given 150 per cent, even if he hasn't performed well. You never really know with some other bike riders, because it's a crazy sport, but he gives everything every time he puts his wheel on the start line.'

Adrien's breakthrough into Europe was, however, marred by news coming from Rwanda: Jock was pulling out of the country.

He was not leaving entirely – he would retain the base in Ruhengeri – but in 2013 he, along with Kimberly and the mechanic Maxime Darcel, started working in Ethiopia and Eritrea with their cycling confederations under the banner Team Africa Rising. The UCI would also give them bicycles to develop a junior programme and the eventual goal was for an all-African team, including Eritrean, Ethiopian and Rwandan riders, to compete in the Tour de France. It was a moment that everyone who had first-hand knowledge of Team Rwanda had feared, but few were surprised. Jock's frustrations were obvious to everyone around him; as far back as 2010, he told me, 'There's not a day that goes past where I don't think of going home – I think about it a lot.' With every trip I made to the country, he seemed to be ageing at an accelerated rate, as if he was living animal years.

Breaking point for Jock came at the Tour of Rio in September 2012. The Tour of Rio did not sound like a taxing assignment, but it's one of the most punishing races in South America. There are 125-mile stages through the mountains and the field is packed with experienced Colombians and Brazilians. On their debut in 2011, Team Rwanda just about held their own: they finished the five-day event fourteenth out of eighteen teams, and Nicodem Habiyambere placed thirty-eighth. When they returned the following year, Jock set his sights on a top-ten team finish.

The trip, however, was in parts farcical and chastening. South African Airways lost half of their luggage, so Jock had to call in favours to borrow a pair of bicycles and water bottles. On the opening day, the six-man squad had four crashes, Joseph Biziyaremye abandoned and Janvier Hadi was their best-placed rider in fifty-eighth. Jock had selected an experienced line-up – Abraham Ruhumuriza, Nathan Byukusenge and Nicodem

Habiyambere among them – but they did nothing to rescue the situation. Coming so soon after Adrien's resilient showing at the Olympics, the team management was crushingly dispirited.

'The Tour of Rio plunged me from the highest pinnacle of my three years in Rwanda to one of my lowest,' recalled Kimberly. 'The team was a disaster. As much as Adrien had risen to ride the race of his life, the rest of the team simply lay down and gave up, literally. I was left trying to figure out how we could be so right and good and so wrong and pathetic in the span of ten days. All the fight Adrien showed at the Olympics was vanquished in the six riders who raced Rio. It was tragically disappointing. Crash after crash and not one got on their bike to fight to get back in the pack. By the end of the race, two riders were in the car and the other four occupied the back of the peloton.'

As the race wound up, Jock, Kimberly and Maxime drove at the rear of the race caravan – a position that reflected the team's overall standing – and discussed their future. Jock had long dreamed of running his own squad of African riders in the Tour de France that could include Rwandans but also Eritreans and Ethiopians. Now felt like the time to move on: they had achieved as much as they could in Rwanda. 'The Ethiopians, talent rivals and perhaps surpasses the natural God-given talent of Rwandans,' said Kimberly in her online journal. Still, she insisted, 'We are not leaving Rwanda. However, it's time for the riders to step up and take responsibility for their team. We have given them all the tools to be successful; they must now seize the reins.'

It was hard to be too optimistic about the future of Team Rwanda. Training would now be in the hands of visiting coaches, some of them from Carmichael Training Systems, and they would need to become quickly attuned to the athletic and cultural needs of the riders. Jock had hoped to hand over the management of the team directly to Rwandans, but it remained a work in progress. Throughout the 2012 season, Rafiki Uwimana assisted Maxime as a mechanic, but he was unreliable and had a habit of turning his phone off when he knew he was in trouble. Obed Rugovera, meanwhile, made a smoother transition. As a rider, he rarely caught the eye, but he was dependable and never complained. Then, when a New Yorker called Megan Leigh visited Ruhengeri and gave the team yoga lessons, Obed proved to be a natural. He retired from racing in 2012 and spent the summer travelling around the United States learning to teach yoga and massage, and practising his English. He would be the perfect *soigneur* for the team. Jock clearly hoped that Adrien would assume the main coach's role, but he was only in his mid-twenties and planned to ride for at least another five years.

Before he moved on, Jock made some changes to how the team was run. These came after another lacklustre display from the riders, this time in the Tour of Rwanda in November 2012. Again in their home race, the Rwandans failed to win an individual stage. After dominating the team competition in 2011, they slumped to fifth place; Adrien, game but clearly exhausted from an unrelenting year of riding, was the best-placed Rwandan in ninth overall. Jock decided that in 2013 they needed to bring through younger riders. For the Tour of Amissa Bongo in Gabon in January, the team was anchored by thirty-three-year-old Nathan, but the rest of the riders were twenty-two or under. The most promising of them, twig-thin Valens Ndayisenga and Bonaventure Uwizeyimana, were born in 1994 and 1993 respectively. Bonaventure, from Gisenyi, had a cleft palate; when he started training with Team Rwanda, Kimberly found that many of the other riders equated the prominent scar on his upper lip with stupidity. There remains an enduring stigma to disability in the country, despite the huge numbers that suffered profound injuries in the genocide. But Bonaventure was clearly resilient: he first tested for the team in 2011, then again in early 2012 before borrowing a bashed-up training bike from his local cycling federation and finally making the grade at the end of that year. No one had ever come back three times and made the team. Within two years, he'd won a stage of the 2014 edition of La Tropicale Amissa Bongo in Gabon, ahead of a field of established European professionals.

Another of the young prospects was twenty-two-year-old Hassan Rukundo, son of Omar Masumbuko, who won the first two editions of the Tour du Rwanda. There were great hopes, too, for Eugene Gashiramanga, Emmanuel Turatsinze's sixteen-year-old son (and Adrien's cousin), who was already completing hundred-mile races with the seniors. Once again, the apple had not fallen far from the tree.

Jock also determined that the training camps, instead of running Monday to Friday up to thirty weeks a year, should become full-time, boarding affairs. Mostly he had lost patience with riders turning up with stomachs full of parasites after a weekend at home, or hopelessly out of shape following the longer breaks. The new system made even greater demands on Team Rwanda's fundraising. For just a four-day camp, Jock estimated that eighteen riders went through 300 eggs, twelve bags of pasta, five bags of brown rice, ten bars of soap, twenty rolls of toilet paper and 150 litres of clean water. That cost around £50 for each rider. Now they had to find even more money.

While these initiatives were mostly positive and necessary, some fallout was inevitable. One worried for a fragile figure like Gasore Hategeka. He had enjoyed a return to form of sorts at the 2012 Tour of Rwanda: demoted to the 'B' squad, he finished in thirteenth place overall, the second-best Rwandan after Adrien. JP Van Zyl, who watched him during the race, was determined that he should not fall by the wayside. 'I believe in Gasore and I believe he can make it,' he said. 'I think he has neglected the cycling and you just need to tell him: *Forget about the money, forget about what's happening at home, focus on the cycling*. But they are very sensitive, these guys. You have to be very careful with Rwandan and African kids, because you put them down once and it takes another three months to build them back up. But I won't give up on Gasore.'

Producing world-class cyclists from Africa will require patience. Everyone was rushing to send them to the Tour de France, but that was only one definition of success for JP. 'People come in and they do this fantastic thing, in a different place, and it's just about numbers: "I'm going to find the next good one, the next one, the next one . . ."' he said. 'You have to invest in people.'

JP stopped short of criticising Jock's decision to move on, but only just. 'I have my opinion and I don't think I'm going to give it to you,' he said, with a smile. 'For Ethiopian cycling it will be a fantastic thing for Jock to go there. I also think it will be almost scary for Rwandan cycling to see if it will continue. But our ambitions are different, me and Jock. I want to see Africans get to a level where they can compete in Europe, not necessarily professionally, but at an Olympic Games. Jock has ambitions to have his own African professional team, so I think he saw there's an opportunity to have better athletes in Ethiopia and that the Rwandans got to a plateau.'

And there was still one final twist. In December 2012, just after the Tour of Rwanda, Adrien noticed a swelling, almost a hardness, in his right calf. He was not riding very much at the time, so he asked around and figured that with some massage his leg would probably go back to normal. But when he returned to South Africa, he did a disappointing physiological test and he finally admitted the soreness he was feeling to his coaches. The day before he was due to fly to Lucca to start the European racing season, in February 2013, he was sent for scans by Dr Jon Patricios, MTN-Qhubeka's team physician. These showed that he had a deep vein thrombosis and the blood clot had moved through his body to become a pulmonary embolism in one of his lungs. The timing of the diagnosis may have just prevented permanent disability or even saved his life. 'They reckon he could have died on the flight to Italy,' said Douglas Ryder.

As Adrien spent ten days in hospital, there was much sympathy for him but also some suspicion. Within a day, an American reporter contacted Douglas to ask if the condition was related to doping, through either EPO use or a blood transfusion. 'He asked, "Is there something funny going on?"' Douglas told me. 'I was like, "Are you shitting me? Honestly, he's a Muslim, he'd rather die on a sword than steal or cheat." But then I realised, "That's just where the sport is unfortunately."' This defence has some scientific credibility: endurance athletes, because of their slower resting blood flow, are at a particularly elevated risk of stagnant blood leading to clotting; according to one study, up to eighty-five per cent of sufferers of venous thrombosis are 'athletic'. Douglas is also justified to point out that the treatment Adrien received in Rwanda was far from ideal. 'The guys there were saying, "We'll just massage it,"' he said. 'Massage a clot straight to his brain and he'll flipping die.'

When Adrien stabilised, his doctors were reluctant to put a date on a comeback. He would be taking the anticoagulant warfarin to break down the blood clots, and in the short term would not be able to travel or even train outdoors, because of the risk that he could crash and potentially bleed to death. Ultimately MTN-Qhubeka announced that they expected Adrien to be sidelined for six to nine months; the team did not expect him to ride in 2013. 'I am disappointed but grateful that this was discovered sooner rather than later,' Adrien said in a prepared statement. 'I was looking forward to testing myself against some of the biggest riders in the world. I will use this time to rest and reflect on my career and what I've achieved so far.'

It must have been difficult for Adrien to extract too many positives from the situation, but a break from competition could have some welcome benefits. Since 2007, his years had been bookended by the twin trials of the Cape Epic mountain bike race in March and the Tour of Rwanda on the road each November. Then, during the European summer, he had competed as normal or prepared for the Olympics. While other professional cyclists had time to recover and recuperate, he had sustained a punishing twelve-month schedule for more than five years. Now his reconfigured programme for 2013 involved a temporary move from the outskirts of Johannesburg to Potchefstroom, so he could live with the other African riders on the feeder team and take lessons to improve his English-language skills. He was also involved in handouts for Qhubeka, the charity that gives bicycles to South African children in return for them doing work to improve their community. Finally, he would keep a long-distance eye on the Adrien Niyonshuti Cycling Academy that he set up in his hometown of Rwamagana in late 2012, independent of Jock's work with Team Rwanda. The academy, which was paid for by donations and his own personal investment, gave a group of Rwandan children – both boys and girls, some as young as ten – a decent meal each morning on their way to school and then opened up again in the afternoon for them to pick up their bikes and go on a ride.

In fact Adrien made his comeback in November 2013 at the Tour of Rwanda. He rode mostly as a training exercise, but he was still proud and determined enough to finish ninth. Knowing his history, Douglas thought only a fool would write Adrien off either in his cycling career or afterwards. 'He'll be incredible, I really believe that,' he said. 'We know his talent and his drive. Hopefully he'll be in the Tour de France and the Giro d'Italia in 2014. Anything he believes he can do, he will do it.'

A neater version of Team Rwanda's story might have wound up at the Olympic Games in 2012. Rarely can a Sunday afternoon in Essex have felt so uplifting. So unlikely, too. It needed Tom Ritchey to pick Rwanda, practically at random, to host his midlife crisis. It needed him to arm-twist Jock into going to the country. It needed Jock to be at such a cavernously low place in his life that dropping everything to live the middle of Africa made sense. It needed him to find an individual athlete of extreme resilience and no little ambition. Rwandans simply didn't qualify by right for cycling events at the Olympics before Team Rwanda landed. The fact that Adrien went on to hold his own in one of the most skilled, technical disciplines in the Games stretched the imagination.

But situations in Africa are rarely, if ever, neat. Politically, socially and economically, the continent defies simple categorisation of success and failure. President Kagame vacillates between hero and tyrant in the Western press. Team Rwanda created hope across the country but it also left some Rwandans disappointed and disenfranchised. It changed lives, but it had not yet discovered the secret of doing so sustainably.

A recurring grumble about Jock was that Team Rwanda existed to bring about his own redemption. He always denied it. It was pure chance that he ended up in Rwanda, a country that had sunk to its own depths in 1994. 'Miraculously, with Rwanda, I found a place – or it found me – where I can really feel like my life was not wasted,' he told me. 'I love helping people. My mindset is such – to give you a little insight – I don't even know why I do it, but if I see a broken-down boat, the first thing I think about is, *How can I fix it up into a beautiful boat?* If I see a fat person, I look at that person and I'm thinking, *Man, if he could just ride a bike, eat properly, that guy would be a real fit person*. I look at everything in terms of their potential, of what they can become. If that person gives me a chance, I will do anything to help them out.'

Jock could be high-handed and there was a disconcerting whiff of neo-colonialism about the authoritarian white man who arrived in Africa and set the locals to work. Team Rwanda was also not shy of twisting the narrative to suit its purposes. When talking about their new project in East Africa, Kimberly declared, 'We want to take riders from Ethiopia and Eritrea, countries that are at war, and show that through sport, through cycling, these countries don't have to be fighting.' This didn't entirely stack up: Jock was never interested in global affairs; he was obsessed with cycling and the creation of world-class athletes. He only engaged with geopolitics when it stood in his way.

But would it make a difference if Jock was driven by some cosmic penance? Adrien, for one, was grateful that he had come. 'The first thing I can say is that I love him because he has helped me a lot,' he told me in 2010, when we had just met. 'If Team Rwanda had not come, I would not be riding a bike, because it was not easy. No spares, no bike, nothing.

I remember that in 2005 I get a problem with the tyre and I could not get a tyre for my bike in the country. Sometimes I call him my dad, because if someone helps you for nothing, he looks after you all the time, you have to give him respect.'

A project that at times had wanted to outfit a million Rwandan coffee farmers with a two-wheeled Technicolor Hummer and dreamed of sending a Rwandan team to the Tour de France had alighted on a smaller but still meaningful goal. 'I'm always disappointed, but finding one jewel out of a hundred makes it worth it,' said Jock. 'I pray that I affect one life and that prayer has already been answered, and after that . . .' He did not quite know how to finish the sentence – the truth was that no one knew what came next.

ACKNOWLEDGEMENTS

I would like to thank Team Rwanda, MTN-Qhubeka, the organisers of the Tour of Rwanda and everyone who agreed to be interviewed for this book. I am especially grateful to the riders and their families, many of whom invited me into their homes and spent hours patiently telling me their stories.

While in Rwanda, I was indebted to the guidance and wisdom of Liberal Seburikoko. Ayuub Kasasa Mago was also of great help with translation. Additional assistance came from Jean Bosco Safari, Eric Kayiranga, Prudent Gatera and Gloria Murekatete.

My understanding of the country was exponentially increased by the writing of Philip Gourevitch, specifically his book *We Wish to Inform You that Tomorrow We Will Be Killed With Our Families: Stories From Rwanda* and his 2011 *New Yorker* article on Team Rwanda, 'Climbers'. The work of Jean Hatzfeld, Steve Bloomfield, Jason Gay, Steve Friedman, Scott Nydam, Tom Southam, Jeffrey Gettleman, Jason K. Stearns and Adam Hochschild was also of considerable assistance. It is an honour to have Dominic Nahr's photographs featured in this book.

Matt Phillips at Yellow Jersey was invaluable in encouraging the project and shaping the text. Likewise, it was a pleasure working with Laura Hassan, Fiona Murphy, Matt Broughton and Alison Tulett at Random House.

David Godwin's support from day one was unstinting. Nicholas Waddell was beyond generous with advice, analysis and hospitality. Thanks also to Alex Bilmes for his enduring friendship and encouragement, Alex Lewis for some nifty work at Hadleigh Farm and the staff of Swiss Cottage Library.

Last and most, I thank Miranda Collinge, who has influenced and improved every page of this book; and Greta for giving me a deadline that I finally had to stick to.

LIST OF ILLUSTRATIONS

All photos courtesy of Dominic Nahr/Magnum Photos